THE MYTH OF CONSENSUS

CONTEMPORARY HISTORY IN CONTEXT SERIES
Published in association with the Institute of Contemporary British History

General Editor: Peter Catterall

Peter Catterall and Sean McDougall (*editors*)
THE NORTHERN IRELAND QUESTION IN BRITISH POLITICS

Wolfram Kaiser
USING EUROPE, ABUSING THE EUROPEANS: Britain and
European Integration, 1945–63

Paul Sharp
THATCHER'S DIPLOMACY: The Revival of British Foreign Policy

The Myth of Consensus

New Views on British History, 1945–64

Edited by

Harriet Jones
Senior Lecturer in Contemporary British History
University of Luton

and

Michael Kandiah
Senior Research Fellow
Institute of Contemporary British History

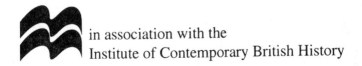 in association with the
Institute of Contemporary British History

First published in Great Britain 1996 by
MACMILLAN PRESS LTD
Houndmills, Basingstoke, Hampshire RG21 6XS
and London
Companies and representatives
throughout the world

A catalogue record for this book is available
from the British Library.

ISBN 0–333–65073–5

First published in the United States of America 1996 by
ST. MARTIN'S PRESS, INC.,
Scholarly and Reference Division,
175 Fifth Avenue,
New York, N.Y. 10010

ISBN 0–312–16154–9

Library of Congress Cataloging-in-Publication Data
The myth of consensus : new views on British history, 1945–64 / edited
by Harriet Jones and Michael Kandiah.
p.   cm.
Includes bibliographical references and index.
ISBN 0–312–16154–9
1. Great Britain—History—George VI, 1936–52.   2. Great
Britain—History—Elizabeth II, 1952–   3. Consensus (Social
sciences)   I. Jones, Harriet.   II. Kandiah, Michael, 1962–
DA588.M96   1996
941.084—dc20
96–20934
CIP

Selection and editorial matter © Harriet Jones and Michael Kandiah 1996
General Editor's Preface © Peter Catterall 1996. For individual chapters see
acknowledgements.

10   9   8   7   6   5   4   3   2   1
05   04   03   02   01   00   99   98   97   96

Printed in Great Britain by
The Ipswich Book Company Ltd
Ipswich, Suffolk

Contents

Contents

Notes on Contributors

Nick Ellison is lecturer in sociology and social policy at the University of Durham. His publications include *Egalitarian Thought and Labour Politics: Retreating Visions*, published by Routledge in 1994.

Martin Francis is a lecturer in modern history at the University of Wales, Aberystwyth. He was formerly a lecturer in modern history and politics at Corpus Christi College, Oxford. He is the author of *Building a New Britain: Ideas and Politics under Labour, 1945–1951*, to be published by Manchester University Press in 1997.

Harriet Jones is a senior lecturer in contemporary British and European history at the University of Luton. Her recent publications include (edited with Brian Brivati) *What Difference did the War Make?* and *From Reconstruction to Integration: Britain and Europe since 1945* and (edited with Lawrence Butler) *Britain in the Twentieth Century. A Documentary Reader, Volume I, 1900–39;* and *Volume II, 1939–70*. Her next work, *The Welfare Game: Conservative Politics and the Welfare State, 1942–57* will be published in 1997 by Oxford University Press.

Michael Kandiah is a senior research fellow at the Institute of Contemporary British History and teaches British political history at the University of London. A specialist on the history of the postwar Conservative Party, he is currently writing a biography of Lord Woolton, forthcoming with Scolar Press.

Helen Mercer is a lecturer in social and economic history at the London School of Economics. Her study of the history of British competition policies, *Constructing a Competitive Order. The Hidden History of British Antitrust Policies*, was published by Cambridge University Press in 1994. Her recent work has included studies of the relationship between the Labour governments of 1945–51 and private businessmen.

Nicholas Owen is Fellow and Praelector in Politics, The Queen's College, Oxford. A specialist on decolonisation, he is completing his monograph on the Labour Party and Indian independence, forthcoming with Oxford University Press.

Neil Rollings is lecturer in economic and social history at the University of Glasgow. A specialist on early postwar economic policy, his publications include *Economic Planning 1943–51* (HMSO, 1992); and *Labour Governments and Private Industry* (Edinburgh, 1992).

Noel Whiteside is Reader in Public Policy at Bristol University. She has published extensively on labour markets and labour market policies in the twentieth century. Her books include *Casual Labour* (with Gordon Phillips), published by Oxford University Press in 1986; and *Bad Times: Unemployment in British Social and Political History* (Faber, 1991). She is currently completing *Wages and Welfare* (with Humphrey Southall), which is forthcoming with Macmillan.

Ina Zweiniger-Bargielowska is a lecturer in economic and social history at the University of Wales, Aberystwyth. She is working on a monograph entitled *Austerity in Britain: Rationing and State Controls, 1939–1955,* which will be published by Oxford University Press.

General Editor's Preface

What is contemporary history? It is a phrase which has come increasingly into vogue. There have even been suggestions that it might be applied to describe, like mediaeval history, a distinctive, if necessarily imprecisely dated period. In the 1950s Geoffrey Barraclough suggested in his *An Introduction to Contemporary History* that changes around 1890 were sufficiently marked to characterise them as the start of a new, contemporary era. It is certainly true that there were important developments in society and culture and in long-term economic trends, not to mention the rise of socialism in Western societies and in nationalism against the West around that point. Whether they are sufficient to mark a new era is another matter. Barraclough's definition is far from commanding universal support, at least as far as the practice of contemporary historians is concerned. Far from being applied to a generally agreed period, there is not even much consensus over the chronological parameters to which contemporary history is addressed. The German *Institut für Zeitgeschichte* is largely concerned with the exploration of the Nazi period. For some, contemporary history is the period within living memory, an elastic timeframe which might extend as far back as oral historians' continuing work in the Edwardian era, or even the 1890s. For other contemporary historians their period begins with some convenient great event, such as the termination of the Second World War in 1945.

Instead of being understood as a distinctive period, contemporary history seems in practice more to involve the bringing of historical approaches and rigour to the analysis of the contemporary, however it is delineated. As such, contemporary history has a long and honourable tradition, going back, as R.W. Seton-Watson pointed out, to the time of Thucydides. Through exploring contemporary developments historically, identifying the causes, circumstances, processes and consequences of change over time, it not only makes its own distinctive contribution to our understanding of the contemporary. Contemporary history, at the same time, also informs the exploration of the contemporary undertaken by colleagues in other disciplines using other methodologies, such as sociology or political science.

Contemporary history not only brings historical methods to bear upon the examination of the contemporary. It also sets out to explore it in depth, to provide a longer perspective within which to scrutinise and seek to understand it. Otherwise there is a danger of looking at recent events purely from one end of the telescope. An example cited by Barraclough is the way in which the Korean War was treated in contemporary comment 'simply as an episode in the postwar conflict between the communist and the "free" worlds and the fact that it was part of a far older struggle, reaching back almost a century, for a dominating position in the western Pacific was passed over without so much as a word'. Later, the revisionist view of the Cold War similarly suffered from being derived from contemporary political perspectives, rather than a longer historical context or detailed document-based research. The structural changes which have shaped the present cannot be fully understood without this historical input. The aim of this series is to supply this need; to put, through both edited collections and monographs drawing on new research, **Contemporary History in Context**.

The notion of a 'postwar consensus' is another example of contemporary political perspectives skewing understanding of contemporary history. Developed to explain apparent continuities in policy from the Wartime Coalition to Labour to Conservative governments in postwar Britain, it has become an orthodoxy which exerts a dominant influence on readings of the period. At its crudest, it divided postwar Britain into a consensus phase and, from the mid-1970s, a Thatcherite reaction, a dichotomy the lady herself was happy to play up.

Historical generalisations can be useful as a convenient shorthand for generally agreed phenomena. However, as this book shows, the idea of 'consensus' obscures much more than it illuminates. Such policy continuities as there are might be more plausibly explained by constraints, economic, electoral or international to name but a few, rather than by the voluntaristic and generous impulses implied by the word consensus. Certainly the latter does not seem to have been the intention of the political parties.

Undoubtedly the postwar period does see the creation and maintenance by governments of different hues of the Welfare State, the cardinal element, for its supporters, of the 'postwar consensus'. This should not, however, obscure the fact that its form was contested. Indeed, the very introduction of key elements of the Welfare State, such as the National Health Service, was shaped by a long pre-history of conflicts, its final form reflecting perhaps compromise rather than consensus. Such developments need to be understood in the light of the very different histories and emotional baggage brought to them by the parties involved. Their creation and survival through the years of Conservative rule, 1951–64, should be seen not so much as a result of consensus as despite the differences between the two main parties. In such circumstances the idea of consensus does not help to illuminate such continuities as do occur.

This book provides a timely challenge to the consensus thesis. The dust has settled somewhat on the Thatcher era, allowing a less emotionally charged exploration of the idea of a 'postwar consensus'. More importantly, the government papers up to 1964 are now available at the Public Record Office. It is now possible because of this to examine the documentary evidence for consensus and continuity from the Attlee governments of 1945–51 to the Conservative administrations of 1951–64. The importance of this work is that it is the first detailed, document-based study to do so, drawing on both these government papers and the archives of the main parties and of major political figures. The result is a challenge to the validity of consensus across a whole series of policy areas. Consensus is at best a gross oversimplification. Instead, this work points to a much richer and more detailed undertanding of the dynamics of politics in postwar Britain.

Peter Catterall
Institute of Contemporary British History
September 1995

Introduction

'Consensus' has become the central paradigm used to explain British politics during a period extending from the second world war until the 1970s. It is a term which has always been used more readily by political scientists than historians; the former are fonder of general models to describe behaviour, while the latter – especially in Britain – tend to be wary of such tidy explanations. But because there is such an understandable overlap between political science and contemporary political history, it has been natural for historians to take the idea of consensus as their starting point, subjecting it to the rigours of empirical analysis as archives have been opened under the thirty-year rule. As research has progressed over the past decade, and we have had some time now to digest the fruits of the Public Records Office and other archives, historians have, however, become increasingly uneasy and sceptical about the usefulness of the consensual model to explain politics and policy-making in early postwar Britain. In this volume, a number of different strands of this growing body of revisionist work is brought together for the first time. Taken together, the new research on the early postwar period provides a serious challenge to the orthodoxy.

In the beginning, for contemporary British historians, there was Paul Addison. His study of wartime politics, *The Road to 1945,* is still widely and justifiably judged to be the seminal work in the field.[1] Addison was the first historian to attempt to explain the genesis of contemporary politics in terms of a war-generated elite consensus, the existence of which had gained widespread currency in the political debates of the 1970s. Addison argued that the Second World War acted as a kind of crucible out of which emerged a new agenda for domestic reform. The experience of the Coalition government, brought together to fight a common external enemy in the extreme circumstances of near-defeat, he argued, had powerful and long-lasting consequences on the shape of postwar political debate. While acknowledging that political conflict – particularly at a popular, grass-roots level – remained profound, the pressures and experiences of the home front led to the emergence of a *Whitehall* consensus around an agreed framework of core values. The welfare state; the mixed economy, the acceptance of Keynesianism, became the objectives of policy-making after the war – a 'postwar settlement' – which explained the apparent ease with which successive Labour and Conservative governments took power in the 1940s and 1950s. Thus, when Labour was elected in 1945 with an overall majority for the first time, it foresook the opportunity to engineer a peaceful socialist revolution in order to complete the programme for reform laid down in a series of White Papers, which had been sponsored and approved by the Churchill coalition. Similarly, when the Conservatives were returned to power in the autumn of 1951, they accepted the basic framework of reforms passed under the Attlee administration. The postwar settlement was not seriously challenged until the 1970s, when stagflation and industrial unrest eroded the basic assumptions upon which it had rested.

As is so often the case, the argument of the seminal work was accepted unquestioningly in a number of subsequent studies. In the decade following the publication in 1975 of *The Road to 1945*, virtually no work on the period was published which took issue with Addison's interpretation. The subtleties of his argument, moreover, were lost in many studies, particularly those aimed at undergraduates or a public audience. The concept of consensus became reduced and simplified to such an extent that virtually no significant differences of approach or policy were allowed for, while Addison's original intention had been to highlight the extent of political conflict during the war and to trace the resolution of those differences. At the same time, the planks of the perceived consensus were widened to include a far broader field of policy, including, for example, industrial relations, foreign policy and decolonisation. Consensus politics involved the imposition of 'a set of parameters which bounded the set of policy options regarded by senior politicians and civil servants as administratively practicable, economically affordable and politically acceptable'.[2] It 'implies a set of common assumptions and a continuity between both the main parties when they were in office'; although there were many disagreements, 'differences in the policies practised when the parties were in office were relatively small rather than fundamental'.[3]

With hindsight, there were two forces at work to shape this powerful body of historiography and political analysis. First, of course, the consensus paradigm was emerging in the late 1970s and 1980s, at a time when Thatcherism was the defining force of political debate. The chasm between the values and approaches of the two major parties was never greater than it was after 1979, inevitably influencing analysis of the early postwar period. It seemed that the basis for any common ground between the parties had irrevocably broken down, and that contrast with what had gone before provided both an obvious and fascinating focus for contemporary historians. Throughout the 1980s an inordinate amount of time was taken up with explaining why early postwar politics were comparatively less confrontational than they became from the mid-1970s. Now that the dust has settled on the Thatcher era, however, and the extreme rhetoric which then characterised both Conservative and Labour debates has moderated, our interpretation of the early postwar period has shifted. The consensus model, as Peter Catterall rightly points out in the Preface to this volume, now seems a good example of the way in which contemporary political developments can skew the interpretation of events in the recent past.

Secondly, and perhaps not so widely appreciated, is the powerful hold which the experience of the Second World War has had and continues to have on British culture. Understandably so, for the war had a profound effect, not only on the role of Britain in the world, but as a 'total' war in a sense not approached by the First World War, on popular culture and social relations. In the historiography of contemporary Britain, however, there is a tendency to trace policy developments in the early postwar period firmly back to the war, sometimes overlooking the influence of other contemporary developments, such as the Cold War. Thus, beginning with Addison, consensus – or what has been perceived as consensual behaviour – has been explained in terms of the legacy of the home front; the 'fair shares society' which led to a widespread acceptance of collectivist solutions to social and economic problems. The most recent and obvious example of this tendency has been Professor Hennessy's history of the Attlee administrations, with the resonant title *Never Again*. The war years are, in this study as in many others, seen as the key to explain the acceptance of the policies associated with the consensus: 'postwar Britain cannot be understood at all without a proper appreciation of *the* great formative experience which shaped it and dominated its economics, its politics and its ethos for at least three decades – the war itself'.[4] Addison himself has recently acknowledged that 'the impact of the Second World War in the making of the postwar state was less decisive, in some respects, than I supposed'.[5] Nevertheless, for many historians early postwar political history remains a rather straightforward story; war engendered consensus and there is little else to be brought into the equation.

What emerges in the new research on the 1945–64 period, by contrast, reveals a far more complicated and interesting picture. The essays collected here do not represent a new agreement, but rather a variety of approaches which suggest that a number of factors were at work to explain the genesis of policies pursued under Attlee, Churchill, Eden and Macmillan. First, as Addison himself has pointed out in the epilogue to the 1994 edition of *The Road to 1945*, several of us have focused on the continued primacy of ideology and party in the politics of the 1940s.[6] Thus in the following chapter, I argue that by the end of the 1940s the

Conservative Party was pursuing a clearly articulated and distinctively Conservative approach to social policy, which was grounded in a rejection of the use of the state as an agency to achieve egalitarian ends. Nick Ellison examines the notion of 'equality' in Labour debates in the 1940s and 1950s, pointing to competing visions of a socialist society within the party, all of which were incompatible with Conservative objectives. Martin Francis argues that Labour policy in practice was closely tied to its socialist goals, owing less to the wartime experience than to a commitment to ideology.

Most of the chapters in this book take issue with the assumption that there was an elite consensus and give examples of fundamentally conflicting approaches. Michael Kandiah, for example, points to a number of areas in which Conservative policy in the 1950s represented a rejection of the goals pursued under Labour. On more specific issues, Ina Zweiniger-Bargielowska reminds us of the intense disagreement over the continuation of rationing and reduced consumption and the extent to which popular disaffection with austerity contributed to Conservative revival after 1949. Neil Rollings discusses the relationship between Butskellism, the managed economy and consensus, concluding that much ambiguity remained in the management of the economy in the 1950s and that the consensual argument that economic policy was dominated by a Keynesian harmony of opinion is misplaced. Noel Whiteside takes up the subject of industrial relations, arguing that the traditional view of Conservative appeasement of the unions in the 1950s masks the Conservative abandonment of an unwritten social contract between Labour and the unions which inaugurated a painful period of union militancy. Nicholas Owen surveys colonial policy in the period, and argues that Conservative resistance to decolonisation has been underestimated and misunderstood.

There has been little consideration of the impact which the emerging cold war had on social and economic policy in Britain, a result in part of the tendency to focus on the effects of the Second World War. Helen Mercer argues that an elite consensus did in fact emerge in the 1940s, but on radically different terms from those the orthodox historiography has suggested. She sees the reorganisation of the ownership of industry, and regulatory policy in terms of a consensus in favour of the preservation of a capitalist economy, and ties the development of such a consensus very firmly to the Cold War which lay simmering under the surface of the Grand Alliance. Cold War politics from 1946 certainly add to our understanding of the context in which policy was conducted in the period and will undoubtedly become an increasing source of research and debate on the early postwar period.

As more pieces of the jigsaw are turned up, the picture which emerges looks far richer and more complex than earlier studies of the 1945–64 period have suggested. The vast archival resources of the period have only been available for a few years and it is already clear that the consensus paradigm as articulated since Addison is seriously flawed. But there is no consensus yet on what alternative approach can be satisfied empirically. Revisionist work on the early postwar period is by no means the last word on the subject; rather, it signals the beginning of a new generation of historiographical analysis and debate.

Harriet Jones
University of Luton
March 1996

NOTES

1. Paul Addison, *The Road to 1945. British Politics and the Second World War*, 1975, London, Jonathan Cape.
2. Dennis Kavanagh and Peter Morris, *Consensus Politics from Attlee to Thatcher*, 1989, Oxford, Blackwell, p. 13.
3. Bill Jones *et al.*, *Politics UK*, 2nd edn, 1994, Hemel Hempstead, Harvester Wheatsheaf, p. 42.
4. Peter Hennessy, *Never Again. Britain 1945–51*, 1992, London, Jonathan Cape, p. 2.
5. Paul Addison, *The Road to 1945. British Politics and the Second World War*, 2nd edn, 1994, London, Pimlico, p. 286.
6. *Ibid.*

1 A Bloodless Counter-Revolution: The Conservative Party and the Defence of Inequality, 1945–51

Harriet Jones

The development of Conservative Party policy in the early postwar years has provided one of the keystones upon which the 'house' of consensus has been built. According to the traditional narrative, the Party responded to the combined experiences of war and electoral defeat in 1945 first, by broadening its membership base and promoting a younger, more progressive generation, and secondly, by accepting the broad strands of what is often called 'the postwar settlement':[1] the mixed economy, the welfare state, full employment policy and Keynesian economic management. Indeed, it has been argued that this was already the case in the spring of 1945, and that the 'trouble was that people did not believe that the Conservatives meant what they said, whereas they thought on the whole that Labour did'.[2] This credibility gap was closed by R.A. Butler, who oversaw the development of a 'new Conservatism', which he later explained as a 'humanised capitalism', 'adapted to the needs of the postwar world'.[3] Lord Blake has explained that

> Once in office the Conservatives had a golden opportunity to show that they were not only the party of freedom but that they could combine it with full employment, rising prosperity and the preservation of the welfare state....[T]he Party did not throw away its advantage. Whatever long term opportunities were missed in terms of restructuring British industry and taking the lead in Europe...Tory freedom did appear to work. Restrictions were relaxed. Living standards rose. Taxation fell. Employment remained high. The welfare state was not dismantled. The housing pledge was fulfilled.[4]

This view – essentially derived from Conservative self-evaluation and passed on through memoirs and official publications – is misleading, uncritical and glosses over both internal Party debates and crucial points of conflict with Labour policy developments between 1945 and 1964. The orthodoxy deliberately exaggerates the extent of policy consensus after the war. This was originally necessary to make Conservatism electable. Later, it became a convenient hook for the 'New Right' and the Centre for Policy Studies, which was anxious from the mid-1970s to distance 'Thatcherism' from what it presented as a weak and flabby consensual Conservatism.

But in the absence of independent primary sources, most historians have tended until recently to accept the broad outlines of this story. Indeed, Paul Addison's *The Road to 1945*, which argues that the wartime Coalition was the progenitor of a postwar consensus between the Parties, set out to explain why 'the 1940s were the decade when the Conservatives were obliged to integrate some of Labour's most important demands into their own philosophy'.[5] The opening of important archives over the past decade, however, has enabled researchers to explore the history of policy development in this period in greater depth. John Ramsden was the first historian to examine the Party archives, providing the basis for his subsequent monograph on the Research Department in 1981.[6] In 1987 he read a paper to the Royal Historical Society which questioned the extent to which the Conservative Party had actually changed as a result of the 1945 election, in which he argued that many of the structural and policy changes put in train after 1945 had their roots in the interwar years, and that a Conservative election manifesto of 1939 or 1940 would have included proposals in advance of current practice in social policy.[7] The most disruptive effect of the war, he argued, was organisational. Constituency associations and Central Office virtually ceased functioning during those six years, except in a most *ad hoc* and chaotic fashion. This breakdown in the Party's machinery was bound to make the post-1945 recovery look spectacular; but he suggested that there were important strands of continuity between pre- and postwar Conservatism, which should not be overlooked. This is a legitimate and important point, and suggests that historians of modern Conservatism should consider the wartime and early postwar history of the Party from a slightly different perspective. The war did not engender a sudden interest in social welfare within the Party; there is a Disraelian tradition of concern for 'the condition of the people' which indeed, early postwar Party propaganda was at pains to emphasise. A distinctively *Conservative* social policy was already in place, which had a long and established pedigree.

Thus it is crucially important to understand that the point is not that Conservatism accepted the 'welfare state' during and after the war, but rather to trace the influence which the Conservative Party had on the shaping and evolution of that intricate network of taxation and benefits which determines how power and wealth in society are distributed. There is no doubt that the Party suffered a profound shock at the extent of its defeat in 1945. But ultimately, the fight against Labour's brand of socialism was taken up with vigour. In fact, although it is true that the combined experiences of war and defeat caused the Conservative Party to flounder for a few years, within a remarkably short period of time a coherent and distinctively Conservative alternative to Labour was articulated and translated into a clear policy agenda, based around the reassertion of the values of the free market and property ownership. The planks of this agenda were constructed, not simply by a group of 'Wets' operating out of a Butler-dominated Conservative Research Department, but rather as the result of rigorous debate and cooperation between activists representing a broad spectrum of belief. The spur was not, however, a new set of principles which emerged out of the Churchill Coalition. On the contrary, it was the agenda set by the Attlee Cabinet, which focused on the nationalisation of key industries, universalism in the social services and the suppression of consumer demand through a continued policy of austerity which led to a clear and unified Conservative response. The supposed 'new Conservatism' which emerged in the late 1940s was in essence an effective anti-socialist front, intractably opposed to the permanent imposition of controls inherited from the war.

The striking feature of British Conservatism in the age of mass democracy has been the way that it has managed and absorbed social change. In particular, the Party has weathered the challenge of socialism in the twentieth century with remarkable success, particularly by comparison to the Conservative elite groups of the other major European powers. There was no opening for a fascist mass movement in Britain in the interwar years, for example, because the Conservative Party under the leadership of Baldwin held widespread popular appeal.[8] In short, the British Conservatives could win elections. The political history of Britain in the past century has been dominated by long stretches of uninterrupted Conservative rule, and the Party's approach to domestic policy has proved over time to be more persuasive to the electorate than has that of the Labour Party. The Party's approach to social and economic policy, moreover, has been broadly consistent and centres upon the question of equality and the distribution of wealth. Conservatism has adopted as a central goal the defence and justification of an economic system which is based on economic inequality in an age in which the Party has depended for permission to rule upon the votes of the earners as well as the owners. This has been accomplished through a skilful combination of reform and appeasement (what is often loosely described as a 'Tory' approach) on the one hand, and a commitment to minimal intervention and market forces (the 'liberal' approach) on the other. As Robert Eccleshall has put it, 'what distinguishes conservatism is its persistent tendency to glamorise social and political inequalities by endowing them with an aura of righteousness'.[9] That is, from Balfour to Baldwin, Churchill to Macmillan, Heath to Major, we see the evolution of a domestic strategy which has met demands for reform with a formula for change which was normally persuasive enough to carry the public, but which at the same time fulfilled the Party's ideological goals, by fending off the tide of egalitarianism.

Looked at from this perspective, the war should be understood as the single most persuasive egalitarian challenge of the twentieth century. To the extent that there was a leftward shift in political culture between 1939 and 1945, it was the Party's task to meet that challenge. This was understood clearly during the war. Almost from the outset, there was a clear determination within the Party to limit any politically unacceptable consequences of the transition to a total war economy to the war itself. Particular concern was expressed over taxation and the distribution of wealth. The 4th Marquess of Salisbury, for example, wrote in 1941 that 'the right and power to make and preserve a private fortune must be jealously guarded as the key incentive for men to sacrifice leisure to industry and thereby secure the prosperity of the Country and the welfare of the poor as well as of themselves....if taxation is maintained at its war level all incentive to industry and frugality will be destroyed.'[10] The tax issue was a key element in the Party's response to Beveridge in the following year. The Postwar Problems Central Committee's (PWPCC) *ad hoc* committee on the Beveridge Report, chaired by Ralph Assheton (who became Party Chairman in 1944), concluded that 'a reduction of taxation is vitally necessary if trade is to revive after the war....No steps should therefore be taken which makes this impossible and the Beveridge Report should be examined in this light.'[11] While anxiety over the future implications of wartime innovations were rife within all sections of the Party, however, there was disagreement over what positive steps should be taken to present an alternative to the electorate. This was partly due to the breakdown in organisation during the war, which led to an unusual degree of faction-fighting within the Party. By the spring of 1943 a growing frustration was evident over the lack of direction in Conservative policy, which seemed increasingly defensive in character. As Richard Law declared at the small

Party conference in May, 'we have got to re-state the Tory creed in terms of positive action. We have got to create and not prevent; we have got to state, not deny.'[12]

In rough terms, Conservative proposals for postwar reform divided into three groups: authoritarian, Tory and liberal. The first strand, the most alarming but least significant, can be seen in some of the wilder proposals which emerged from the PWPCC, leftover, perhaps, from flirtations with fascist ideology in the 1920s and 1930s, or the influence of continental political philosophy.[13] The second strand was represented primarily by the committee of around 20 backbenchers, which was known as the Tory Reform Group (TRG). The TRG argued that the Party should go further in its acceptance of the Beveridge Report and the expansion of the public services than the majority of Conservatives were inclined to do; as Quintin Hogg (later Lord Hailsham) famously warned his colleagues in the House, 'if you do not give the people social reform they are going to give you social revolution.'[14] In effect, the Tory Reformers were arguing that the Party should carry out a pre-emptive strike in social policy in order to safeguard its electoral future. The bulk of the Party, however, faced the prospect of an election with complacency, not least Churchill himself, who was almost wholly preoccupied with the high politics of the Grand Alliance and the balance of power in postwar Europe. Although a sense of urgency and foreboding was widespread within the Party after the publication of the Beveridge Report, only Butler seems to have shared the Tory Reformers' instinctive appeasement.[15]

The third, liberal, group was by far the largest body of opinion in the Party during the war, and its role in the early postwar period has been consistently underestimated.[16] Churchill himself, as well as the Chairman, Ralph Assheton, the staff at Central Office and the over-whelming majority of the 1922 Committee should be included in this camp, which was determined to seek a reduction of taxation and return to a competitive, market-based economy after the war. Wartime propaganda reflected these concerns by stressing that the first priority of postwar policy must be to revive exports through a return to the free market. Social reform and Beveridge, it was argued, were dependent upon prosperity and no clear promises could be made until prosperity had been achieved. There was, moreover, a clear resistance within this group to the whole idea of 'social security', which it was feared would not only prove to be unaffordable, but would also destroy incentive.[17] In 1944 the liberal Conservatives found their intellectual prophet, the Austrian economist Friedrich von Hayek, whose book *The Road to Serfdom* explained liberal economic theory in layman's terms and warned against the 'socialists of all parties'. The Party's leadership was heavily influenced by Hayek's arguments in defence of the free market and drew largely on Hayekian rhetoric during the general election campaign in the spring and early summer of 1945.[18] That is, electoral strategy was determined by the liberal majority within the Party, which was confident of victory, and reform *à la* Beveridge was not the first focus of propaganda. As the Nuffield Study of the campaign would remark, the election was characterised by a 'battle down the line' over domestic policy, with the Conservatives emphasising a return to free enterprise.[19] Churchill's misjudged Gestapo speech was not, therefore, an aberration, but only a rather clumsy example of this tactic.

This approach was clearly not persuasive with the voters, who, it has been argued, were primarily concerned to ensure that the Beveridge proposals were implemented and that reconstruction was not dropped as it had been after the First World War.[20] The extent of defeat was largely unexpected within the Party, and Churchill's preoccupation with the diplomacy of the Grand Alliance meant that there was no single figure to give a clear policy lead in the months immediately following the election either. For about two years the basic Tory/liberal faction fighting which had made the work of the PWPCC so ineffective during the war continued to hamper policy development. As Viscount Hinchingbrooke (who had been a prominent member of the TRG during the war) would reflect in 1947:

> 1945 was by far the worst philosophical disaster that has ever overtaken the Tory party....I do not...know of any occasion in history when a landslide of votes has been accompanied by the seizing from the dispossessed party of its political aegis, leaving it a vacant, wondering, and wandering collection of earnest, public-spirited souls in search of a new philosophy and faith.[21]

A new intellectual framework for policy development, however, was not long in coming, and provided a basis for Party unity from the end of the decade. The basis of the formula was anti-socialism; the core of the argument against socialism (although by no means the only intellectual objection raised to it) was the threat of egalitarianism posed by the Attlee government's social and economic policy. The Party was in no sense reconciled to the 'welfare state' in the years following the war. Instead, there developed a vigorous rejection of the universalism and redistributive elements of the Labour programme. A new consistency in the Party's approach was apparent by 1949 and will be illustrated here at three different levels: the philosophy of postwar Conservatism, electoral strategy and propaganda, and policy development.

After the 1945 election there were numerous calls from within the Party and in the press for a restatement of Conservative principles and philosophy. Among the attempts to take up this challenge, two texts in particular can be identified as major contributions to Conservative thought in the early postwar period: Quintin Hogg's *The Case for Conservatism* and Richard Law's *Return from Utopia*.[22] A comparison of the texts is revealing because the two ostensibly represented different wings of the Party, and yet their treatment of the question of egalitarianism are based on similar points, underscoring the intellectually consistent common ground which was emerging within the Party at this time. The underlying argument of both texts was the urgent need for economic expansion, which could only be provided through the abolition of controls, the lowering of taxation and the reintroduction of clear incentives and 'rewards' for productivity and innovation. Hogg's book was the first to appear. As a young wartime Tory Reformer, his statement of faith was meant to provide a popular declaration of modern progressive Conservative thought. The focus of his concern was the urgent need for economic expansion following the crippling expense of war, which all could agree was the nation's priority at this time. The passion in Hogg's argument against socialism comes from the belief that a society based on egalitarianism would prove to be inherently unable to generate new wealth:

> Conservatives see in Socialism a squalid struggle for ever diminishing shares of a rapidly disappearing cake....Conservatives condemn Socialism in peace time for the same reason that they acquiesced in, or even applauded, some Socialist measures in war....the object in war is the equal sharing of burdens, hardships and privations, but our first object in peace should be the abolition of hardship by the creation of new wealth.[23]

For Hogg, poverty was a basic human condition: *'poverty has no origin, since it is the primeval condition of the race'*. The story of economic progress was one based on the incentive to be wealthy, and 'to create wealth and to use it wisely must be the aim of the true statesman'.[24] Progress from poverty over time was the result of endeavour, which must be encouraged through incentive. This contrasts sharply with what Hogg describes as the socialist theory of poverty as a consequence of the unjust distribution of economic resources. 'According to the Socialist, the interest of the classes in a nation is profoundly and irreconcilably different. The poverty of one is caused by the wealth of the other, and until the wealth of the one is terminated by murder or force (communism) or legal expropriation (Socialism) poverty and misery will be the lot of the majority.'[25]

Hogg asserted throughout the text that poverty was not the result of the uneven distribution of wealth, and that the current focus on questions of redistribution was having disastrous consequences for economic growth and recovery from the war:

> Conservatives will not deny that there was great poverty in this country before the war....what the Conservative denies is that the poverty was the *consequence* of the inequality, or that the true remedy for the poverty consists in levelling down incomes to a common level. The Conservative therefore distinguishes between the *fact of poverty*, which he admits to be an evil, and the *fact of inequality*, which he does not necessarily regard as an evil at all, but which he regards as something which must inevitably result from a state of society in which differential rewards are paid to skill and professional qualifications.[26]

He repeatedly stressed the importance of reducing taxation and restrictions on the economy because 'it is in the public interest that incomes should differ'.[27] The concentration of wealth in the hands of the state which is the result of socialism, moreover, involves a dangerous erosion of individual rights, 'a step straight in the direction of tyranny'.[28] Private property could thus be justified as strengthening democracy and the freedom of the individual. 'Just as political democracy and political freedom mean the diffusion, the sharing of political power, so economic democracy, economic freedom, means the sharing, the diffusion, of economic power, that is property, as widely as possible throughout the community.'[29] This provided the intellectual basis, of course, for 'property-owning democracy', discussed below. But Hogg also justified the ownership of large fortunes, which he did not see as contradictory to the interests of his economic democracy:

> Conservatives believe that the incentive to possess property by legitimate means is one of the most valuable aids to the production and increase of wealth. Provided that others are not thereby impoverished or harmed they consider that the possession of large fortunes is a good – a good both absolutely and relatively because it tends to the diffusion of economic power and away from its concentration in the hands of the government.[30]

In *The Case for Conservatism* Hogg thus argued that economic inequality is necessary both to generate new wealth and to preserve individual freedom.

Richard Law wrote the manuscript for his *Return from Utopia* during roughly the same period, although the volume was not published until late

1950. In spite of the fact that he was never to hold a Cabinet post, Law (later Lord Coleraine) is remembered as being one of the most influential backbench MPs of the 1940s and 1950s. His instincts in the early postwar period were confrontational and combative; it was Law, for example, who led the Conservative opposition to the National Health Service Bill in the House in 1946, at a time when the Party's research and information departments were still in a state of disarray. Law was one of the most important members of what could loosely be described as the Party's right wing after the war; along with, for example, the economist Diana Spearman, who became a central figure in the economic policy section of the Research Department. He was implacably opposed to any compromise with collectivism. Hayek had aroused widespread interest within the Party, but for Law, *The Road to Serfdom* became something of a mantra. His quintessentially liberal beliefs inspired *Return from Utopia*, which he hoped would form a basis for a distinctively Conservative domestic policy. In fact, the book was widely and favourably reviewed when it did appear and generated a good deal of interest both within the Party and in wider political circles. For the purposes of this argument, however, what is noteworthy is not so much the Hayekian or proto-Thatcherite rhetoric in the text, but rather the underlying similarities between Law's arguments against socialism and those of Quintin Hogg, in spite of the latter's credentials as a Tory Reformer. For Law, as for Hogg, the heart of the argument against socialism was the issue of wealth-creation: 'the free economy, with all its inconveniences and all its inequalities of income, is yet more productive of wealth and general well-being than any other system that has been devised.'[31] Law explains the importance of incentive in rather more blunt terms than Hogg: 'To weaken or destroy incentive is to take away the mainspring which energises the machine and, at the same time, to make competition meaningless – because, in practice, men do not compete except for a prize.'[32] Law does concede the need to operate some degree of redistribution:

> an industrial society will not hold together if the distribution of wealth is left only to the operation of market forces. While we can admit that the more skilled player is entitled to take more out of the pool than the less skilled (for otherwise the game becomes meaningless), we should regard it, very properly, as intolerable if he were to end up with all the chips at his end of the table.

But in his view the operation of a modern mixed economy was nonsensical because it attempted to operate an economic system which depended upon incentive while taking those incentives away: 'the burden of taxation is so heavy as effectively to destroy the incentives which are the condition of the free economy.'[33]

> There are arguments, which seem to me to be valid, for a free economic system based upon the price mechanism. There are arguments, which seem to me to be less convincing, for a planned economy, based upon compulsion and control. But for a free economy which is not based upon monetary incentives there are no arguments at all.[34]

Thus for Law, as for Hogg, the implication of the concentration of economic power in the hands of the state is the erosion of freedom: 'political liberty, which depends upon the widest possible diffusion of power and responsibility, cannot easily be reconciled with an economic system in which both must be centralised in the highest degree.'[35] Again, whereas for Labour 'economic democracy' could only be secured through nationalisation, for Law the opposite was true. The planned economy in his view 'represents a kind of middle way between anarchy and dictatorship', and economic freedom 'consists in the widest practicable diffusion of power, not in its concentration'.[36] For Law then, as for Hogg, the continuation of an economy based on incentive was vital both for the purposes of wealth-creation and for the preservation of freedom. These essential ingredients of the Conservative argument against egalitarianism did not represent any seismic shift in the Party's philosophy; both men were restating and reasserting theories which had been consistently applied for many decades.

These really very conventional Conservative arguments against socialism presented the case at a time when Labour's economic and social policy – based upon concepts of social justice and equality – were beginning to wear thin with the electorate. As Zweiniger-Bargielowska demonstrates in chapter 5, there was precious little bipartisanship after the war on the subject of rationing and austerity. From the late 1940s, Conservative policy-makers began to stress a form of capitalism, which emphasised the widespread ownership of property and a departure from controls, which was specifically designed to appeal to the middle-class floating voters who had chosen Labour – and immediate implementation of Beveridge – in 1945. In propaganda terms, it was the catchphrase 'property-owning democracy' which was seized upon. The phrase has its origins as far back as the 1920s and was used as early as the autumn of 1945 in Party speeches. But in the months following the election, 'property-owning democracy' was thought of in the context of industrial policy and nationalisation, as a counter to what Labour called 'economic democracy'. The Conservative argument, as described by the 5th Marquess of Salisbury in 1946, went like this:

We want economic democracy, to balance political democracy. The more people who have personal property and personal responsibility the better we shall be pleased. Why we hate Socialism is that it is a move in exactly the opposite direction. It is taking away all individual initiative and responsibility from the ordinary citizen and merely making him into a cog in a vast machine. It is in fact a move in the direction of the slave state, wholly retrograde and destructive of all that our fathers have fought for over so many centuries.[37]

'Property-owning democracy' was subsequently stressed in a series of speeches written by Reginald Maudling for Anthony Eden in the campaign against nationalisation, and was gradually widened to encompass social policies as well, particularly housing. 'A nationwide property-owning democracy', declared Eden in a speech at Plymouth in October 1946, 'can only be achieved by a great increase in the production of wealth, and by ensuring that its distribution is closely related to ability and effort, and that savings, when won, are protected against the dissipating force of unemployment or ill-health.'[38] Great play of the phrase was made in both the 1950 and 1951 election campaigns to highlight the proposed freeing of the housing market, which could give a slice of property for those who could afford to buy instead of renting a council-owned dwelling. As David Eccles put it in the spring of 1948, 'Ownership of property is an institution which can have a creative and decisive effect upon character.'[39]

Eden's words, quoted above, are qualified at the end by his reference to the safety net of universal benefits. He was speaking in 1946, at a time when the Party's line on universalism was not altogether clear. A new emphasis on social policy was evident from 1948, however, as the Party turned away from industrial issues (which had been given initial priority). Unease over earlier assurances on welfare was heightened by economic crisis from 1947 and Labour's determination to use control of consumer expenditure rather than cuts in services to contain spending. This policy, of course, simply exacerbated the basic differences in approach between the parties. The Conservatives in this period became increasingly determined to reduce taxation and to cut public spending, themes which were targeted at the middle class; as David Clarke, the Director of the Research Department, argued in the summer of 1948:

The floating vote is mainly middle class (incomes £700–£1,200 *per annum*). These people are now finding it impossible to live. The chief fear of the middle-class voter is being submerged by a more prosperous working class. Our whole appeal must be in this direction. We cannot reduce prices – we cannot materially increase lower scale salaries – but we can reduce taxation by economies; also revise the basis of taxation (*vide chamber*). No pledges in this direction can be too strong. We must discuss this *ad nauseam*.[40]

Of course, in theoretical terms, the reduction of taxation would raise productivity by providing greater incentives, and indeed, as Butler emphasised, was 'the principal instrument' by which incentives in society could be raised.[41] This argument was a central theme in the years preceding the elections of 1950 and 1951. In practical terms, it was realised that the only way to accomplish such reductions would be by rethinking the Labour concept of universal social services. Within the Research Department it was Iain Macleod who was responsible for designing a new policy framework in the first half of 1949. In a memorandum written in the early spring of that year, Macleod argued:

> It is necessary, if only for our own intellectual satisfaction, that we should re-define our whole attitude towards the social services. Increasingly, they are being used not for the relief of destitution, or misfortune, or ill health, but as a means to redistribute wealth, and as a means to realise in the end a Communist society. Increasingly, the citizens pay into a common pool in proportion to their means and take out an equal share of benefit. Not only the social services proper, but the food subsidies and the new Housing Bill show this tendency....the conception of a minimum standard is disappearing in favour of that of an average to which ability and thrift are irrelevant. Perhaps we have gone too far along this road to retreat now. If we can erect road blocks they must be the twin ones of a minimum standard and a personal test of needs.[42]

Quintin Hogg, in the meantime, was busily drafting the policy statement which would become *The Right Road for Britain*. Macleod's notes to him for the section on the social services stressed that 'the Conservative Party does not regard the true function of the social services to be either the provision of an average standard or the redistribution of wealth. It approves the historic function of the social services as the relief of the unfortunate...'[43] Party rhetoric in these final months of opposition, both in propaganda and in Parliamentary debate, came increasingly to stress the urgency of targeting those in greatest need. In this way, the Party found a new confidence in its argument for greater social inequality, an example of Eccleshall's 'aura of righteousness', which portrayed Labour's social policy as one of unreasonable greed and irresponsibility. When Butler gave his instructions to the Conservative Candidates Association in 1950, the Party's confident new line was already well entrenched. Mr Churchill, he explained, wanted to provide a basic safety net of benefits on top of which 'everybody shall be allowed to build a greater and better future for themselves than they are allowed at present....to give people rewards for extra labour, and the encouragement, and not derision of the profit motive'.[44] The work of the One Nation group of MPs, including Macleod and Powell, first elected in 1950, provides a further illustration of this new approach. 'Socialists', One Nation declared, 'would give the same benefits to everyone, whether or not the help is needed, and indeed whether or not the country's resources are adequate. We believe that we must first help those in need.'[45]

By the end of the 1940s, therefore, the Party had developed a consistent and firm response to Labour's domestic policy approach, based upon the rejection of the use of the state as a tool to redistribute wealth or to maintain the egalitarian trends introduced during the war years. The emphasis of Conservative policy development before the elections, and indeed of the Churchill administration after 1951, was placed squarely upon finding ways to reduced public expenditure and taxation, and on reorienting social policy around the question of need. This was clear by the end of the 1950s in a variety of policy areas. In the NHS, the Party espoused the adoption of charges and an expanded role for the private sector; in education, policy was aimed at defending secondary school organisation, which would target needs and talents in a tripartite system; in the social insurance/national assistance scheme, the Party supported a shift of emphasis towards means-testing; there was general opposition in principle to raising universal pensions in line with the cost of living; and in housing, perhaps the most obvious example, the Party vigorously opposed its incorporation as a branch of the public sector and campaigned with considerable success around the assertion that returning housing to the private sector would increase productivity and enable those who could afford it to buy into the property-owning democracy.[46] By 1949, Macleod would remark, there was already a 'distinct cleavage of opinion' between the Conservative and socialist approach to the social services.[47] In practice, of course, it proved to be virtually impossible to curtail public expenditure to the extent that in theory was acknowledged to be desirable, a dilemma which was underscored by the resignation of the Government's Treasury team in 1958. But the objective of Conservative social policy after 1951 was based on a firm rejection of egalitarianism; by cutting taxes and reorienting the social services around the question of need, by lifting controls and returning to a broad emphasis on consumerism and the free market, the Conservatives were rejecting the values that had governed the country during the war and the Attlee years. Superficially, there may have been little dramatic change when Churchill came back to power. But the rejection of the role of the state as the agent of profound redistribution, implicit in Conservative philosophy and policy by the end of the 1940s, was based upon a rejection of egalitarian values inherent to Conservative political philosophy. This is a rather obvious point, but one which is central to our understanding of the failure of the Attlee revolution.

ACKNOWLEDGEMENTS

I would like to acknowledge the Master and Fellows of Churchill College for the use of the papers of Lord Swinton and Lord Hailes. The papers of Lord Swinton I have cited with the kind permission of the Earl of Swinton. The papers of Lord Hailes have been cited with the kind permission of Sir Nicholas Hedworth Williamson. I am grateful to Lord Clitheroe for permission to quote from the papers of his father. I would also like to thank Lord Coleraine for permission to cite his father's papers. Material from the Conservative Party Archives has been reproduced with the permission of the Conservative Party.

NOTES

1. The term was coined by Paul Addison, several years after the publication of *The Road to 1945*; see 'The Road from 1945', in Peter Hennessy and Anthony Seldon, eds., *Ruling Performance. British Governments from Attlee to Thatcher*, 1987, Oxford, Blackwell.
2. Robert Blake, *The Conservative Party from Peel to Churchill*, 1972, London, Fontana, pp. 254–5.
3. Lord Butler, *The Art of the Possible. The Memoirs of Lord Butler*, 1971, London, Hamish Hamilton, pp. 134, 137.
4. Blake, 1972, p. 269.
5. Paul Addison, *The Road to 1945. British Politics and the Second World War*, 1975, London, Jonathan Cape, p. 278.
6. John Ramsden, *The Making of Conservative Party Policy. The Conservative Research Department since 1929*, 1980, London, Longman.
7. John Ramsden, '"A Party for Owners or a Party for Earners?" How far did the British Conservative Party really change after 1945?', *Transactions of the Royal Historical Society*, 5th ser., 27, 1987.
8. See Bruce Coleman, 'The Conservative Party and the Frustration of the Extreme Right', in Andrew Thorpe, ed., *The Failure of Political Extremism in Interwar Britain*, 1989, Exeter, Exeter University Press.

9. Robert Eccleshall, 'English Conservatism as Ideology', *Political Studies*, 25, 1, March 1977, p. 62.
10. The papers of Lord Swinton, Churchill College, Cambridge. MS.SWIN 270/5/1, 'Postwar Conservative Party at Home and in External Relations', June 1941.
11. Conservative Party Archives, Bodleian Library, Oxford [hereafter CPA], CRD2/28/6, 19 January 1943, Report on the Beveridge Proposals.
12. The papers of Lord Coleraine, private possession. MS.CLRN, 31 March 1943.
13. See, for example, the surviving records of the 'Watching Committee' in MS.SWIN270/5; or the proposals of the PWPCC education sub-committee contained in 'Looking Ahead: A Plan for Youth', London, PWPCC, 1942.
14. *Hansard*, 5th ser., 16 February 1943, 386:1614.
15. See, for example, Lord Butler, *The Art of the Possible*, 1971, London, Hamish Hamilton, pp. 126–7.
16. The only major study of Conservative social policy during the war estimates that some 90 per cent of the parliamentary party could be described as 'liberal' in this sense of the word. See Hartmut Kopsch, 'The Approach of the Conservative Party to Social Policy during the Second World War', unpublished doctoral thesis, London 1970. Some analysts use the terms neo-liberal or libertarian in order to avoid confusion with the Liberal Party, or with the National Liberals.
17. See, for example, Report on the Beveridge Proposals, 1943.
18. Harriet Jones, 'The Conservative Party and the Welfare State, 1942–55', unpublished doctoral thesis, 1992, London, pp. 103–9; see also Richard Cockett, *Thinking the Unthinkable. Think-Tanks and the Economic Counter-Revolution, 1931–1983*, 1994, London, Harper-Collins, chapter 2.
19. R.B. McCallum and Alison Readman, *The General Election of 1945*, 1947, London, Oxford University Press, pp. 99–101.
20. Steven Fielding, 'What did "the People" Want? The Meaning of the 1945 General Election', *The Historical Journal*, 35, 2, 1992.
21. Viscount Hinchingbrooke, 'The Course of Conservative Politics', *The Quarterly Review*, 1947, CCLXXXV, 574, p. 489.
22. Quintin Hogg, *The Case for Conservatism*, 1947, London, Penguin; Richard Law, *Return from Utopia*, 1950, London, Faber and Faber.
23. Hogg, 1947, p. 133.
24. *Ibid.*, p. 184.
25. *Ibid.*, p. 147.
26. *Ibid.*, pp. 171–2.
27. *Ibid.*, p. 181
28. *Ibid.*, p. 182.
29. *Ibid.*, p. 63.
30. *Ibid.*, p. 101.
31. Law, 1950, p. 113.
32. *Ibid.*, p. 110.
33. *Ibid.*, p. 111.
34. *Ibid.*, p. 116.
35. *Ibid.*, p. 93.
36. *Ibid.*, p. 92.

37. The papers of Lord Clitheroe, private possession. MS.Clith, 14 May 1946, Salisbury to Assheton. Note the Hayekian language here, which permeates so much Conservative discussion in this period.
38. CPA CRD2/8/1, 26 October 1946, Eden speech at Plymouth.
39. CPA CRD2/23/7, Spring 1948, draft by David Eccles.
40. CPA CRD2/50/10, Summer 1948, Clarke notes on general policy.
41. CPA CRD2/9/14, 1949, Butler memorandum on priorities in economic policy.
42. CPA CRD2/27/2, 7 March 1949. This was sent by the CRD as a 'Statement of Social Services Policy' to the Consultative Committee on 18 March 1949.
43. *Ibid.*, 4 April 1949, Macleod to Hogg.
44. The papers of Lord Hailes, Churchill College, Cambridge. MS.HAIS 2/8, 23 January 1950.
45. C.J.M. Alport *et al., One Nation: A Tory Approach to Social Problems,* 1950, London, CPC, p. 9. Other prominent members of the group were Enoch Powell, Iain Macleod, Angus Maude, Robert Carr, Gilbert Longden and Edward Heath.
46. For a detailed account, see Jones, 1992.
47. CPA CRD2/27/5, PMC(49)5, 19 May 1949.

2 Consensus Here, Consensus There ... but not Consensus Everywhere: The Labour Party, Equality and Social Policy in the 1950s

Nick Ellison

A good deal has been written about the existence, or not, of a 'postwar consensus'.[1] While many contemporary historians treat the period from 1940 through to, at least, the early 1960s as one marked by common agreement about the basic objectives and principles of government amongst the leaders of both major political parties, others believe the level of consensus has been overstated.[2] 'Consensus' on this second view exists more in the mind of those who look back nostalgically to a pre-Thatcherite past where, to echo L. P. Hartley, things were done differently – and with less rancour. Much depends, of course, on how 'consensus' is defined. This chapter will employ two separate but equally plausible interpretations, one 'procedural' the other 'substantive', in order to demonstrate the difficulties associated with efforts to treat Labour's approach to social policy in the 1950s in consensual terms.

It is important to be clear about the very different attitudes to politics and policy-making that these two approaches imply. Construed procedurally, 'consensus' conveys little more than broad agreement amongst political elites about the basic direction of policy-making. As Addison has suggested, 'settlement' may be a better word, indicating an acceptance of the parameters within which 'policy' is debated.[3] A substantive interpretation goes further. It is one thing for political parties to agree about general frameworks, but quite another to go beyond them to a deeper ideological identification of purpose about the aims and objectives of specific policies.

Adopting the procedural definition for the moment, it would be foolish to deny that certain basic features of policy were broadly agreed. The 1944 White Paper, *Employment Policy*, with its pledge to maintain 'a high and

17

stable level of employment' together with the acceptance of Keynesian demand management techniques for the fulfilment of this ambition, stands as an example of a defining socio-economic objective accepted by both parties. Again, there was common recognition of the need for a more comprehensive approach to social policy, at its most visible in the Coalition government's acceptance of the Beveridge Report and the passing of the 1944 Education Act.

The Labour government which came to power in 1945 interpreted these ambitions in a particular way. Welfare legislation between 1946 and 1948, alongside other measures to extend central state control over the economy, gave the settlement a collectivist character, which proved sufficiently electorally popular to make it difficult for the Conservatives to promote an avowedly anti-collectivist programme in the two general elections in 1950 and 1951.[4] To seek votes on the basis of pre-Keynesian economic orthodoxy and social retrenchment would have been to risk electoral defeat, as Tory strategists recognised.[5] Churchill's last administration and subsequent Conservative governments consequently upheld the principle of state welfare, pursued a broadly Keynesian macroeconomic policy complete with the commitment to full employment and even retained 20 per cent of British industry in public ownership.[6]

Electoral pragmatism was underpinned by at least three further considerations, which sustained this prevailing sense of political agreement. First, certain civil servants who had gained senior positions during the Attlee regime continued to favour the broadly Keynesian macroeconomic policy Labour had pursued in its last two years of office, and their influence was felt, particularly in the early 1950s. In the early years of Churchill's government the Chancellor, Rab Butler, retained Sir Edwin Plowden, Chief Planning Officer and Chairman of the Economic Planning Board created by Sir Stafford Cripps in 1947, as an adviser on macroeconomic policy. After Plowden's retirement in 1953, Sir Robert Hall, a close colleague who had directed the Economic Section in the late 1940s, became Economic Adviser to the government. Anthony Seldon has noted that 'both were Keynesian and also "economic"', and both, moreover, 'thought ... in macro-economic terms about full employment and balance of payments stability'.[7] If 'Mr Butskell' had any foundation, in reality, the caricature lay more in the activities and opinions of civil servants than in those of the two Chancellors who unwittingly gave their names to the mythical figure.[8]

Second, the Conservatives were fortunate in their timing. Although the internal economic situation they inherited on coming to power in 1951 initially looked bleak, the Korean War, which had so distorted economic strategy during Labour's last year in office, ended in the summer of 1953, easing the demand on public spending accordingly. For the rest of the decade economic growth, rising living standards and a growing sense of affluence produced a 'feel good' factor, which drew the sting of inter-party political argument – as socialists like Tony Crosland and Richard Crossman recognised.[9] Underlying indicators were not entirely favourable but, in the words of one commentator, 'the fact of affluence was by 1955 incontestable'.[10] Wages had risen, home ownership had increased and by 1957 exports had reached record levels. By the 1959 general election, indeed, 'the material prosperity of the British people proved the only real issue', even committed left-wingers like Bevan believing that Labour's defeat was due to fears that the Party might destroy the prosperity over which successive Conservative governments had presided.[11]

Third, if the Conservatives endorsed full employment and the welfare state for the reasons outlined above, it is only now becoming clear that a further factor also contributed to the general desire to maintain these institutional symbols of the early postwar world. Britain was hardly alone in developing and maintaining a system of state welfare in this period. Western European nations from Scandinavia through West Germany, Austria and France increased welfare spending for electoral and other reasons rooted deeply in their respective histories,[12] but they did so too as an outcome of the developing Cold War between East and West. In the words of one Labour intellectual, 'if a progressively improving and juster economic and social system can be established in the West ... it can confidently leave communism to wallow in its suspicions and abuse, its terror and enforced confessions.'[13] Western governments, then, were in a position to offer 'welfare', in the context of a mixed economy, as the capitalist alternative to communist claims that poverty could be eliminated by a combination of command planning and state-controlled collective consumption.

RETHINKING 'CONSENSUS'

Yet, whatever the strength of these 'underpinnings', the prevailing settlement was at best superficial and never achieved a substantive character. Indeed, on this latter criterion it is open to question whether any real understanding had ever existed between the two parties. Stephen Brooke raises this doubt in his account of the Labour Party during wartime, claiming that debates about reconstruction within the Coalition 'invariably fell along party lines' and that 'in terms of policy and ideology Labour retained a distinctive programme'.[14] This claim is subsequently projected into the future, Brooke contending that 'there is ... much that can be said for the argument that consensus ... in the post-1947 era was not a linear development but a series of erratic blips, occasions when the paths of the competing political parties crossed, rather than a constant narrowing of parallel lines.'[15]

'Erraticism' fits the image of consensus in the 1950s rather well, although perhaps not quite in the manner alluded to by Brooke. Despite levels of agreement that can undoubtedly be observed across a number of policy areas, these extended neither to the specific details of, nor to the ideological assumptions underlying, policy formulation. Indeed, the closer the examination of a particular area, the murkier the image of consensus becomes – elements of agreement existed, to be sure, but always in a context of prevailing conflict.

The 'settlement' never threatened to subdue political argument as the briefest survey of the period will demonstrate. In policy terms, the Conservatives clearly differed from their Labour predecessors: they denationalised iron and steel and road haulage, and were plainly antipathetic to the expansion of the public sector. Less significance was attached to economic planning and, although accepting the fact of the welfare state, Conservative governments were reluctant to embrace the spending levels its maintenance, let alone expansion, seemed to imply. The National Health Service, for example, the most potent symbol of Labour's governmental achievements, was 'consolidated' rather than further developed and the Ministry demoted from Cabinet status. In housing, too, after an initial spate of council house building, the Conservatives encouraged more private sector interest and a 'mixed economy' housing market.[16] Continuing scepticism about the need further to redistribute wealth and the state's capacity to increase public spending on social services found a voice in the stated inclinations, if not always the actions, of Conservative Chancellors at key moments throughout the decade.[17]

Different policy objectives were indicative of clear ideological differences between the parties. Conservative governments in the 1950s generally stressed the need to economise where possible on welfare spending not just because eliminating 'waste' was good economic management but because many Tory politicians and intellectuals hardly endorsed the statist, egalitarian and redistributionist character attributed to it by Labour.[18] If never compounded into a single coherent theory, the Conservative outlook consistently stressed the inevitability – indeed the desirability – of continuing inequality, arguing that the policy implications of this stance suggested, *inter alia*, the fostering of individual opportunity, targeting state provision on those most in need and support for continued private provision for those able to pay for it.[19]

It is, of course, possible to reduce these differences merely to ones of emphasis in an all-embracing environment of political agreement, but this involves overlooking a major shortcoming of the 'procedural' definition of consensus. Those favouring this interpretation understand consensus in terms of 'continuity': Conservative administrations in the 1950s pursued the macroeconomic and welfare strategies associated with the Attlee governments of the late 1940s, which in turn had drawn their inspiration from wartime proposals. Though comparatively new, the Keynesian 'rules of the game' were generally accepted and understood – indeed, ever less painlessly in the environment of rising economic growth, higher living standards and greater social stability.

But to cast consensus in terms of what Labour had done and subsequent Conservative accommodations to it leaves the development of either Party's beliefs during the 1950s out of account. While the Conservative Party could never be described as happy about the extent of state involvement in welfare and economy – the Thorneycroft resignation in 1958 being an obvious sign of disquiet – potentially unsightly outbursts could be minimised, partly by the very fact of being in government and partly by the anaesthetic properties of economic growth. Labour, however, experienced much more significant difficulties. Focused on the re-emergence of earlier debates about the nature and direction of socialist doctrine, sustained intra-Party political argument throughout the 1950s (and beyond) not only testified to the Party's changed character but also demonstrated just how far removed from Conservative thinking Labour politicians actually were. Where social policy is concerned, the existence of a number of competing interpretations of 'equality' could have a quixotic and sometimes paradoxical effect on the level and nature of consensus.

LABOUR AND THE 'PROBLEM' OF SOCIAL POLICY

Labour's Doctrinal History – an Excursus

Wider disagreements about the nature of socialism have always affected the Labour Party's approach to social policy, the main bone of contention being disputes about the meaning of equality. Here three strands of thinking dating back to at least the 1930s competed for pre-eminence. The aftermath of the collapse of Ramsay MacDonald's second minority government in 1931 found Labour not only leaderless but bereft of ideas. An essential part of the recovery process proved to be the ideological reconstitution of the Party as various groups moved to produce new interpretations of socialist doctrine.[20] The first strand was 'technocratic'. Left-wingers like Harold Laski and E.F. Wise regarded public ownership and centralised planning as the means to a greater equality of economic power holding and that, in the absence of state control, private ownership of the means of production would always result in a basic inequality of power between owners and producers. Most visible in the dramatic, though unsuccessful, demands emanating from the Socialist League in the early 1930s, the technocratic initiative found more solid expression in Hugh Dalton's efforts to furnish Labour with credible policy proposals through a series of newly-created NEC sub-committees.[21] Co-opting younger intellectuals like Evan Durbin and Hugh Gaitskell from the New Fabian Research Bureau (NFRB), Dalton presided over the creation of a 'centre-left' version of technocratic socialism which regarded public ownership and planning as essential preconditions for social reform, though not for the class war which those further to the left appeared to favour.

The second strand was 'Keynesian socialist'. With some pedigree in Hobsonian theories of underconsumption, it really emerged after the publication of *The General Theory* in 1936. Keynesian socialism stressed the importance of demand management and the state's role as fiscal manipulator, and enjoyed direct support from younger Keynesians like James Meade and Douglas Jay. Hardly a major influence on Party policy in the 1930s, Keynesian socialism had begun, by the end of the decade, to offer distinctive policy proposals based less on public ownership and 'physical' forms of control than on budgetary techniques and taxation as the major requirements of greater social equality.[22]

Lastly, 'qualitative socialists' like Cole and Tawney, from an earlier generation of Party intellectuals, employed a number of policy options ranging from public ownership and central planning (Cole) to welfare reform (Tawney) not so much because they were wedded to specific policy solutions but because they believed such measures to be capable of realising a society based upon human fellowship and a basic equality of condition. Not a loud voice in Party debates during the 1930s, this line of thought nevertheless maintained the hopes that had underpinned the ethical socialism of Labour's founding fathers. Qualitative socialism became a central motivating force in the outlook of a number of social policy analysts in the 1950s.

These strands of thought are important because of the order of priority they accorded social policy. Keynesian socialists like Douglas Jay and

Colin Clarke, as well as qualitative socialists like Tawney, were content to adopt demand management strategies accompanied by social reform, but their convictions were hardly shared elsewhere. Technocrats, whether left or centre-left, believed that economic transition had to precede 'social amelioration'. They believed it necessary, in Durbin's words, to put 'the acquisition of power before the abolition of privilege, control before benefits, the pill before the jam, in social legislation'.[23]

This interpretation of priorities found expression in Labour's official policy statements. Labour's *Immediate Programme* (1937), drafted by Durbin and Dalton, gave precedence to the ownership and control of finance as well as a number of basic industries and services, emphasis being placed squarely on the takeover of the 'commanding heights' of the economy. Although proposals for extending welfare were included, these were regarded as secondary measures intended for implementation in the wake of economic reconstruction. As Attlee said of the *Programme*, it was 'a table of priorities showing what will be done first'.[24] 'No socialist government', he argued, 'can neglect fundamental change for immediate patchwork reform.'[25] The formula was neat enough, but circumstances forced Labour to abandon this newly-created sense of priorities. By creating a popular egalitarian mood, further stimulated by the publication of the Beveridge Report and other plans for social reform, war did not necessarily alter Labour's understanding of the kind of measures needed for reconstruction, but it forced a rethinking of the order in which they might be implemented. Social reform moved up the agenda.

The Party came to power in 1945 charged primarily with responsibility for the implementation of significant welfare legislation – about which sections of the Left were uncomfortable to say the least.[26] Despite attempts to reaffirm the commitment to public ownership,[27] wartime perceptions of priorities, together with the important intellectual changes they produced amongst moderate sections of the Party including centre-left figures like Durbin,[28] forced the Attlee governments to attempt economic reform and social amelioration simultaneously. If the heroic achievements of Labour's first three years were the result – for which all sections of the Party were happy to take credit – the abiding question of priorities, what socialism really ought to be about, remained unresolved.

APPROACHES TO SOCIAL POLICY IN THE 1950S

Technocrats, Keynesians and qualitative socialists understood the legacy of 1945–51 in very different ways. No faction simply wanted to maintain the 1940s settlement, if by this was meant, in Tony Crosland's words, 'Keynes-plus-modified-capitalism-plus-welfare-state',[29] without furthering it and to this extent the conscious pursuit of consensus exercised no over-whelming priority in policy-making. Rather, each wanted to advance its particular vision of the egalitarian society in terms of how that vision could best be developed to meet the demands of the new decade. Attitudes to the nature and purpose of social policy, particularly in the developing climate of 'affluence', played a defining role.

Technocratic Socialism

Technocrats of left or centre-left persuasion, though differing amongst themselves about industrial policy (specifically the emphasis to be placed on public ownership as opposed to indicative planning), did not believe that social reform should displace the extension of physical state control over the economy. In their view, greater equality could only be guaranteed by, in the words of one Bevanite, 'the bulk of property and hence the full direction of savings and investment [coming into] public hands'.[30] Social reform was merely icing on the socialist cake.

Although the Bevanite left increasingly split into 'Tribunite' and centre-left groupings after 1954,[31] neither fragment regarded social policy as having much to do with socialist objectives. Typically enough, Bevan railed against 'socialist revisionists ... who [wanted] to substi-tute novel remedies for the struggle for power in the state',[32] while centre-left intellectuals like Thomas Balogh distinguished, in more mea-sured terms, the Party's stated commitments to higher social spending from 'anything which is specifically socialist'.[33] For Balogh and his col-leagues, Harold Wilson and Richard Crossman, the real issues for a Labour government concerned concentrated industrial investment and indicative planning to combat what they saw as the temptations of affluence. These centre-leftists feared that a complacent and decadent Britain would become uncompetitive and so vulnerable to overhaul by swiftly developing nations like Germany and efficient command economies in the Eastern bloc, where the state had the power to invest and plan for growth.[34]

Keynesian Socialism

In contrast, Keynesian socialists, effectively the group gathered around Hugh Gaitskell in the early 1950s, conceived greater social equality as the important socialist objective, achievable primarily through fiscal and ameliorative measures. From its infancy in the 1930s, this perspective took some time to mature fully. The late 1940s and very early 1950s saw Gaitskellites-to-be condoning further instalments of public ownership and committed to certain elements of physical planning,[35] but as early as 1952, with the publication of *New Fabian Essays*, there were signs of a sea-change. Crosland's seminal essay, 'The Transition from Capitalism', claimed that what the Left still hoped for had in fact come to pass – the capitalist system had been transformed by the effective elimination of private economic power.[36] As he wrote four years later in *The Future of Socialism*, capitalism had been permanently changed because 'the passive state had given way to the active, or at least the ultimately responsible, state; the political authority has emerged as the final arbiter of economic life.'[37] The path to social equality, in other words, lay open.

These views were echoed by Roy Jenkins, Douglas Jay and Gaitskell himself. For the greater part of the 1950s this group attempted to recast earlier assumptions about priorities to reflect their concerns about greater social equality. Crucially for the future of this strand of thought, the Gaitskellites disagreed amongst themselves about precisely how to define the idea but they were nevertheless clear that the fruits of economic growth had to be used for egalitarian purposes.[38] Redistribution through taxation together with social reforms, particularly in education, could result in the greater equality of opportunity and social justice demanded by the Keynesian socialist vision. These opinions brought them into direct conflict with left-wingers and also contrasted, though less sharply, with the qualitative socialist position.

Qualitative Socialism

A number of different perspectives can be associated with qualitative socialism in the 1950s but most significant from the social policy view-point is the work of the Titmuss group. Richard Titmuss, one-time Liberal Party supporter, member of Sir Richard Acland's Common Wealth Party and, from 1950, Professor of Social Administration at the LSE, had been much impressed by the manifestation of the collectivist spirit in the provision of universal state services during the war.[39] In his view the social solidarity expressed during the war could only be maintained as a basic feature of British society if the welfare state could be reconstructed in such a way as to foster a basic equality of status among individuals. His broad analysis of the role of the welfare state in the mid-1950s suggested that, far from a high degree of redistribution from rich to poor as many Conservatives, some Labour sympathisers and certain social scientists

claimed (with varying degress of enthusiasm), welfare as presently constituted actually perpetuated social divisions.[40]

To remedy the situation Titmuss argued that social policy must become
a much more active weapon for equality in the state's hands than Labour
had originally envisaged. Far from endorsing Keynesian socialist opti-
mism about economic growth as a potential 'facilitator' of future social
equality, Titmuss and his colleagues, Peter Townsend and Brian Abel-
Smith, regarded capitalist materialism as corroding solidaristic and communal values. As Townsend wrote in 1958, 'if a ... classless society
means anything it is a society where differences in reward are much nar-
rower than in Britain today ... but also a society where a respect for
people is valued most of all, for that brings a real equality.'[41] The statement summarises the qualitative socialist position: if it was 'about equality', it was also about a wider vision of human fellowship.

LABOUR, SOCIAL POLICY AND 'CONSENSUS'

These differing perspectives could produce two possible outcomes in
Party discussions about specific social policy proposals. In certain cases –
usually where doctrinal interests were not perceived to be at stake or
where the factions involved could find something in policy proposals to
suit their particular prejudices – Labour could act as an opposition to some
effect. The Party's general egalitarian ethos was plain to see in such
instances; it clearly contrasted with Conservative positions, demonstrat-
ing the absence of substantive consensus.

Where particular factions believed policy proposals compromised their
interpretation of egalitarian principles, however, internal strife could lead
to confusion and a policy vacuum. Here, although this state of affairs
made no contribution to consensus as such, the absence of internal agreement arguably hindered Labour's ability to act as an opposition, consequently conveying an impression of greater inter-party agreement than
actually existed. Three examples must suffice to demonstrate these points.
The Party's deliberations about a new national superannuation scheme and
the development of its ideas about comprehensive schooling show Labour
effectively displaying egalitarian policies distinct from Conservative positions. The various approaches to private education within the Party all
stood in marked contrast to the Conservative approach, but internal disagreements resulted in the failure to produce a coherent policy towards
the private sector, so reducing the salience of a clearly non-consensual
issue.

National Superannuation

It is unnecessary to go too deeply into the history of Labour's super-annuation proposals save to say that, by the mid-1950s, the Party found itself facing incompatible demands from different wings of the movement about the future of social insurance. At the 1955 conference, the trade unions asked for an assurance that a future Labour government would increase the value of national insurance benefits only to find themselves opposed by Bevan, a long-time critic of the 'insurance principle'.[42] The Executive, in the shape of Richard Crossman,[43] recognising that benefits could only go up if contributions were also increased, and foreseeing a damaging split with the unions over both the level of contributions and the insurance principle itself, turned in some desperation to ideas for a new national superannuation scheme, mooted by Titmuss and his colleagues, designed to produce greater equality in old age.[44]

The details of the scheme were excessively complex and changed over time, and in truth, Labour never really mastered them – despite national superannuation being a manifesto commitment for nearly 15 years. In the 1950s, however, different Party factions recognised their respective conceptions of equality in the scheme and therefore were willing to lend it their support. Technocrats approved of those elements which criticised private insurance companies and seemed to address the class inequalities in the welfare system 'discovered' by Titmuss.[45] Crossman himself referred with enthusiasm to the possibility of taking the companies into some form of public control (if not outright ownership), declaring in typically technocratic fashion that 'we should not forget the enormous economic power that those who invest in these private insurance schemes exert on the community.'[46]

For the Titmuss group, the driving vision behind the idea was twofold. First, less inequality in contributions – the abolition of Beveridge's flat-rate principle – and greater equality in old age, which in the group's view would lead to a more solidaristic community.[47] Second, Titmuss and his colleagues, like technocrats, wanted to see the 'irresponsible' power of the insurance companies curtailed lest 'individual gain and political quietism, fostered by the feudalism of the corporation may substitute for the sense of common humanity nourished by systems of non-discriminatory mutual aid'.[48]

The Gaitskellites were the most doubtful about national superannuation, Jay, for instance, criticising Titmuss's desire to nationalise the entire insurance sector at a meeting of the Study Group on Security in Old Age in July 1956.[49] But the group could not appear too hostile to the idea. The scheme was demonstrably more egalitarian than existing arrangements and for individuals who believed socialism to be synonymous with social equality it was difficult to oppose the ambition of higher and more equal pensions. As Crosland stated in conversation with Crossman, although he remained sceptical of the latter's more fanciful ideas about the national superannuation fund acting as a wellspring of economic investment, he was nevertheless keen on the scheme as a 'social service' financed by its own contributory 'tax' system.[50]

If unity did not stretch right across the movement – the unions remained sceptical about the abolition of 'egalitarian' flat-rate payments – the policy attracted an impressive level of intra-party agreement. The confidence showed. Armed with a proposal promising greater equality in old age from a universal system of national superannuation based upon graduated payments, freedom of choice between the state and private schemes and the index-linking of contributions, Crossman found himself in a strong position to condemn Conservative counter-proposals, hastily concocted in 1957. It was 'a swindle' because, unlike Labour's scheme, it was not inflation-proofed and, furthermore, because additional pension was strictly related to additional contributions it was inegalitarian.[51] Crossman remained ebullient in the face of rather fuller Tory plans in 1959, noting that 'the trouble for the Government is that the Opposition is fighting this Bill', and again, that 'it was we who were making precise, detailed, expert speeches'.[52] According to Crossman, at least, the PLP's morale was raised as a result.

Education in the 1950s

After the passing of the Butler Act in 1944, education has generally been understood as an area of consensus *par excellence*. The Attlee governments did their best, within existing resources, to implement the Act, particularly in so far as this involved raising the school-leaving age from 14 to 15, making secondary education compulsory and beginning the long process of improving school buildings, reducing the size of classes and ensuring sufficient teacher recruitment. All of these initiatives lay well within the parameters set by the Coalition government.

Although on their return to power in 1951 the Conservatives did not immediately give education a high priority matters improved after 1954.[53] Sir David Eccles, appointed Minister of Education in October of that year, brought a surer touch to the Education Ministry. He tackled the issue of the reorganisation of all-age schools – a central promise of the 1944 Act – and also instigated a shift towards technical education.[54] With none of these initiatives did Labour quarrel. But there were two issues – comprehensive schooling and the future of private education – on which the Party's egalitarian perspective contrasted markedly with Conservative education policy. Only in the former, however, was this contrast translated into serious debate between the parties.

Agitation for the 'multilateral' and, later, the 'comprehensive' school had existed in the Labour Party since the late 1920s. However, because the abiding objective of Party policy was compulsory secondary education for all, Party leaders displayed little interest in the nature of school organisation. To facilitate its passage onto the statute book, the 1944 Act contained nothing precise about the structure of the secondary school system, despite a series of reports recommending a tripartite structure of grammar, modern and technical schools, entrance being governed by the child's ability as determined by the 11-plus exam.[55] After the war, both Labour's Education Ministers, Ellen Wilkinson and George Tomlinson, supported by a number of Labour local education comittees, proved more than happy to interpret the Act in a tripartite spirit, arguing that the grammar schools offered the best opportunity for working-class children to succeed academically, while maintaining that every child, irrespective of which school he or she attended, would be treated in terms of a 'parity of esteem'.

Tripartism came under increasing attack in the late 1940s, however. By 1952, following pressure from the National Association of Labour Teachers (NALT), the Party had committed itself to comprehensive re-organisation. Although, typically enough, different Party factions interpreted comprehensivisation in rather different ways much common ground existed over the issue.

Left-wing technocrats, in so far as they were interested at all, argued for wholesale reorganisation and the abolition of the grammar schools. A pamphlet published in 1958 by the Tribunite splinter group, Victory for Socialism (VFS), confirmed the Left's chariness of any division of schools which could be interpreted as a division of prestige.[56] VFS demanded 'a complete system of comprehensive schooling in every county and county borough', although it acknowledged that 'the methods of grouping the schools should be a matter for local decision'.[57]

This thinking went further than the Gaitskellite position, but did not entirely contradict it. For the close-knit coterie around Gaitskell as well as for other 'moderates' like Jim Griffiths, Chuter Ede and Michael Stewart, the benefits of the grammar schools must not to be lost amidst enthusiasm for comprehensivisation.[58] Some, like Jay, warned that 'socialists should beware of making the comprehensive school an exclusive dogma'.[59] Others dissembled. Comprehensives, in Roy Jenkins' view, would

probably be the best method of organisation 'if we were constructing our
state secondary system afresh', but there were 'some very good, well-
established grammar schools' and he hoped that 'where they were of adequate size, in reasonable buildings, and with a good tradition they will be
left undisturbed'.[60]

Gaitskell himself was no less sceptical. Like many of his colleagues he
disliked the 11-plus but confided to his old headmaster that there was 'no
question of our throwing away the tradition of the grammar schools'.[61]
Again, at a meeting with Lancashire and Chesire grammar school head-
masters in October 1955, he recorded: 'I was rather astonished to hear them
say, one after another, that Labour was against the Grammar schools.'[62]

However, Gaitskellite chariness on this issue should not be read as an
unwillingness to contemplate change. It was just that existing arrangements should be incorporated where these were of proven worth. In this
instance, if no other, Gaitskellites enjoyed the support of centre-leftists
like Crossman and Wilson, both of whom were keen to see the education
system maximising the production of highly trained and educated individuals able to spearhead the technological revolution their economic policies
were intended to create. In some contrast to the Tribunite Left, both
groups embraced a meritocratic equality of opportunity in preference to a
more radical 'equality of outcome'.

But these differences of emphasis were slight. While the issue of equality in education would become more heated in the future, Labour agreed
upon a formula which advocated the extension not of grammar schools
but of the 'grammar school tradition' to many more children, in a 'comprehensive' context. One point in particular was crucial. Griffiths told the
1958 Party conference that the ambition to make grammar school education more widely available implied the abolition of the 11-plus – and it
was this, above all, that each faction wanted to hear.[63]

Though not entirely satisfactory, the formula put distance between the
two parties in an area otherwise characterised by a good deal of procedural
agreement. The differences were displayed in the debate over the
Conservatives' education White Paper in 1958.[64] While the Education
Minister, Edward Boyle, regarded comprehensive schools as potentially
interesting experiments, he stopped well short of Labour's position.
Arguing that 'opportunity' meant the chance 'in all secondary schools' for
boys and girls 'to go forward' to the limits of their ability,[65] Boyle was
emphatic that this should not imply a fundamental reorganisation of the
secondary system let alone the abolition of the 11-plus. All would be well
so long as children of 'middle range' ability could get suitable courses in
the schools they were already attending.

For their part, Labour spokesmen argued that more pupils must benefit from a 'grammar school education'. As Chuter Ede, a key figure in the drafting of the 1944 Act, put it: 'I support the comprehensive school system because I believe it will increase the number of our children who will receive a grammar school education who are fitted for it.'[66] Griffiths argued in similar vein. 'We do not intend to destroy grammar school education', he stated, 'but to extend its traditions and its opportunities to many more children.'[67] Underlying these statements was the common belief among Party intellectuals and policy-makers that equal opportunities could only be effectively enhanced if each and every school had the facilities to offer children 'grammar school' courses. Anything less would risk limiting a child's developing potential.

Such cohesion was not apparent in Labour's debates about the fate of the private sector. Ironically, there was general agreement that the presence of an elite private sector furnished, in Margaret Cole's words, 'a powerful instrument for preventing the creation of a classless society'.[68] The difficulty came in agreeing how best to deal with the private schools. Primarily concerned with the improvement of the state system, the 1944 Education Act had left private schools out of account. The Attlee governments, moreover, concentrated on the main task of creating, staffing and equipping a proper secondary school system, and devoted little time to the issue of private schooling. Though Labour was formally committed 'to end privilege in education', as *Challenge to Britain* put it in 1953,[69] the search for an acceptable solution foundered in a mire of alternatives based upon competing understandings of equality.

The issue was debated at the 1953 conference where fierce exchanges took place between Gaitskell and Jennie Lee about the validity of adopting the Fleming Committee's (1944) recommendation to grant a percentage of free places in the public schools.[70] It simmered thereafter, giving way to more dramatic disagreements about public ownership, but surfaced again in 1958. Three positions can be discerned. First, the Tribunite case, advanced in VFS's *Equality in Education*, demanded an end to 'the private purchase of privileged education'.[71] Rejecting 'Flemingism' as simply a different form of elitism, VFS argued that responsibility for the successful public schools should be vested in the Minister for Education, admission 'for suitable pupils' becoming the concern of the Minister and local authorities.[72] Tribunite demands for a greater equality of economic power informed this perspective. As Bevan put it, 'in a class society ... it is impossible wholly to prevent class education' because different levels of income would find expression in different standards of expenditure. The 'permanent solution [was] greater equality in the distribution of wealth', in his view the only way to alter 'long-run economic trends' significantly.[73]

Centre-left views were much less rigid. As a member of Labour's Study Group on Education, Richard Crossman acknowledged the right of parents to have their children educated outside the state system, but argued that a private sector should not be permitted to give children unfair advantages.[74] 'In British democracy', he declared, 'a socialist system of state education must leave room for a private sector. All we are entitled to do is to take steps to prevent this private sector becoming a privileged sector.'[75] He, too, refuted the Fleming solution as this statement implies.

Privilege *per se* was not Crossman's only concern. He was anxious about increasing economic competition from Germany, Japan and the Eastern bloc, and maintained that the public school system ill-equipped the country to deal with it. Public schools created an 'anachronistic and elite education system', which fostered an Establishment with a 'set of cultural values hostile to technology and applied science'.[76] They were, in other words, bad for economic efficiency and detrimental to the principle of equality of opportunity that should inform new educational priorities.

To redress the situation a much greater concentration on technological education would be required, combined with changes in university entrance arrangements to favour state school applicants. Furthermore, raising the academic status of redbrick universities and institutes of technology would increase the proportion of their graduates obtaining key posts in the Establishment. Borrowing ideas from Brian Abel-Smith, Crossman also suggested that the state should not be in the business of subsidising those who sent their offspring to public schools through tax concessions for children in full-time education (the value of which rose by income).[77] If parents wished to use the private sector, they should pay the full cost of it.

These views contrasted with a third approach. The Gaitskellites broadly favoured the Fleming solution. In a letter to his daughter, Gaitskell wrote that the intention behind Fleming was to 'throw open "public" schools like Winchester to merit not wealth'[78] and found support from Jay and Jenkins, both of whom declared a preference for the scheme.[79] In this instance, however, the Gaitskellites were not only internally divided – Crosland providing a very different interpretation of the Fleming proposals[80] – but they did not get their way either with the Study Group or with the Party as a whole.[81] Adopting the Fleming solution, as representatives of both left and centre-left pointed out, would create elitism in one part of the system just as Labour was advocating its removal in another.

This stand-off resulted in a decision to postpone consideration of the matter. *Learning to Live*, the Party's policy statement on education, published in 1958, simply stated that no scheme for taking over the public schools showed sufficient merit to justify the large diversion of public money required – and besides it would constitute an invasion of liberty to prevent parents from spending their money in the manner they chose.[82] Resorting to an old argument that improved state schooling would diminish the perceived need for private education, the Party declared that, outside the drive for comprehensive schooling, a Labour government would concentrate on reducing class sizes, recruiting better qualified teachers and providing better school equipment – similar priorities to those voiced by the Conservatives. The 'decision' – effectively a decision not to decide – focused the force of Labour's egalitarian concerns on the state sector, depriving the Party of an issue on which it clearly differed from Conservative governments.[83]

CONCLUSION

This consideration of Labour's social policy adds a cautionary note, if not a knock-out blow, to assumptions about consensus in the 1950s. To return to Stephen Brooke's point about 'erraticism', social policy debates illustrate the complex reality surrounding argument about detailed proposals – a reality made all the more complex, and erratic, by Labour's capacity for damaging internal disagreement. And it is important to take account of detail, for it is only in doing so that the kernel of political argument can be discovered. While elements of agreement can always be observed in the broad sweep of policy proposals, they lose significance as underlying differences are exposed.

None of the above should be taken to imply a denial of a notable level of procedural consensus, however. The overarching objective of full employment remained a key concern to Conservative governments throughout the 1950s, and the 'welfare state' generally remained safe in Conservative hands, marked by common agreement about many pragmatic aspects of social provision. However, the contention here has been that accounts of the period have focused too exclusively on this procedural dimension and have consequently obscured important substantive differences. When explored, these disagreements provide evidence of a degree and quality of political argument much more richly textured than procedural accounts acknowledge.

Why, then, if clear instances of inter-Party disagreement existed in the 1940s and 1950s, is it only comparatively recently that the prevailing acceptance of the immediate postwar period as one of unusual consensus has been challenged? Outside a general warning against the temptation to assume that the past is always and forever cosier than the present, there is particular reason at the present time, if not to destroy, then to reappraise earlier perceptions in the light of changed circumstances. Two separate but related factors have made a reassessment necessary, both concerned with the growth of instability and uncertainty in contemporary society. First, economic change since the early 1970s associated with deindustrialisation and the emergence of increasing global competition has had a profound impact on the domestic economies of Western nations.[84] As the capacity of nation-states to 'manage' their own economic destinies has declined in the face of demands for ever-greater 'flexibility' in the face of expanding and highly competitive international markets, so hallowed principles like 'full employment' have come to be considered as no longer sustainable. Social change arising from these new imperatives, fostered by high levels of unemployment, the receding prospect of permanent or lifetime employment for many people and the erosion of welfare provision, has been accompanied by growing political confusion as these underpinnings of procedural consensus disintegrate.

A second factor has lent additional weight to this general climate of uncertainty. The sudden end of the cold war, far from creating greater security as was initially supposed, has created less. As Eric Hobsbawm has written,

> the end of the cold war suddenly removed the props which had held up the international structure and to an extent not yet appreciated, the structures of the world's domestic political systems ... what was left was a world of disarray and partial collapse, because there was nothing to replace them.[85]

And it is uncertainty (rather than instability) that currently suffuses contemporary political argument. Without the familiar landmarks of full employment and 'welfare' sustained, at least in part, by an international context which lent them additional meaning, the way ahead is not clear. In such circumstances it becomes more difficult to suspend our sense of disbelief about perceived levels of political agreement a generation and more ago. Received impressions of the economic, social and political environment of the immediate postwar period clash so sharply with contemporary experience that a reassessment of the postwar settlement has become inevitable.

NOTES

1. See, for example, Paul Addison, *The Road to 1945*, 1975, London, Jonathan Cape; Paul Addison, 'The Road from 1945', in Peter Hennessy and Anthony Seldon, eds., *Ruling Performance: British Governments from Attlee to Thatcher*, 1988, Oxford, Blackwell; Anthony Seldon, *Churchill's Indian Summer: The Conservative Government 1951–55*, 1981, London, Hodder and Stoughton; Dennis Kavanagh and Peter Morris, *Consensus Politics: from Attlee to Major*, 2nd edn, 1994, Oxford, Blackwell; Keith Middlemas, *Power, Competition and the State, vol. I, Britain in Search of Balance, 1940–1961*, 1986, Basingstoke, Macmillan.

2. See Ben Pimlott, 'The Myth of Consensus', in L.M. Smith, ed., *The Making of Britain: Echoes of Greatness*, 1988, Basingstoke, Channel Four/Macmillan. Stephen Brooke's *Labour's War: The Labour Party During the Second World War*, 1992, Oxford, Clarendon Press, also questions the existence of consensus in the wartme Coalition government.

3. Addison, 'The Road from 1945', p. 6.

4. In some contrast to the 1945 contest of which the *Evening Standard*'s Charles Wintour said that 'real hatred and venom were abroad'. See Kenneth O. Morgan, *Labour in Power, 1945–1951*, 1984, Oxford, Clarendon Press, p. 485.

5. While, inevitably, elections generate a good deal of oppositional rhetoric, the Conservative Research Department had been preparing for a more interventionist role in economy and society since, at least, the early 1940s. Policy documents like Macmillan's 'Industrial Charter' spoke, for example, of the need 'to convince the great postwar electorate that we accepted the need for full employment and the welfare state'. See Seldon, 1981, p. 422.

6. Contemporaries certainly noted these similarities with Labour's 'golden age'. See Donald Chapman, 'What Prospect for the Labour Party?', *Political Quarterly* 25, 1954; Samuel Beer, 'The Future of British Politics: An American View', *Political Quarterly* 26, 1955.

7. Seldon, 1981, p. 165.

8. Philip Williams, *Hugh Gaitskell*, 1979, London, Jonathan Cape, pp. 312–18 for a discussion of 'Butskellism'. Kenneth O. Morgan also challenges the accuracy of the depiction in *The People's Peace: British History 1945–1989*, 1990, Oxford, Oxford University Press, pp. 118–19.

9. C.A.R. Crosland, *The Future of Socialism*, London, Jonathan Cape, 1956, p. 517; Janet Morgan, ed., *The Backbench Diaries of Richard Crossman*, 1981, London, Hamish Hamilton and Jonathan Cape, 1981, p. 437.

10. Morgan, 1990, p. 123.

11. John Barnes, 'From Eden to Macmillan, 1955–1959', in Hennessy and Seldon, 1988, p. 137.

12. The emergence of welfare states in Western Europe and the particular social, economic and political factors which gave rise to them are discussed by Gosta Esping-Andersen, *The Three Worlds of Welfare Capitalism*, 1990, Cambridge, Polity; Peter Baldwin, *The Politics of Social Solidarity*, 1990, Cambridge, Cambridge University Press, and by a variety of authors in Peter Flora, ed., *Growth to Limits: The Western European Welfare States Since World War Two*, 1986, Berlin, De Gruyter.

13. Thomas, Balogh, *The Dollar Crisis: Causes and Cures*, 1949, Oxford, Basil Blackwell, p. xxxvii.
14. Brooke, 1992, pp. 9–10.
15. *Ibid.*, p. 342.
16. Rodney Lowe, *The Welfare State in Britain Since 1945*, 1993, Basingstoke, Macmillan, pp. 247–48.
17. For instance, Butler's desire to float the pound in early 1952, attacked by Lord Cherwell, Eden and others on the grounds of the social dislocation such a policy could cause. The resignation of the Thorneycroft Treasury team in the wake of the Cabinet's failure to support a deflationary package to contain rising inflation in January 1958 stands as the best example of an attempt to steer a Conservative government in the direction of avowedly free market policies.
18. Enoch Powell, 'Conservatives and Social Services', *Political Quarterly* 24, 1953, claimed that it was inaccurate to assume that rank-and-file Toryism welcomed the system of state welfare that had emerged in Britain during the twentieth century and which had reached its apogee in the creation of the 'welfare state' in the late 1940s.
19. Ian Macleod and Enoch Powell, 'Social Services: Needs and Means', 1952, London, Conservative Political Centre.
20. Nicholas Ellison, *Egalitarian Thought and Labour Politics: Retreating Visions*, 1994, London, Routledge, ch. 1.
21. Dalton's influence in the creation of a number of NEC policy committees is discussed by Ben Pimlott, *Hugh Dalton*, 1985, London, Jonathan Cape, pp. 212–24.
22. See Douglas Jay, *The Socialist Case*, 1937, London, Faber and Faber.
23. E.F.M. Durbin, *The Politics of Democratic Socialism*, 1940, London, Routledge and Kegan Paul, p. 306.
24. *Labour Party Annual Conference Report* (hereafter *LPAC*), 1937, p. 83.
25. *Ibid.*, p. 181.
26. Bevan's anxiety about the Beveridge proposals stemmed from his fear that an insurance system would simply mean that the working class would effectively pay for its own benefits.
27. For example, the famous debate at the 1944 Party conference. See *LPAC*, 1944, pp. 161–3.
28. For Durbin's intellectual progress during the war, see Brooke, 1992, pp. 250–1.
29. C.A.R. Crosland, *The Future of Socialism*, 1956, London, Jonathan Cape, p. 115.
30. J.P.W. Mallalieu, *Tribune*, 4 April 1952.
31. Ellison, 1994, ch. 3.
32. *Tribune*, 13 June 1952. Other leading Tribunites such as Michael Foot, Barbara Castle or Jennie Lee, echoed these sentiments in countless *Tribune* columns and elsewhere; see, for example, Castle, *Forward*, 31 August 1956; Lee, *Tribune*, 22 November 1957; Foot, *Tribune*, 27 March 1959.
33. *New Statesman*, 19 December 1953, pp. 784–6.
34. Balogh and Crossman were particularly worried about this prospect. See R.H.S. Crossman, 'The Affluent Society', in *Planning for Freedom*, 1965, London, Hamish Hamilton, pp. 97–8.

35. Crosland, writing in 1950, claimed that nationalisation continued to have a role to play in Labour Party policy because of its capacity to influence the redistribution of wealth. *Socialist Commentary*, February 1950, p. 30.

36. C.A.R. Crosland, 'The Transition from Capitalism', in R.H.S. Crossman, ed., *New Fabian Essays*, 1952, London, Turnstile.

37. Crosland, 1956, p. 63.

38. This much was clear from the policy statement *Towards Equality*, 1956, London, Labour Party, the product of the heavily Gaitskellite Study Group on Equality, set up by Gaitskell after his leadership victory in 1955.

39. See R.M. Titmuss, *Problems of Social Policy*, 1950, London, HMSO.

40. R.M. Titmuss, 'The Social Division of Welfare', reprinted in *Essays on the Welfare State*, 1963, London, Allen and Unwin.

41. Peter Townsend, 'A Society for All', in Norman MacKenzie, ed., *Conviction*, 1958, London, MacGibbon Kee, p. 120.

42. *LPAC*, 1955, p. 96.

43. Crossman's comic account of this episode is contained in R.H.S. Crossman, *The Politics of Pensions*, 1972, Liverpool, Liverpool University Press.

44. The ideas were initially published by Abel-Smith in *The Reform of Social Security*, Fabian Research Series, 161, 1953, London, Fabian Society.

45. See Barbara Castle, *Tribune*, 19 September, 1958.

46. *LPAC*, 1955, p. 202.

47. See Titmuss's verbal contribution to the Study Group on Security in Old Age on 27 June 1956. Labour Party Archives, Box 28.

48. R.M. Titmuss, 'The Irresponsible Society', in Titmuss, 1963, p. 243.

49. At a meeting of the Study Group on Security in Old Age, 4 July 1956. Labour Party Archives, Box 28.

50. Morgan, 1981, p. 763.

51. Crossman claimed that over a period of time, inflation would erode the value of the pension, meaning that contributors would actually receive less in real terms than they had paid in – see *ibid.*, p. 625.

52. *Ibid.*, pp. 736–8. See also *Hansard*, 5th series, 1 December 1958, 598:994ff.

53. Churchill's first Education Minister, Florence Horsbrugh, did not get a Cabinet seat until 1953 and the education budget was not expanded during the first three years of the government.

54. Seldon, 1981, pp. 274–9.

55. The Spens Report (1938) and, more infamously, the Norwood Report (1943) had endorsed the tripartite system on the grounds that intelligence could be accurately measured and children allocated to the schools most appropriate to their intellectual capacities.

56. Victory for Socialism [hereafter VFS], *Equality in Education*, 1958, p. 4. The sentiments expressed in the pamphlet were echoed in speeches by left-wingers during the debate on Labour's education policy statement, *Learning to Live* at the 1958 Party conference. See, for example, Tam Dalyel's speech, *LPAC*, 1958, p. 96.

57. VFS, 1958, p. 4.

58. Crosland's was a notable exception to the Gaitskellite norm of caution in education policy. See Crosland, 1956, pp. 275–6.

59. Douglas Jay, *Socialism in the New Society*, 1962, London, Longman, p. 247.

60. Roy Jenkins, *The Labour Case*, 1959, Harmondsworth, Penguin, pp. 98–9.

61.   Quoted in Williams, 1979, p. 466.
62.   Philip Williams, ed., *The Diary of Hugh Gaitskell, 1945–1956*, 1983, London, Jonathan Cape, p. 328.
63.   *LPAC*, 1958, p. 88.
64.   The White Paper admitted that pupils were receiving education in schools that differed widely in quality but nevertheless the Conservatives remained committed to 'a substantial element of selection'.
65.   *Hansard,* 5th series, 27 November 1958 598:537.
66.   *Ibid.*, 26 November1958 598:462–3.
67.   *Ibid.*, 27 November 1958 598:527–8; see also Griffiths' contribution to *Learning to Live* debate, *LPAC*, 1958, p. 88.
68.   Margaret Cole, 'Memo on LP Policy for Education', Re 161, May 1957, p. 7. These sentiments had already been expressed in Labour's policy statement *Towards Equality*, published in 1956 (see p. 6).
69.   The statement actually said that little could be done about the private sector in the first ten years of a Labour government – which angered left-wingers like Jennie Lee.
70.   See the debate on *Challenge to Britain*, *LPAC*, 1953, pp. 173–4.
71.   VFS, 1958, p. 10.
72.   *Ibid.*, p. 11.
73.   *Tribune,* 7 January 1955.
74.   R.H.S. Crossman, 'Suggested Framework for a Section of the Education Policy Statement Dealing with the Private Sector', Re 240, November 1957, p. 1. Study Group on Education, Box 32, Labour Party Archives.
75.   R.H.S. Crossman, 'Some Notes in Elite Education with Special Reference to the Problem of Universities', Re 211, October 1957, p. 3. Study Group on Education, Box 32, Labour Party Archives.
76.   Crossman, Re 211, pp. 4–5.
77.   Brian Abel-Smith, 'Educational Maintenance Allowances', Re 224, November 1957, pp. 4–5. Education Study Group, Box 32, Labour Party Archives.
78.   Williams, 1979, p. 468.
79.   See Jay, 1962, p. 250; Jenkins, 1959, p. 87.
80.   See Crosland, 1952, pp. 275–6. He argued that a weighted version of Fleming should be implemented with places not allocated to the brightest but to 'a wide cross-section' of the population. The point was pursued by Tawney in one of the last pieces he did for the Party before his death. See T.H. Tawney, 'Memorandum on "Public" and Other Independent Schools', Re 238, November 1957, p. 2.
81.   See Alice Bacon's speech at *LPAC*, 1958, p. 110.
82.   Final Statement of the Education Study Group, Re 369, pp. 29–31. Following a proposal from Tawney, the Party suggested that a Commission might be set up to examine the issue of the public schools.
83.   As Alice Bacon put it to the 1958 conference, 'let us not forget that there is as much inequality within the State system of education as there is between the State system and the private system ... . There is even a great deal of inequality between one local authority and another...the next Minister of Education has a real job of work to do in evening out these inequalities within the State system.' *LPAC*, 1958, p. 111.

84.   These issues are discussed by, *inter alia*, David Harvey, *The Condition of Postmodernity*, 1989, Oxford, Blackwell; Scott Lash and John Urry, *The End of Organised Capitalism*, 1987, Cambridge, Polity.

85.   Eric Hobsbawm, *Age of Extremes: The Short Twentieth Century, 1914–1991*, 1994, London, Michael Joseph, p. 255.

3 'Not Reformed Capitalism, But ... Democratic Socialism':[1] The Ideology of the Labour Leadership, 1945–1951

Martin Francis

The Labour Party's leadership in the 1940s, in contrast to its successors in the 1980s and 1990s, never felt self-conscious or embarrassed about seeing the label 'socialist' applied to their policies. Indeed, the 1945 Labour manifesto, *Let Us Face the Future*, explicitly informed the electorate that the Party's ultimate purpose was 'the establishment of a Socialist Commonwealth of Great Britain – free, democratic, efficient, progressive, public-spirited, its material resources organised in the service of the British people.'[2] But did such statements reflect a wholehearted desire by the Labour government of 1945–51 to transform British society along fundamentally socialist lines? Or were they merely a rhetorical ornament, intended to hide the leadership's essential opportunism from a much more radically inclined rank and file? Paul Smith once argued that Disraeli's political ideas 'were not the motive force of his performance, but rather the costume which he wore in deference to the susceptibilities of his audience'.[3] Many authorities would conclude that a similar characterisation should be applied to the Attlee government which, they argue (especially after the crises of 1947) eagerly embraced a cross-party consensus constructed along lines dictated by Beveridge and Keynes.[4]

The failure of the existing literature to take Labour's postwar socialism seriously reflects an unwillingness to analyse the relationship between the governments' policies and Labour's ideology. Too many studies of the Attlee years reflect the continued, if diminishing, myths about the uni-ideological nature of British political culture and the tendency to 'write history with the ideas left out'.[5] Moreover, many historians have been over-reliant on the official government records deposited at the Public Record Office. Such records are obviously vital to an understanding of government policy and decision-making, but civil service notions of continuity have meant that the records of discussions at both Cabinet and ministerial level have frequently been denuded of any explicitly socialist content. The partisan nature of Labour's policies is much more obvious if the wider hinterland of the governments' policy-making is restored – in particular, the memoranda and minutes of the NEC's Policy Committee, the Party's Research Department and of independent bodies such as the Fabian Society. If the ideological dimension to the governments' policies is given fuller appreciation, it becomes more obvious that Labour ministers frequently applied specifically socialist precepts to the exercise of power. Of course, it has to be conceded that this statement can be applied to some ministers much more easily than to others, and that to some it cannot be applied at all. *Let Us Face the Future* claimed that 'the Labour Party is a Socialist Party, and proud of it'.[6] In fact, it would have been more accurate to have said that the Labour Party was not so much a socialist party, as a party which contained socialists. For despite the apparent adoption of a 'socialist objective' in the 1918 constitution, the Party in the 1940s effectively remained the 'federal alliance' between socialists and trade unionists which had been created in 1900.

And of course, the character of Labour's policies was not exclusively dictated by ideological considerations. Like any other government, the Attlee administration had to take many decisions for purely pragmatic and administrative reasons and address issues that were wholly unrelated to questions of political philosophy. Moreover, the relationship between government policy and socialist ideas was consistently framed, and occasionally circumscribed, by a number of structural constraints. The most obvious of these constraints was Britain's precarious economic situation, but recent research has added the persistent hostility of business leaders and a vigorous opposition from the Conservatives in parliament and local government.[7] It should also be made clear that such claims for the essentially non-consensual nature of the Attlee governments' policies are based on an assessment of their domestic programme. When it came to foreign affairs, the government believed that this was an area of policy which was largely at the mercy of outside developments, and so it would be impossible to sustain a distinctly socialist approach. This belief formed the basis of Bevin's policy at the Foreign Office, and was developed at a more theoretical level in the writings of the head of the Party's International Department, Denis Healey.[8]

Nevertheless, while the above qualifications should always be borne in mind, it can still be confidently asserted that in many key areas the governments' policy was moulded, not by pragmatism and expediency, but by the dictates of socialist ideology. Labour ministers offered a variety of definitions of what they meant by 'socialism'. In 1949 Bevan defined socialism as 'the language of priorities', while in 1950 Morrison argued that it meant 'the assertion of social responsibility for matters which are properly of social concern'. However, that there was a broad consensus in the Party about what socialism entailed is evident from the 1949 policy statement *Labour Believes in Britain*, which was accepted by both the NEC and party conference. This policy statement insisted that Labour's socialism was based on four basic principles: the pursuit of equality, the transfer of economic power to the nation through public ownership and physical planning, the release of productive capacities which had been constrained under capitalism, and the compatibility of the Party's objectives with Britain's democratic traditions. *Labour Believes in Britain* also reflected Labour's belief that socialism should be concerned with individual moral transformation, with improving the 'quality of life' in its widest sense, not merely with questions of material improvement and economic power.[9] These specifically socialist principles underpinned a range of Labour's policies in the 1945–51 period.

Recent research would suggest that this claim is certainly justified in the field of macroeconomic policy. It is true that after the economic crises of 1947, the Labour government increasingly utilised Keynesian expedients, in particular influencing the level of demand through the budget. However, this did not represent a straightforward abandonment of socialist planning in favour of the politically neutral, or indeed potentially anti-socialist, creed of demand management. For up to 1951 planning through the price mechanism was still supplemented by the more specifically socialist expedient of physical controls. As Rollings has demonstrated, despite the 'bonfire of controls' of 1948, leading Ministers, such as Morrison, Gaitskell and Wilson, frequently reiterated their belief that planning by means of fiscal techniques would have to be supplemented by a minimum number of permanent controls.[10] The minutes of the Cabinet's Economic Planning Committee on 19 January 1950 were explicit that the consensus among senior ministers was that, so long as full employment was maintained, 'controls were inevitable'.[11] Labour's positive valuation of controls is given added significance when it is juxtaposed with the Conservatives' professed desire to 'set the people free', and their deliberate exploitation of growing public discontent with rationing, shortages and unnecessary bureaucratic interference.[12] However, Labour's desire to invest their policies with a specifically socialist character was not confined only to economic planning. It can also be seen in a number of other policy areas, which will be discussed in the brief survey which follows. These areas include public ownership, health and education.

Herbert Morrison, speaking to the party conference on the eve of the 1945 general election, argued that 'the real controversy and the real fight between the Labour Party and its Conservative opponents will be as regards ... the future of British industry .... You cannot get a quart of socialist prosperity out of a miserable pint capitalist pot.'[13] These words implied that Labour had a distinctive policy towards industry, one which could be easily differentiated from that of their opponents. This distinctive element was to be the advocacy of the public ownership of key industries and services. Indeed *Let Us Face the Future* presented nationalisation as central to Labour's attempt to rebuild Britain on socialist lines, proposing to transfer to state ownership coal, cable and wireless, gas, electricity, the Bank of England, civil aviation, road transport, railways and steel. Those who endorse the consensus model have been unimpressed by this dramatic commitment to extend the public sector in Britain to around 20 per cent of the total economy. They point to the fact that in subsequent general elections, Labour's nationalisation programme was much more modest. The so-called 'shopping list' of industries and services for which nationalisation was proposed in the 1950 manifesto was much smaller, and included far fewer key points in the economy, than its 1945 counterpart, listing as it did merely water supply, cement, meat, sugar refining and industrial insurance. The 1951 manifesto made no explicit public ownership pledges at all.[14] Advocates of consensus also point out that Conservative opposition to many of Labour's nationalisation measures was half-hearted and ineffectual, and that, on their return to office in 1951, they were content to restore only two industries – road haulage and steel – to private ownership.[15]

There certainly was a relative downgrading of public ownership in Labour's programme by the end of the decade. This was partly the result of concern that further substantial waves of nationalisation might prove to be a vote loser or might prejudice continued military and economic assistance from the United States. It also reflected a lack of enthusiasm for nationalisation among trade union leaders in the major industries which were still in the private sector.[16] Nor can the influence of Keynesianism be ignored here. Even the relatively modest utilisation of demand management undertaken after 1947 seemed to demonstrate that many of Labour's long-cherished objectives, especially full employment, were less dependent on nationalisation than had once been thought. However it is unwise to exaggerate the potency of this Keynesian challenge. Those figures in the government, notably Gaitskell, who are seen as being most comfortable with the new budgetary approach to economic planning, felt nationalisation of key industries could still play a critical role in the coordination and control of production, distribution, investment and pricing policy. Gaitskell would also have been receptive to the insistence of his close friend, Evan Durbin, that public ownership was a vital means of improving labour relations in many industries.[17] Not surprisingly, a continued commitment to nationalisation is even more evident among the older generation of ministers – Dalton, Attlee, Bevan and even Morrison. Morrison's notion of 'consolidation', to which the government subscribed after 1947, was intended to allow the government to take stock: to consider ways of improving the efficiency of, and the scope for increased participation by producers and consumers in, the newly nationalised industries.[18] It did not imply a permanent retreat from public ownership, as Labour's renewed extension of the state sector in the 1960s and 1970s was to show. The relative absence of further nationalisation measures in the 1950 and 1951 manifestos needs to be set against the way the official party policy statements, *Labour Believes in Britain* (1949) and *Labour and the New Society* (1950), still credited the public ownership programme of 1945 with making a decisive contribution to Labour's postwar achievement.[19]

Nor should too much be made of the Conservatives' failure to reverse the bulk of Labour's nationalisation measures after 1951. For although public ownership *per se* was not an ideological line of demarcation between the two parties, the Conservatives and Labour perceived nationalisation in very different ways. For while the former identified it as a tactical expedient for one or two crisis-ridden industries, the latter saw it as a superior form of economic organisation. This fundamental difference has been partly obscured by the way Labour's nationalisation programme was presented in 1945. The justification for each of the individual acts of public ownership specified in *Let Us Face the Future* were all based, not on the need to redistribute economic power so as to secure social justice, but on the need to promote greater economic efficiency. For example, coal nationalisation would 'bring great economies in operation and make it possible to modernise production methods', while the takeover of gas and electricity would 'prevent competitive waste, open the way for coordinated research and development, and lead to the reforming of uneconomic areas of distribution'.[20] When, in 1948–9, the Labour leadership began to draw up a programme for the next general election, many industries – including Unilever, oil distribution, the motor industry and aircraft manufacture – were rejected as potential candidates for nationalisation simply because they could not be proved to be inefficient under private ownership. A document drawn up in the Party's Research Department in

November 1946 identified the 'criteria for nationalisation' as facilitating new investment, improving management and allowing greater co-ordination.[21]

This essentially technical case for public ownership obviously seems much less partisan and much more consensual than blood-curdling cries about seizing the 'commanding heights of the economy'. However, it would be extremely misguided to interpret it as an abandonment of social-ism in favour of pragmatism. Labour's case for state ownership of industry had always rested as much on increased efficiency as on social justice, drawing as it did on three different traditions of British socialism: the ethical prerogatives of the ILP, a (well-diluted) Marxist appreciation of the nature of economic power and the technocratic priorities of the Fabians.[22] The Fabian influence on Labour's justification for public ownership is obvious in the implication in *Let Us Face the Future* that nation-alisation was essential to secure the necessary modernisation and rationalisation of British industry which private ownership had apparently failed to accomplish. This was a claim that very few Conservatives, and their allies in the business community, would have been willing to endorse.[23]

Moreover, Labour had no desire to express its motives for nationalisa-tion exclusively in terms of the promotion of greater economic efficiency. For while *Let Us Face the Future* might have justified the nationalisation of individual industries or services in terms of promoting economic efficiency, its uncompromising tone and the extensive list of industries it singled out for takeover reflected an alternative motive for public owner-ship: the redistribution of power, both within industry and in society as a whole. In 1951 John Strachey, the Marxist theorist turned government minister, argued that nationalisation played a critical role in Labour's efforts to narrow the gap between rich and poor. For although it was true that the compensation of former shareholders meant that nationalisation would not abolish large unearned incomes, by reducing step by step the amount of industry in private hands, it 'progressively dries up the source of unearned income'. Further, 'the redistribution of the national income, without any extension of public ownership, would have been merely a measure of social reform, of patching up the existing capitalist structure while in no way altering the structure itself'. Strachey concluded that the redistribution of wealth and power was

the real point of nationalisation; we betray the whole tradition of our Movement if we ever forget it. And we do sometimes forget it. We sometimes let people get away with the suggestion that after all, the only possible reason for nationalising an industry is if it can be proved that its efficiency will increase.[24]

Strachey did not elaborate further on which 'people' he had in mind here. If he was talking about the party leadership he was being extremely unfair, since they certainly had no desire to 'get away' with only stating the 'efficiency' justification for nationalisation. *Labour and the New Society* in 1950 emphasised that nationalisation was 'a way of dealing with industries in which inefficiency persists and where the private owners lack either the will or the capacity to make improvements'. However the statement also contained a long passage relating public ownership to the achievement of social justice and the redistribution of power:

> Big business men ... bankers and merchants directed the economic life of the nation .... The whole nation was imperilled by private control of the economy .... Therefore the public will must be supreme .... Public ownership is the most effective way of public control because it makes industry directly accountable to the people.[25]

Crucially, the inclusion of the public ownership of iron and steel in Labour's 1945 programme made it ultimately impossible for Labour (even if it had wanted to) to discuss nationalisation in terms that excluded its contribution to the redistribution of power. For the Attlee government knew that the steel industry under private ownership could not easily be condemned as inefficient. This had not stopped the 1945 manifesto from trying, for the takeover of the steel industry was presented there as an antidote to the way private monopoly had 'kept inefficient high-cost plants in existence'.[26] But Labour acknowledged that the productive performance of the industry, both during the war and (after 1946) under the Iron and Steel Control Board, had been quite impressive, and its expansive character had been symbolised by the opening of a new plant at Port Talbot. As *Tribune* pointed out in 1947, 'unfortunately the "efficiency argument" has provided the opponents of nationalisation with some apparently plausible retorts'. For although the industry 'may have been inefficient in the past ... it is so no longer'. *Tribune* concluded that the government would be more likely to win over public opinion if it simply argued that the steel industry in its present form 'continues to represent a dangerous and undemocratic concentration of economic power in private hands'.[27]

This judgement was not confined to the Party's left wing. *Socialist Commentary* asserted that the efficiency argument provided a case for rationalisation, not nationalisation, and that the real justification for a change in ownership was 'the issue of power. Steel represents the largest concentration of power in the economic system.'[28] Indeed, this was the case made by those ministers (most notably Bevan and Dalton, and to a lesser extent Cripps) who pressurised their somewhat reluctant colleagues into maintaining the government's commitment to nationalise steel. The Cabinet's eventual decision to press ahead was influenced by a number of considerations, including the industry's importance to the export drive and the need to retain electoral credibility.[29] However George Strauss, the Minister of Supply, chose to introduce the Steel Bill to the Commons as a 'great reform [which] removes from the private sector of our economy to the public the industry which is the citadel of British capitalism. It transfers to Parliament and the community the power to dominate the economic life of this country which now resides with the steelmasters at Steel House.'[30] With a substantial portion of party opinion believing 'steel is power', and with the government ultimately upholding its commitment to nationalise the industry, it would have proved impossible for the Labour leadership to present the public ownership programme as a whole as merely a technical exercise in rationalising and modernising a number of failing industries. In fact, given that the rhetoric of Strachey and Strauss was far from uncommon among ministers, it is extremely unlikely that the government had even the slightest intention of neglecting the ethical and political, as opposed to the merely economic, motives for nationalisation.

Labour's decidedly non-consensual approach to the pursuit of social justice was even more evident in taxation policy, where the government had a consistent commitment to reducing inequalities of both income and capital. In 1946, Hugh Dalton promised a Fabian audience that 'in the course of the next five years ... we are going to do a lot of equalising.'[31] Hugh Gaitskell told the 1951 Trades Union Congress, 'I am a Socialist and have been for the past 25 years, because I want a much fairer distribution of wealth and income, because I want the class structure to progressively disappear.'[32] During the war there had been a dramatic increase in, and a steepening of the gradient of, income tax. The Attlee government retained this steeply progressive tax structure after 1945. In 1949–50 the income and surtax structure was much more progressive than it had been in 1938, although income tax concessions between 1945 and 1950 meant it was slightly less progressive than it had been at the end of the war.[33] Labour Chancellors increased the tax burden on the wealthy to even higher levels than had obtained during the war. In Dalton's first budget, although the rate of income tax was cut to 9 shillings in the pound, surtax was increased on all incomes over £2500 p.a. On incomes over £20 000 the rate went up from 9s 6d to 10s 6d in the pound. When this was added

to the 9s in the pound income tax, the total tax paid on these high incomes
had risen to 19s 6d in the pound. In 1955, Rogow and Shore concluded
that Labour had effectively imposed a ceiling on post-tax incomes of little
more than £6000.[34] Dalton also attempted to ensure his income tax structure would shift the burden from 'the poorer to the richer' by raising the
income tax exemption level, thereby removing around three million of the
poorest from liability. This progressive income tax structure remained a
key feature of the Attlee years, despite the preference expressed by Dalton
(who hoped 'Philip Snowden does not turn in his grave') and his successors for indirect over direct taxes.[35] There was nothing remotely consensual about such redistributive policies, despite the fact that they had
been initiated by the wartime Coalition. The Conservatives were pledged
in 1945 to make 'an early reduction in taxation', and Labour was
definitely breaking with precedent in continuing wartime tax levels into
peacetime; this had certainly not happened after the Napoleonic, Crimean
or First World Wars.[36]

Indeed Labour's income tax policies were so progressive that by the end
of the decade it was widely accepted that the limits of income redistribution
had now been reached. As early as December 1946, Christopher Mayhew
was arguing that the scope for raising the lowest incomes by reducing the
highest was very small. For even if the government, 'in a burst of class
consciousness', decreed a maximum net income of £1000 for everyone,
and distributed the surplus of incomes above this level to wage earners,
less than 5 per cent would be added to wages. Similar assertions were made
by Roy Jenkins and James Callaghan in the years which followed.[37] Some
government statements seemed to suggest that the only solution to this
problem was the creation of more distributable wealth. Cripps stressed that
any further redistribution of income would have to await a general increase
in productivity and export levels. Until then, there was 'only a certain sized
cake to be divided up'.[38] However, others argued that, since the limits of
income redistribution had been reached, the next step should be to tackle
the unequal distribution of property which had produced the inequality of
income in the first place. *Socialist Commentary* declared in June 1951 that
'we have moved a long way towards levelling incomes, but steps to ensure
a fairer distribution of property are essential for any further advance
towards the equality of opportunity which is basic to socialism.'[39]

Such pleas did not go unanswered, and Labour's leadership did give
some serious attention to the redistribution of property. In the 1930s
Dalton had declared that the 'limitation of inherited wealth is the principal
gateway' through which Labour's attack must pass if it was 'to carry the
inner citadel of capitalism'.[40] In his April 1946 budget, Dalton attempted

to rationalise the incidence of death duties, which had remained largely unchanged since they were first imposed by Harcourt in 1894. Some smaller estates were exempted from estate duty, while the rates on those estate between £2000 and £7500 were lowered. However the rate of duty on estates over £12 500 was sharpened, with the maximum rate on the largest estates rising from 65 to 75 per cent.[41] This attack on inherited wealth continued under Cripps, who raised the highest rate of duty to 80 per cent. Both the government and its supporters were aware that death duties could never be the ultimate solution to the unequal distribution of property. As Roy Jenkins pointed out, they only brought benefits over a period of 30 or 40 years, since only a handful of rich people died in a single year.[42] One alternative was a capital gains tax, which was certainly being given serious consideration by Gaitskell in his final months at the Treasury in 1951.[43] Indeed, Labour's election manifesto in 1951 promised that Labour would 'take measures to prevent large capital gains', although it gave no specific details on how this might be accomplished.[44]

The Labour leadership were also giving serious consideration in 1950–1 to the introduction of a capital levy, at least as a long-term policy. Many in the Party had had their appetites whetted by the mild form of capital levy introduced in Cripps' April 1948 budget: the so-called once-and-for-all 'Special Contribution', levied from investment incomes of over £2000. Michael Foot and Richard Crossman both demanded the imposition of a capital levy in Parliament in 1950, while the following year Roy Jenkins produced a detailed plan of how such a levy could be put together.[45] That such demands were received sympathetically by some of the Party's leading policy-makers is evident from the NEC's approval in June 1951 of a Research Department memorandum, 'The Distribution of Income and Wealth', which came out strongly in favour of a capital levy.[46] The capital levy was a radical measure, which even a Labour government with a renewed electoral mandate might have baulked at. Nevertheless, although such a levy was not specifically referred to in the October 1951 manifesto, a promise was included that Labour would 'increase taxation on the small minority who own great fortunes and large unearned incomes'.[47] When Labour left office it had, in Roy Jenkins' words, 'hardly yet scratched the surface' of the maldistribution of property. Even the 1951 manifesto conceded that 'half of Britain's wealth is still owned by one per cent of the population'.[48] However, Labour was clearly aware of this problem and was beginning to take steps to remedy it. It has often been stated that in the late 1950s, Crosland and Gaitskell attempted to redefine socialism in terms of the notion of 'equality'.[49] In fact, the amount of attention given to the redistribution of capital in the last months in power demonstrates that even before 1951 many figures in the Party had already placed the pursuit of equality at the forefront of Labour's objectives.

The egalitarian motif is also evident in the establishment of the National Health Service. The NHS's leading historian has argued that, while Labour never sought a consensual line on health, its attempt to implement specifically socialist policies was checked by the medical profession, who exacted significant concessions from the Minister of Health. Bevan allowed GPs in the new state service to retain private patients, agreed to the presence of pay beds in NHS hospitals, dropped his initial insistence that doctors should be paid entirely by salary and failed to promote the cause of the local health centre, which had promised to substitute cooperation for competition among doctors. As a result, 'the policies for socialized medicine evolved by the Labour Party over three decades were abandoned to such an extent that the NHS was reduced to an empty shell. Although for the sake of pride formally represented as a socialist measure, in reality the NHS had become the captive of corporate interests.'[50] Certainly, the left-wing pressure group, the Socialist Medical Association, expressed disappointment over the shape of the new service,[51] but they were an uninfluential fringe of Labour opinion, increasingly discredited by their long-standing links with the Communist Party. The rest of the Party accepted that, even though concessions had been made in some areas, Bevan's new service contained a number of features which were held to be distinctly socialist.

Bevan's decision to create a unified state hospital service by means of the nationalisation of both voluntary and local authority was welcomed as a sign that the NHS would mark a new order in health: as he told Parliament in April 1946, no longer would the standard of health care received depend on whether one lived in a wealthy or a poor local authority. How far such a genuine equalisation of services was ever practicable is open to question, but this was a concern few raised at the time.[52] The main objection to nationalisation came from those, notably Morrison, who were concerned about the negative effect the disappearance of municipal hospitals would have on local democracy.[53] However, these fears were offset by the expectation that the disappearance of voluntary hospitals would banish the stigma of charity and remove from the Conservatives what Bevan termed an important source of 'political and social patronage'.[54] The nationalisation of hospitals was welcomed by the Party as a radical step, effecting a high degree of direct ownership and employment by public bodies in the social field to parallel that taking place in the industrial sphere.

Moreover just as industry, both publicly and privately owned, was ostensibly subject to centralised 'planning', instead of being allowed to respond solely to the pull of the market, health care too would be properly planned. This was most obviously seen in the way doctors were to be subject to 'negative direction', under which they could be refused permission to set up practice in an already over-doctored area. This parallel between industrial and health policy was stated by both Bevan and Arthur Woodburn, responsible for the health service in Scotland, in Parliament.[55] In fact, taking the NHS as a whole, government planning of health care provision proved to be just as uneven and inconclusive as it had been in regard to industry. But the implementation of 'negative direction' did hold out the promise of the reconstruction of health care along more scientific and rational lines. It also raised the hackles of the Conservatives, who opposed the exclusion (made on the grounds that these areas were already adequately catered for) of GPs from the south coast resorts to which many people moved in their old age.[56] The Conservatives were also opposed to Bevan's decision to prohibit the buying and selling of practices in the NHS. As with the nationalisation of hospitals, this decision broke with any wartime consensus. For in May 1945 Bevan's Coalition predecessor, Henry Willink, had announced that the sale of goodwill would not be abolished in the short term.[57] Bevan partly justified the measure in terms of its contribution to the direction of GPs, but he added an ethical motive, criticising what he felt had been 'tantamount to the sale and purchase of patients'.[58] Arthur Greenwood welcomed the end to a situation which was reminiscent of 'hucksters in the market place', and Bevan was certainly not offended when the BMA accused him of running a 'Ministry of Morals'.[59]

Even Bevan's critics in the SMA had to concede that, whatever concessions he might have made, he had succeeded in ensuring that the new service was based on 'free access', and had thus satisfied the most important socialist maxim of all: that health care should be geared to need rather than to means.[60] What particularly impressed contemporaries was the range of free services: not just hospital and GP services, but supplementary services such as dental and ophthalmic care. At this stage, charges were effectively restricted to minor services such as home helps. Attlee's press secretary described the NHS as a 'significant pointer to the new pattern of society which is coming into existence ... in which, although some differences in income will continue, such differences will no longer be a factor in determining claims on essentials.'[61] Bevan himself went further and argued that the NHS could make an important contribution to the redistribution of income, because (in contrast to national insurance) it was not based on contributions, but was paid for out of general taxation.[62]

Bevan not merely sought to establish a free health service which would be available to all; he also wanted to make the best possible service available to all. He insisted that the poor had a right to expect the same quality of life as the better-off, even if they lacked the purchasing power which a free market economy would have regarded as essential to support such a standard of living. To ensure the highest quality service in the NHS it would be necessary to have the top doctors at least partly inside the service, and this was why Bevan made the concession to allow NHS doctors to retain private patients.[63] The Minister of Health's emphasis on high quality social services is also evident in his housing policy. Bevan insisted that new council houses should be buildings of a much higher standard and placed in a much more salubrious environment than had previously been required for municipal housing. The spaciousness of Bevan's council houses – he proposed that a three-bedroomed house should be in the order of 900–50 square feet – exceeded even the recommendation of the 1944 Dudley Committee, seen at the time as unprecedented in its generosity on the question of size.[64] Such insistence on quality would certainly not have been a priority for a Conservative Minister. Opposition spokesmen (and indeed some of Bevan's Cabinet colleagues) demanded that quality be sacrificed in order to speed up completion rates of council houses. Bevan replied that the lack of interest in quality shown by the Tories was a reflection of class bias, in that they were not concerned about the type of accommodation working-class people had to inhabit, since they would not have to live in it themselves.[65] The distinct lack of consensus such exchanges reflect was also evident in the ominous noises about the need to cut 'waste' in the social services, which were prominent in Conservative rhetoric in the 1950 and 1951 elections.[66]

There is one area of Labour's social policy where one might assume the case for consensus would prove more resilient. In health and housing the government could argue that the plans and blueprints of the wartime Coalition should in no way bind a government which had been elected in 1945 on a self-professed socialist programme. By contrast, in the field of education, the scope for moulding a social service in line with distinctly socialist requirements seemed much more limited. For in 1945 the legislative framework of Labour's education policy was already in place, in the form of the 1944 Butler Act. Indeed Labour's two postwar Education Ministers, Ellen Wilkinson and George Tomlinson, have frequently been censured for their failure to do little more than implement the 1944 Act, and in particular for their reluctance to challenge the assumption (implicit rather than explicit) in the Act that secondary schools should be organised on tripartite rather than comprehensive lines.[67] It is certainly true that, while both ministers considered setting up individual experimental comprehensive schools, they had no desire to see the establishment of a national comprehensive system. However, it seems unfair to place the responsibility for the failure to introduce comprehensive schooling in the immediate postwar years solely at the door of the government. Labour-controlled LEAs also had little enthusiasm for comprehensive schools, and by 1950 only 100 mixed ability schools had been proposed in the development plans forwarded to the Ministry of Education by local authorities.[68] If Wilkinson and Tomlinson had turned their back on a specifically Labour response to secondary education, then the vast majority of the Party in the country were willing to go along with them.

But had the two ministers in fact done any such thing? Their guilt is dependent on the assumption that only an education policy based on the comprehensive school has a right to be labelled 'socialist'. In fact, few in the Labour Party of the 1940s would have accepted such a premise. The implementation of the 1944 Act ensured the achievement of Tawney's 'free secondary education for all' and 'equality of educational opportunity'. For most sections of Labour opinion, these nostrums, rather than any vague concept of 'common schools for all', were felt to be the fundamental tenets of a socialist educational policy. What party members saw as a priority was making the provisions of the 1944 Act a working reality by ensuring an adequate supply of teachers and proper school buildings.[69] This approach did not imply the embrace of consensus. Labour convinced itself that it alone could be relied upon to fulfil the promises of the Butler Act, and that, if a Conservative government had been in power, the raising of the school leaving age to 15 would have suffered the same fate as the 'day continuation' clause of the 1918 Fisher Act.

If the extent of the influence of socialist ideas on education policy is not to be underestimated, it is important to avoid any tendency to view Labour's ideology in 1945–51 with the benefit of hindsight. It is necessary to appreciate the contemporary vitality of definitions of socialism which later generations were to find primitive and inadequate. In 1956 Crosland argued that 'equality of opportunity' was not the same thing as genuine equality, but was a 'limited goal', which was not, 'from a socialist point of view, sufficient'. For, there was a danger that 'under certain circumstances the creation of equal opportunities may merely serve to replace one remote elite (based on lineage) by a new one (based on ability and intelligence)'.[70] There was nothing dramatically novel about such an argument, and Crosland himself had made similar claims at the Fabian 'Problems Ahead' conferences in 1949–50.[71] However, for the vast majority of the party, Crosland's arguments had limited resonance in the years before 1951. Labour's attachment to tripartism in 1945–51 reflected a continued satisfaction with 'equality of opportunity'. Educational equality was perceived largely in terms of providing children from all social backgrounds with the same opportunities in the competitive system which had previously been monopolised by the middle classes. The abolition of fees under the 1944 Act would now allow the brightest boys and girls from working-class families to take advantage of a grammar school education.[72]

Far from pursuing the politics of consensus, in the areas of economic planning, public ownership, taxation, health, housing and education, the Attlee government invested its policies with a specifically socialist character. This was understood only too well by the Conservative opposition, which is why they responded with rage and hostility to so much of Labour's programme.[73] The essentially partisan nature of Labour's policies was also appreciated by supporters and opponents alike among the British public. The unprecedented levels of turnout in the 1950 and 1951 elections (84 and 82.5 per cent respectively) and the high membership levels of political parties in this period suggest that the electorate needed little convincing that which of the major parties was in power did matter.[74] Of course, Labour was keen to refute Conservative claims that their policies were alien or doctrinaire. They constantly reiterated their commitment to a democratic vision of socialism, which sought, in Morrison's words, 'to combine freedom with planning; liberty with order'.[75] However, they made no effort to deny that their programme was intended to serve as the first instalment in the transition to a future socialist society, albeit one which was compatible with, and indeed celebratory of, the British political tradition. As Attlee himself declared in his memoirs:

> The old pattern was worn out and it was for us to weave the new. Thus, the kind of reproach levelled at us by Churchill, that we were following a course dictated by social prejudice or theory, left us completely unmoved .... Our policy was not reformed capitalism, but progress toward a democratic socialism.[76]

NOTES

1. I would like to thank Paul Addison, Steven Fielding and Ina Zweiniger-Bargielowska for useful comments on an earlier draft of this paper.
2. F.W.S. Craig, ed., *British General Election Manifestos, 1918–1966*, 1970, Chichester, Political Reference Publications, p. 101.
3. P. Smith, *Disraelian Conservatism and Social Reform*, 1967, London, Routledge, p. 12.
4. See, for example, P. Addison, *The Road to 1945*, 1975, London, Jonathan Cape. Even those who have argued for a distinct lack of consensus during the war, have also claimed that there was a retreat from collectivism after

1947: K. Jefferys, *The Churchill Coalition and Wartime Politics, 1940–1945*, 1991, Manchester, Manchester University Press, pp. 214–16; S.J. Brooke, *Labour's War: the Labour Party During the Second World War*, 1992, Oxford, Oxford University Press, especially pp. 329–35; K.O. Morgan, *Labour in Power, 1945–1951*, 1984, Oxford, Oxford University Press, passim.

5. This phrase comes from P.F. Clarke, 'The Progressive Movement in England', *Transactions of the Royal Historical Society*, 5th series, 24, 1974, p. 159.

6. Craig, 1970, p. 101.

7. For example, the contributions to N. Tiratsoo, ed., *The Attlee Years*, 1991, London, Frances Pinter.

8. For example, Labour Party, *Cards on the Table*, 1948, London, Labour Party.

9. Labour Party, *Labour Believes in Britain*, 1949, London, Labour Party, pp. 3–4. For further elaboration of this definition, see M. Francis, 'Economics and Ethics: The Nature of Labour's Socialism, 1945–1951', *Twentieth Century British History*, 6, 2, 1995. See also, S. Fielding, 'Labourism in the 1940s', *Twentieth Century British History*, 3, 2, 1992, pp. 138–53.

10. N. Rollings, '"The Reichstag Method of Governing"?: The Attlee Governments and Permanent Economic Controls', in H. Mercer *et al.*, eds., *Labour Governments and Private Industry: The Experience of 1945–51*, 1992, Edinburgh, Edinburgh University Press, pp. 115–36.

11. Public Record Office [hereafter PRO], CAB 134/224, Economic Policy Committee minutes, 19 January 1950, pp. 5–6.

12. I. Zweiniger-Bargielowska, 'Rationing, Austerity and the Conservative Party Recovery after 1945', *Historical Journal*, 37, 1, 1994, pp. 173–97.

13. *Labour Party Conference Report* [hereafter *LPCR*], 1945, p. 89.

14. For comparison of the three manifestos, see Craig, 1970, pp. 101, 128–31, 148.

15. Addison, 1975, p. 273.

16. K.O. Morgan, 'The Rise and Fall of Public Ownership in Britain', in J. Bean, ed., *The Political Culture of Modern Britain*, 1985, London, Hamish Hamilton, pp. 288–91.

17. H. Gaitskell, *Socialism and Nationalisation*, Fabian Tract no. 300, July 1956, London, Fabian Society, pp. 9–10, 18–23. For Durbin's views, E. Durbin, 'The Importance of Planning' (1935), in his *Problems of Economic Planning*, 1949, London, Routledge, pp. 53–4.

18. For example, PRO: CAB 134/688–92, Minutes of the Socialisation of Industries committee, 1947–51.

19. *Labour Believes in Britain*, pp. 9–10; Labour Party, *Labour and the New Society*, 1950, London, Labour Party, pp. 18–25.

20. Craig, 1970, p. 101.

21. Labour Party Archive, Research Department RD 33, 'Criteria for Nationalisation', November 1946, pp. 2–3.

22. Morgan, 1985, pp. 280–1.

23. Conservative Research Department, *The Campaign Guide: General Election 1950*, 1949, London, Conservative and Unionist Central Office, pp. 93–119.

24. J. Strachey, *The Just Society*, 1951, London, Labour Party, pp. 6–9.
25. *Labour and the New Society*, pp. 20, 18–19.
26. Craig, 1970, p. 101.
27. *Tribune*, 8 August 1947, p. 7.
28. *Socialist Commentary*, 12, 15, December 1948, pp. 338–9.
29. For disagreements in Cabinet over steel nationalisation, see Morgan, 1985, pp. 112–21.
30. Hansard, 5th series, 15 November 1948, 485:78.
31. H. Dalton, 'Our Financial Plan', in Fabian Society, ed., *Forward from Victory!*, 1946, London, Victor Gollancz, pp. 48–9.
32. *Trades Union Congress Annual Report* [hereafter *TUCR*], 1951, p. 370.
33. I.D. Little, 'Fiscal Policy', in G.D.N. Worswick and P.H. Ady, eds., *The British Economy, 1945–50*, 1952, Oxford, Oxford University Press, p. 174.
34. A.A. Rogow and P. Shore, *The Labour Government and British Industry, 1945–1951*, 1955, Oxford, Oxford University Press, p. 119. The average annual income of an adult male in 1951 was around £440.
35. Nuffield College, Oxford, Fabian Society Papers, C 64/2, Item 3, 'Lecture Given by the Rt. Hon. Hugh Dalton, at Central Hall, Westminster, 13 November 1946', pp. 4–5.
36. Craig, 1970, p. 96.
37. C.P. Mayhew, *Socialist Economic Planning*, Fabian Discussion Series no. 1, December 1946, London, Fabian Society, p. 18. For Jenkins, see Nuffield College, Oxford, G.D.H. Cole Papers, B/3/5/E, 'Problems Ahead' Conference, Buscot Park, July 1949, Session II, p. 2. For Callaghan, see his 'Approach to Social Equality', in D. Munro, ed., *Socialism: The British Way*, 1948, London, Essential Books, pp. 147–8.
38. *TUCR*, 1948, p. 362.
39. *Socialist Commentary*, 15, 6, June 1951, p. 126.
40. H. Dalton, *Practical Socialism for Britain*, 1935, London, Routledge, pp. 336–7.
41. Hansard, 5th series, 9 April 1946, 421:1834–7.
42. *LPCR*, 1950, p. 119.
43. P.M. Williams, *Hugh Gaitskell*, 1982 edn, Oxford, Oxford University Press, p. 165.
44. Craig, 1970, p. 150.
45. S.P. Chambers, 'The Capital Levy', *Lloyds Bank Review*, vol. 19, no. 1, January 1951, p. 1; R. Jenkins, *Fair Shares for the Rich*, 1951, London, Tribune.
46. Labour Party Archive, National Executive Committee Minutes, 27 June 1951.
47. Craig, 1970, p. 244.
48. *LPCR*, 1950, p. 119; Craig, 1970, pp. 149–50.
49. G. Foote, *The Labour Party's Political Thought: A History*, 1985, London, Croom Helm, pp. 212–34.
50. C. Webster, 'Labour and the Origins of the National Health Service', in N.A. Rupke, ed., *Science, Politics and the Public Good*, 1988, Basingstoke, Macmillan, p. 199.
51. For example, the editorial in the SMA journal, *Medicine Today and Tomorrow*, 5, 5, March 1946, p. 5.

52. Hansard, 5th series, 30 April 1946, 422:49; C. Webster, _Problems of Health Care: the National Health Service before 1957_, 1988, London, HMSO, pp. 395–7.

53. PRO: CAB 21/2032, 'The Future of Hospital Services: A Memorandum by the Lord President of the Council', 12 October 1945, p. 2.

54. _Hansard_, 5th series, 26 July 1946, 426:468.

55. _Ibid._, 9 February 1948, 447:148–9.

56. _Ibid._, 3 July 1947, 425:1917–46.

57. _Hansard_, 5th series, 3 July 1947, 425:1947–70. Webster, 1988, pp. 90–1.

58. _Ibid._, 30 April 1946, 422:53.

59. _Ibid._, 2 May 1946, 422:398–9.

60. SMA Bulletin, December 1946, pp. 1–4.

61. F. Williams, _The Triple Challenge_, 1948, London, Heinemann, p. 131.

62. A. Bevan, 'July 5th and the Socialist Advance', _Tribune_, 2 July 1948, p. 7.

63. _Hansard_, 5th series, 1 May 1946, 422:19.

64. J. Burnett, _A Social History of Housing_, 1978, Newton Abbot, David and Charles, p. 284.

65. M. Foot, _Aneurin Bevan, vol. 2, 1945–1960_, 1973, London, Davis-Poynter, pp. 78–9.

66. For example, see the Conservatives' 1951 manifesto, Craig, 1970, p. 144.

67. D. Rubinstein, 'Ellen Wilkinson Re-considered', _History Workshop Journal_, 7, 1979, pp. 161–9; C. Benn, 'Comprehensive School Reform and the 1945 Labour Government', _History Workshop Journal_, 10, 1980, pp. 197–204.

68. R. Morley, 'A Job for Mr. Tomlinson', _Tribune_, 6 October 1950, p. 10.

69. For example, the speech of George Thomas, _Hansard_, 5th series, 31 July 1947, 441:690–4.

70. C.A.R. Crosland, _The Future of Socialism_, 1956, London, Jonathan Cape, p. 237.

71. Nuffield College, Oxford, Fabian Society Papers, G 50/3 Item 3, 'Problems Ahead' Conference, Oxford, March 1950, Session II, pp. 10–11.

72. Ellen Wilkinson was quite explicit that this was the guiding principle of her policy, _LPCR_, 1946, p. 189.

73. Zweiniger-Bargielowska, 1994, especially pp. 193–4.

74. D. Butler and A. Sloman, eds., _British Political Facts, 1900–1979_, 1980, Basingstoke, Macmillan, p. 208.

75. H. Morrison, foreword to Munro, 1948, p. 1.

76. C.R. Attlee, _As It Happened_, 1954, London, Heinemann, p. 163.

4 Conservative Leaders, Strategy – and 'Consensus'? 1945–1964[1]

Michael Kandiah

The postwar political consensus 'usually refers to the widespread elite agreement on policy goals and broad continuity of government policy'.[2] This model of political behaviour has been used to explain the Conservative Party's espousal of positive welfarism and for its supposedly newfound acceptance of state intervention in the immediate postwar years; for the apparent continuities between the Labour and Conservative governments during this period; and why there was to be no dismantling of the welfare state during the thirteen years of Conservative rule (1951–64). Consensus theory thus suggests that compromise had triumphed over conflict and, according to some, the appearance of conflict between the political parties and elites was 'often a sham, for parties are not real adversaries and the choices they offer the electorate are imaginary'.[3] This chapter will consider whether Conservative Party leaders' actions really did converge with those of their Labour counterparts and will examine the strategies pursued by Conservative leaders in order to appreciate their political aims and vision and to comprehend the parameters within which they operated.

The 1945 general election campaign revealed the cleavages – not consensus or convergence – between Conservatives and Labour. The Conservative Party fought the 1945 election on a national government platform somewhat reminiscent of the broader political alignments of the 1930s (although, obviously, without the National Labour contingent) in an attempt to perpetuate the idea of continuing national unity in a time of crisis. Churchill was to be the campaign's principal focus and Party publicity urged people to 'Let Him Finish the Job' – that is, finish fighting the war in Asia. While he reiterated his commitment to social welfare reform and attempted to promote his 'Four-Year Plan' for reconstruction, he also strongly defended free enterprise and pursued with great vigour an anti-statist, anti-planning and anti-socialist line, which had distinct hints of the arguments contained in Hayek's *Road to Serfdom* (1944). This was to set the tone for the campaign on the hustings. The Party's election manifesto was written with some speed, between April and June 1945, and it reflected the absence of official Party policy on postwar reconstruction and social welfare. It emphasised the Party's continued adherence to fiscal prudence and, while accepting the Coalition government's White Papers as the basis for postwar actions, it did not explain how, if elected, a Conservative government would effect reconstruction and reform. The Party's platform in 1945 was based on: anti-socialism, the preservation of capitalism (though not necessarily all-out *laissez-faire* capitalism),[4] limited reform and a belief in individual freedoms and opportunity.[5] Within these broad parameters Party leaders were to operate in subsequent years.

According to the consensus paradigm, the 1945 defeat facilitated a transformation in Conservative principles engineered from above. '"New Conservatism" was formally adopted' and 'became the new orthodoxy', according to Nicholas Deakin: 'It was from this point that the postwar consensus became a reality.'[6] However, on closer inspection 'New Conservatism' would appear to be not too far removed from 'Old Conservatism'. In the aftermath of the defeat there were calls for clear policy statements from all sections of the Party. What followed was a sustained and well-publicised review of policy, the results of which were articulated in the series of charters produced between 1947 and 1949: the *Industrial, Agricultural, Imperial* and *Worker's Charters. The Industrial Charter*, the first and most important of the statements, saw the role of the state as strong: it called for 'a partnership between the Government, Industry and the Individual'.[7] But this position did not really represent a transformation in the attitudes of the Party leaders towards the state, it was more a confirmation of past practices. During the 1920s and 1930s Conservative and Conservative-led governments had intervened at the macroeconomic level (for example, with the establishment of the National Grid, the 'cheap money' policy and protectionism) and at the microeconomic level (for instance, the moves to rationalise certain ailing industries like coal and steel). During this period state intervention had occurred for a variety of reasons, including a desire to alleviate sectoral unemployment. These measures may have been *ad hoc*, but the prewar years did not see unbridled *laissez-faire* capitalism in operation. Instead, as Nick Tiratsoo and Jim Tomlinson have suggested, the 1930s witnessed the 'support of cartelisation and market sharing within a protectionist framework'. During the Depression the Conservatives demonstrated a keen awareness of the power of the state, and the National Government had carefully and successfully manipulated the existing (highly selective) welfare system to stem working class political unrest.[8] *The Industrial Charter* looked forward to an elaboration of the methods of state intervention pursued before the Second World War, although with a new Keynesian (or, rather, a quasi-Keynesian) approach. Moreover, private enterprise and wealth-creation were still seen as the key to sustained economic growth. In total, therefore, the policy statements which constituted the 'New Conservatism' were not a dramatic advance on the position which had been put forward in the 1945 general election manifesto and were in no way a repudiation of traditional Conservative precepts. R.A. Butler, the Party's principal policy-maker and one of the prime movers behind the Charters, said that the central purpose of these statements 'was to present a recognizable alternative to the reigning orthodoxies of Socialism – not to put the clock back, but to reclaim a prominent role for individual initiative and private enterprise in the mixed and managed economy'.[9] Therefore, the Charters were meant to mark the assertion, not the retreat or the dilution, of Conservatism and Conservative attitudes and certainly did not signal policy convergence with Labour. Prior to its formal approval at the 1947 Annual Party Conference, there were no guarantees that *The Industrial Charter* would have been accepted either by Churchill, whose interest in policy-making was minimal, or by the party at large. Its presentation at the party conference was carefully managed by Butler and others and, fortu-nately from their point of view, the loudest voice of dissent came from extreme reactionaries like Sir Waldron Smithers. It was approved princi-pally because the Charters were meant to be documents which most people in the Party (aside from perhaps the most diehard or the most com-mitted neo-liberal) could live with, and they were seen by the Party faith-ful and by much of the electorate at large as Conservatism renewed – which was precisely what the Party leaders wanted.

The Charters were also part of a strategy to help promote the Party's appeal across the classes. *The Industrial Charter* stated: 'To the worker, we offer a new charter giving assurance of steady employment, incentives to test his ability to the utmost ... . To the consumer we offer the ultimate restoration of freedom of choice, the prospect of a better standard of living and protection from restrictive practices.'[10] The 1945 result demonstrated that the Party had not secured the support it had hitherto received from the middle classes, the young and the working classes. Most Party leaders were conscious that the fear of unemployment had counted against them heavily and that measures promising constructive postwar reform, particu-larly the Beveridge Report and the White Paper on Health, had had con-siderable cross-class appeal.[11] The primary purpose of the Charters, as Butler said, was to allay fears 'that full employment and the Welfare State were not safe in our hands'.[12] Party leaders had realised that a clear-cut commitment had to be seen to be made that there would be no return to the harsh economic conditions pre-1939 or to life 'on the dole'. This also meant that the Party in government would have to leave the broad outlines of the welfare state intact and accept the goal of full employment. Conservatives were to be on the defensive about their stand on social welfare and employment during the entire period under consideration.[13] During the 1951 general election they had felt very vulnerable to a charge made in the *Daily Mirror* that many social services would be cut if the Conservatives were to win, and a concerted effort from Churchill downwards was made to reassure the electorate.[14] The Liaison Committee, established soon after the Party was returned to power, consistently noted in the early years of the administration that public opinion reports found most people were worried that a Conservative government would mean unemployment, cuts in education expenditure and charges for use of the health service.[15] According to opinion polls, the popularity of the government consistently trailed behind Labour until 1953,[16] when the electorate came to believe that the Conservatives would not cut back on welfare provisions, that high unemployment would not return and that the Conservatives had delivered on their 1951 election pledge to secure economic growth while at the same time 'setting the people free'.

Conservative leaders had appreciated the fact that the Party would have to reconstruct its working-class voter-base if it were to win elections, and this meant addressing not only the needs of particular working-class groups but, perhaps most of all, adopting a more conciliatory, nonthreatening stance towards the trade unions. During the war Churchill knew that he had to work with the unions, and postwar their power and authority were considered to be formidable. One Party strategist noted after the February 1950 election that the Conservatives, whether in opposition or in government, had to attempt to live with the trade unions and that overt hostility was counterproductive: 'the more you attack the Trade Unions, the more wholeheartedly the weight of their whole organisation will be flung into the next election against us, and this will count far more than any odd votes you pick up by attacking them.'[17] This line of thinking had been behind *The Industrial Charter's* calls for cooperation with the unions and the establishment of the Trade Union Committee at the Conservative Research Department. Therefore the Conservatives sought to persuade the unions that the Party would not be harmful to their own and to working-class interests.[18] There were two problems with this strategy. First, as Noel Whiteside argues in this volume, the Conservative government's moves to restore market forces to collective bargaining had worked to destabilise government–trade unions relations. Secondly, the trade unions were exceedingly unpopular with the Party's middle-class supporters. This antipathy would become more marked as the 1950s progressed, as inflation ate away at the benefits the middle classes had enjoyed from the tax cuts since 1951. At the same time, industrial wage demands and strife increased, and the middle classes began to consider that their economic position relative to the working class's was being steadily eroded. *The Sunday Times* spoke on the middle classes' behalf when it commented that in the aftermath of the 1955 budget, they were being squeezed by 'monstrously' high tax rates. From then onwards the middle classes were to be vociferous in their demand for legislation curbing the power of unions, on whom they thought the Conservative government was being too easy.[19] Indeed, the government had been concerned about implications of the so-called 'wage–price spiral', and the 1956 White Paper on *The Economic Implication of Full Employment* called for wage restraint in the face of potentially rising inflation.[20] However, explicit anti-union legislation and imposed wage settlements were difficult to contemplate at this stage because Conservative leaders believed that the 1951 and 1955 general election wins to have been 'undoubtedly' the result of the Party winning substantial trade union votes. Prime Minister Macmillan concluded in August 1957 that it 'would be inexpedient to adopt any policy involving legislation which would alienate this support'.[21] Party strategists had estimated in 1960 that 'it is still from the working-class two thirds that we get more than half our votes – and have to if we are to win an Election'.[22] There was never any question of the government 'taking on the unions' whatever the demands from the Party's middle-class warriors.

Conservative leaders actively and aggressively sought to promote anti-socialism and opposition to Labour through a variety of different strategies in order to revive the Party's postwar electoral fortunes. 'The United Front Against Socialism' was officially inaugurated on 10 May 1947 when it was announced that Lord Woolton, the recently appointed Party Chairman, and Lord Teviot, Chairman of the Liberal National Party (the rump of the Liberal Party which had remained with the National government after 1932), had signed an agreement, the Woolton–Teviot Pact, which urged their respective constituency associations to combine in the fight against socialism.[23] This anti-socialist front was designed to achieve a number of disparate aims. The principal long-term objective was to consolidate the right-wing vote in the Party's favour and to offer the Conservative Party as the sole and distinctive alternative to the Labour Party. The Liberal Party's share of the popular vote in the 1945 general election had been 9 per cent (mainly middle-class voters), and Party leaders believed that winning a substantial portion of Liberal votes in the subsequent elections would make all the difference.[24] Additionally, an internal Party report suggested that the personal profiles of floating voters coincided remarkably with those of Liberals, and capturing one group might mean catching the other.[25] 'Our object', Woolton told all constituencies, 'must be to combine with moderate Liberals wherever they are organised and to attract them individually where no organisation exists.'[26] The Woolton–Teviot Pact was, therefore, an attempt to capture or neutralise the Liberal vote via the Liberal Nationals: all Liberals were told that, in reality, there was now little difference between traditional Liberalism and Conservatism and that the two needed to join forces to defend individual freedoms and the free enterprise system. This appeal was attractive to many Liberals, principally because they were opposed to Labour's nationalisation programme, and efforts were made at various points between 1949 (the passage of the Iron and Steel Act was a significant date[27]) and 1951 to reach some kind of entente between the two parties. However, there was an insuperable difference between Conservatives and Liberals over the issue of proportional representation. The Liberals had no intention of vanishing into the bosom of the Conservative Party as the Liberal Unionists had done and, in the opinion of Lady Violet Bonham-Carter, daughter of the Liberal Prime Minister H.H. Asquith (1908–16), 'It is Electoral Reform which alone can ensure our survival as a Party.'[28] As proportional representation was something few Conservatives were willing to consider discussing, talks between the two Parties stalled by mid-1951. Soon afterwards many prominent Liberals in the House of Lords resigned from the Party and took the Conservative Whip because, they said, a Conservative government was the 'only hope of preventing the national catastrophe of a further and final period of Socialist rule – or misrule as we see it'.[29] The bulk of the Liberal Party, however, did not take this line as they saw themselves both as the third alternative in British politics and as an anti-socialist party. Nevertheless, what these manoeuvres with Liberals reveal is how polarised right was from left, and that Conservative leaders actively sought to utilise and encourage this state of affairs – not convergence or consensus.

Another objective of the 'United Front Against Socialism' was to demonstrate that opposition to the Labour Party was widespread. Party leaders were so anxious to demonstrate that hostility to socialism crossed simple party political boundaries that they insisted that the Liberal Nationals retain a separate identity and continuously rebuffed suggestions which might lead to the formal union of the two parties.[30] Both Churchill

and Woolton dissuaded Lord Simon, a leading Liberal National peer, from
officially joining the Conservative Party in 1948 for fear of weakening his
Party.[31] Similarly, in the same year, Woolton was unforthcoming when
Dorothy Crisp, president of the Housewives League, a non-party organisation formed in 1945 to protest against the maintenance of rationing, suggested formal connection between their respective organisations. He told
her that previously they had both pledged 'that there was no association,
directly or indirectly', between them and was of the opinion that an
alliance would not 'serve any good political purpose'. The League had
done much to undermine women's support for Labour and an official connection would only bring its protest into the party political arena. This
would have diminished the League's effectiveness because its activities
could then have been dismissed as party-inspired agitation.[32] Again,
Conservative leaders' activities suggest that they wished to promote political conflict as much as they could.

   Ross McKibbin has argued that in the 1930s the Conservative Party's
considerable cross-class electoral success depended upon the perception
that it was the Party of 'the public', and in the postwar period there was an
attempt to recreate this situation – although undertaken in entirely different circumstances Conservative leaders appear to have had a similar end in
mind.[33] The Labour Party was always identified as the 'Socialist Party' in
all official Conservative pronouncements. This was meant to encourage
suspicion of Labour by highlighting its ideological basis and because the
word 'socialist' had continental – and therefore, sinister and un-British –
connotations. The 1951 manifesto suggested, 'The attempt to impose a
doctrinaire Socialism upon an Island which has grown great and famous
by free enterprise has inflicted serious injury upon our strength and prosperity.'[34] Woolton said that he had hoped to communicate to the electorate
that 'Conservatism was just common sense' and that the Party was the
defender of civic and personal values.[35] The rationale behind and the
rhetoric of the 'United Front Against Socialism' had been that the Labour
government's policies were 'anti-public': irrational, pernicious and
leading to crisis. The wording of the 1947 Woolton–Teviot Pact was
explicit:

> Today as a result of the war Britain is facing a difficult and dangerous
> situation. The dangers of the situation are being seriously aggravated
> by the politics of the Socialist Government and by their administrative
> incompetence. These policies bear no real relations to the needs of the
> hour, and they are imperilling the liberties, livelihood and well-being of
> the people.[36]

Controls, rationing and austerity were not necessary but were the result, they suggested, of Labour's 'mis-government' and because the Labour Party was ideologically driven – controls were there for the sake of control. Churchill announced that the difficulties which the Labour government had been having in meeting their house-building programme was the result of 'the pedantic, irrational enforcement of socialist prejudice'.[37] During the 1951 election manifesto these ideas were stressed and a subtle connection was made between Labour's socialism and Soviet communism: 'The choice is between two ways of life; between individual liberty and state domination; between concentration of ownership in the hands of the state and the extension of ownership over the widest numbers of individuals.'[38] These Cold War sentiments and the linkage between austerity and socialism were ones which were to find sympathy in the minds of women and the middle classes. This, as Ina Zweiniger-Bargielowska has suggested, was to help the Conservatives 'regain much of the support lost in 1945 and to reconstruct a majority which was strengthened in subsequent elections when "affluence" became the byword of Conservative success'.[39] After 1951 Conservative leaders were to present the Party as the most 'logical' choice for the rational voter and suggested that the collectivist vision had not worked: the 1959 election campaign, for instance, told people 'You never had it so good', and 'Life's better with the Conservatives – Don't Let Labour Ruin It'. As late as 1960, Conservative publicity material sought to mobilise popular support by reminding people about rationing and austerity.[40]

Conservative leaders had by no means accepted the Attlee government's economic and industrial settlement. Some Conservative leaders (notably Macmillan) held the opinion that control of industry and, in particular cases, nationalisation was not undesirable but the two parties had disparate aims. Prominent in Labour's approach was control of the 'commanding heights of the economy'. This was totally at odds with most Conservative leaders' views: they were opposed to the public ownership of key industries which were still in some way financially viable for private enterprise to run, such as the iron and steel industry and road haulage. It was for this reason that they had pledged to denationalise these particular industries (and not industries suffering from long-term decline like coal). By 1947, as the Cold War began to take more definite shape and as international capitalism began to reassert itself under the aegis of the US government, Conservative leaders' position against nationalisation began to harden. When criticising the Iron and Steel Bill in Parliament, Churchill, briefed by the Conservative Research Department, argued that nationalisation was neither efficient nor necessary, and was not beneficial to the consumer. He also pointed out that the industry had been heavily controlled and regulated since the 1930s, a situation which was acceptable both to the owners and to the Conservative Party. Looking at the performance of the nationalised industries – the railways had made substantial losses in 1948, and the coal industry had raised prices to consumers by 20 per cent – he wondered if the price of steel would go up. This, he suggested, would adversely affect Britain's export trade, which in turn would lead to a deterioration of the domestic economy.[41] The Party Chairman Woolton ensured that Conservative propaganda connected the losses made by nationalised industries with privations suffered by ordinary people: it was claimed, for instance, that the £44 million lost by the coal and civil aviation industries in 1948 could have reduced the cost of a pint of beer by 1 1/2 pence, 'built 7 new electric power stations', 'or with the same sum over 30,000 new houses could have been built'.[42] Even though there was to be a 'vogue for planning' in the late 1950s, and the establishment of the National Economic Development Council (NEDC or 'Neddy') appeared to signal a more interventionist phase of government, Conservative leaders had little desire to interfere with the patterns of ownership of British industry.

The consensus model has not accounted for the Party's extra-parliamentary strategy against nationalisation. Conservative leaders established informal links with certain threatened industries and together attempted to work out tactics;[43] they also assured industrialists that the Party was opposed to all nationalisation;[44] and encouraged the establishment of industry-based and funded anti-nationalisation organisations.[45] For example, Woolton had advised the Brewers Society to set up their own anti-nationalisation campaign as the Labour government's 1948 Licensing Bill was thought to be the precursor to nationalisation. Central Office, the Conservative Party's headquarters, provided the brewers with a special liaison officer who coordinated publicity and synchronised their officially separate campaigns. Woolton felt that an extra-parliamentary campaign of this kind was the best way to create and mobilise popular support against nationalisation; a party-inspired campaign could have been dismissed as politically partisan.[46] The Party also liaised with organisations promoting free enterprise, and Woolton urged his friend, Robert Renwick, to set up the 'educational' non-party United Industrialists Association in 1947.[47] Prior to both the 1950 and 1951 general elections Central Office secretly gave support and direction to campaigns undertaken by various industries, such as the sugar manufacturer Tate and Lyle's highly successful 'Mr Cube' free enterprise campaign, and those of right-wing organisations like Aims of Industry.[48] The potential value of this strategy was noted by the Labour MP Peter Shore: 'propaganda for free enterprise reaches the public in a most effective way, for it does not appear to be propaganda, or to have any connection with politics.'[49] Additionally, although these non-party campaigns were supposed to be about anti-nationalisation, people 'could not have been told to vote Conservative more plainly', as a contemporary observed.[50] Thus this extra-parliamentary response also fitted nicely with the 'United Front Against Socialism' strategy which had sought to promote opposition to Labour and help build up the Party's electoral base at the same time.

David Dutton has claimed, 'it is in government that its practitioners learn that politics is indeed the art of the possible', and, given that there were to be no immediate or wholesale revision of government policy by successive Conservative administrations, he has concluded that consensus was vindicated during the years 1951–64.[51] However, the problem with this analysis is that the constraints (and perceived constraints) which limited the actions of Conservative governments have not been properly appreciated. The principal constraint between the 1951 and 1955 elections was the fact that Party had not secured the majority of the popular vote. Even after the 1955 general election, which they were to win by a comfortable majority, the gap between Conservatives and Labour in opinion polls remained within a few percentage points and leaders were not sanguine about the Party's ability to win elections in succession. Macmillan noted in September 1957 that 'Since the first Reform Bill it has been very rare for the same Party to win even two elections running, and to win three is almost a miracle'.[52] Therefore, throughout the period they had to compete with Labour for the small percentage of undecided voters and this meant, Party leaders believed, that adventurous policies would be dangerous to consider.[53] The Cold War also placed constraints on the actions of Conservative leaders. Soon after they came into government in 1951 they had to deal with a balance of payments crisis which, according to the Chancellor, Butler, was 'worse than 1949', when sterling had to be devalued, and 'in many ways worse than 1947', when convertibility had been suspended. He therefore recommended to Cabinet 'an urgent review of all Government expenditure so as to cut out waste, and – far more important – to cut out and slow down expenditure on work which is valuable but not essential in times of crisis'.[54] To ease pressure on sterling Butler put forward the so-called 'Operation Robot', which would have effectively floated the pound. If implemented, the Chancellor told the Cabinet, it 'would have a salutary effect in bringing home to the people of this country the reality of the economic situation in which they were living' by forcing them to alter the domestic consumption agenda and endure a rise in inflation, and would have required that they accept significant cuts in welfare spending. However, the Cabinet rejected the proposal and this rejection has been interpreted by some as a triumph for consensus. However, the multiplicity of reasons for its rejection make this explanation unconvincing. It was judged to have been a Draconian measure which would have a profound and negative effect upon Cold War and Commonwealth alliances and would have disrupted the linkages between the Western economies: it would have destroyed the Bretton Woods system, hastened the demise of the European Payments Union and 'might even be regarded as inimical to the efforts of the North Atlantic Council to establish a sound economic foundation on which to build up the defensive strength of Western Europe'. Most of these outcomes, the Cabinet noted, would 'certainly be distasteful to the United States government'. The minutes also record the Cabinet's view that 'Reliance on monetary measures would be thought to point to large-scale unemployment; and the Government would be exposed to all the well-worn criticisms directed on that account against the Conservative Party'. Additionally, 'Operation Robot' would have penalised certain Commonwealth countries unduly and would have probably smashed the sterling area (which Conservative leaders wished to preserve). Finally, the proposal was likely to be so drastic that it would be extremely unpopular in the country and 'if it were thought possible that an even more grave economic crisis might develop later in the year, it would be unjustifiable to take at this stage a step which might exclude all possibility of forming a National Government to handle the situation'.[55] The latter comment suggests how serious the Cabinet thought the situation was – class and parliamentary harmony had to be preserved during this highly tense period of the Cold War. Favourable world economic conditions were then to work to the Conservatives' advantage, as increased exports boosted domestic earnings and improvements in the terms of trade meant that the Conservatives could pursue tax-cutting strategies while at the same time financing the spending on domestic welfare programmes.

The consensus model has dismissed as mere rhetoric the Conservative Party's 1951 election pledge to promote free markets. The Conservatives did attempt to restore market forces overtly. For example, in 1953 they reopened the Liverpool cotton exchange; by 1954 they had dispensed with most restrictions and physical controls over the economy and had de-rationed most foodstuffs; and in 1964 Resale Price Maintenance was abolished. As Noel Whiteside points out in chapter 7, market forces began to determine collective bargaining in the labour market once the Conservatives were returned to power. Party leaders determination to return to markets underpinned their housing programme. Superficially, a cross-party consensus existed in this particular area: both Labour and Conservatives had agreed that housing was a pressing problem and had placed promises for its provision high on their electoral agendas in 1945, 1950 and 1951; and both had suggested that they would deliver more housing more quickly. However, Conservative leaders believed that free enterprise would be better able to build houses for the nation than state planning – they proclaimed 'Homes for all – but not under Socialism'. The Labour government had hoped to bring about societal change through its housing programme: accommodation was to be provided for 'all members of the community' and not for just the working classes or to implement slum clearance.[56] The Attlee government was also to pursue policies which favoured renting rather than ownership, and which discriminated against private builders. Conservative leaders, however, wished to create a 'property owning democracy' in which the private sector would be the principal supplier of housing. Local authority and council provisions, they thought, should be limited to the working classes.[57] The Party's 1950 Annual Conference enthusiastically agreed to a house building target of 300 000 houses and after the 1951 election Harold Macmillan was put in charge of housing to ensure that target was met. Under his direction, despite initially increasing the number of houses built by local authorities, the industry was gradually returned to the private sector. By 1959 the private builders were building more houses than local authorities.[58]

Limited denationalisation under the Conservatives has been considered a policy convergence with Labour and is supposed to demonstrate consensus politics in operation. However, Conservative leaders' strategies were to be shaped largely by the fear that a future Labour government would simply renationalise the industries the Conservatives had denationalised. This would hardly have been a satisfactory outcome in the long run if free enterprise was to be preserved and confidence in the capitalist system was to be built up. Therefore Duncan Sandys, the Minister of Supply who was put in charge of steel denationalisation, attempted to secure cross-party support by proposing to retain public supervision of the industry, but this proved impossible as Labour insisted that if and when they were returned to government, they would renationalise steel. Divergence between the two Parties could not have been more marked. According to *The Economist* the parliamentary debates which ensued in November 1951 revealed a 'bitterness of feeling between the parties' which had created 'a political situation more full of difficulties and dangers'.[59] The differences between Conservatives and Labour were to be further entrenched when Labour announced in 1953 that it would extend

the scope of its nationalisation programme to include profit-making industries like engineering and chemicals.[60] Meanwhile, the Conservatives went
ahead with the denationalisation of the steel industry. This proved to be a
success; but it was not to be a complete success, for while the first
tranches of industries offered for sale were oversubscribed, the government was to find that the take-up of later share offers was slack
(particularly after 1957). The reason was partly because the portions of
the industry being offered for sale in the final stages were in poor condition and partly because Labour had deliberately sought to scare off
investors by continuing to threaten to renationalise the industry when they
were returned to power.[61] The iron and steel industry had been brought
under government supervision in the prewar period and Conservative
leaders felt that this situation should be recreated in some form. Therefore,
they put into place the Iron and Steel Board. Admittedly this was not a
free market but the important thing from their point of view was that the
state no longer owned an industry which could be run by private enterprise. They were thus to achieve 'a larger political end', as Kathleen Burk
has observed: 'they had struck a blow for the principle of free enterprise,
at the same time setting new boundaries for the proper role of the State'.[62]
The experience and settlement of the denationalisation of road haulage
would prove to be almost identical. While some industrialists thought that
the Conservatives had not gone far enough in restoring private ownership,
others felt that the government had taken the right line. As things were,
one industrialist noted, 'there might be less chance of any Labour
Government trying to reverse the present Government decision[s] at the
cost of dislocating British Industry'.[63] In many ways this end was what the
Conservative leaders had hoped to accomplish with their denationalisation
programme and it was meant to be a significant revision of Labour's
industrial settlement.

   Two Conservative leaders, Woolton and the Lord Privy Seal, Harry
Crookshank,[64] had hoped for more extensive denationalisation, but the fact
this did not occur cannot be interpreted as the validation of the consensus
model. Butler told Churchill that further 'or more effective denationalisation' was not feasible principally because of the country's recurring
balance of payments problems and because of a lack of liquidity in the
economy.[65] Hoping to find evidence of inefficiency and waste, the
Churchill government established a number of official inquiries to assess
the performance of the nationalised industries. Conservatives were to be
disappointed by the various reports' findings: the Ridley Committee recommended in 1952 only a few minor changes to the existing arrangements
on the provision of fuel and power; the Fleck Committee's report (1955)

found that the coal industry should be further centralised; and the Herbert Committee (1956) suggested decentralisation of electricity distribution. None found that nationalised industries had been performing poorly and none recommended denationalisation. Even if denationalisation had been suggested, no nationalised industry was sufficiently profitable for investors to be willing to buy it. Conservatives leaders therefore decided to 'modernise' nationalised industries and placed a new emphasis on competition and an increased significance on efficiency. To this end they established a Select Committee in 1955. Conservative leaders, in particular Macmillan, increasingly came to hold the opinion that industry's competitiveness and efficiency had to be improved *vis-à-vis* the Europeans, who according to OEEC and other international reports had been outperforming the British since at least the mid-1950s (if not since the early 1950s). The emphasis on competition and efficiency would fundamentally alter the *raison d'être* of nationalised industries – implicitly and explicitly market forces were brought into the equation. The nationalised industries which remained under state control were thus to operate along lines which were much more in accord with Conservative thinking. In 1948 Woolton had outlined the Party's position on industry: 'We want to see strong central guidance with the maximum enterprise and opportunity in industry.'[66] This had been Conservative leaders' strategy when in government.

The consensus model has justified its case on the fact that Conservatives maintained high levels of public expenditure during their years in power. After the First World War measures of social reform faced the 'Geddes axe' in 1922 when economic conditions had deteriorated.[67] Nothing similar happened after the Conservatives were returned to power in 1951. The model rejects as only empty words the Party's 1951 manifesto promise to 'cut out all unnecessary Government expenditure, simplify the administrative machine, and prune waste and extravagance in every department'.[68] In fact, as soon as the Conservatives were returned to power they began to consider how to cut public expenditure. Immediate retrenchment would have meant a reduction in public expenditure and cuts to welfare services, but such actions would have been electorally unpopular and were not ones that Conservative leaders were prepared to take.[69] The dilemma Conservative leaders felt they were in is captured in a letter written by Woolton to Churchill a few weeks after the Party had been returned to government:

I have no doubt about the wisdom of making severe cuts in Government expenditure ... . We shall find ourselves in politically difficult waters if we begin by making serious cuts in the social services ... and leave ourselves open to the charge that what we have saved by this means we have later spent in the reduction of taxation.[70]

This dilemma, in one way or another, was to confront Conservative administrations year after year.[71] In January 1957 Iain Macleod (Minister of Labour and National Service) argued against cuts in expenditure on health care because, he told Prime Minister Macmillan, it would not be politically prudent for the Conservative government to be seen to be pursuing policies which 'tax the old and the young and the mad to help the surtax payers', and because such cuts would alienate certain key sections of the middle-class electorate.[72]

However, the problem of ever-rising public expenditure was to remain extremely problematic and Conservative leaders would have liked to have done more to contain its expansion. However, for the reasons outlined in Noel Whiteside's chapter, they were unable to control it. 'The most anxious fact on the home front is I think the alarming increase in the cost of the welfare state,' Anthony Eden noted as he resigned the prime ministership in the aftermath of the Suez crisis in 1956.[73] A similar view would be expressed by Prime Minister Douglas-Home in 1964, when he contemplated the forthcoming general election. He said that he thought 'Beveridge was very costly. Would another enquiry be as bad or if we win [the next election] should we not impose our own scheme?'[74] In 1958 the Chancellor, Peter Thorneycroft, demanded £153 million of spending cuts, but Macmillan was not supportive and the Cabinet could only agree to cuts amounting to £105 million. This precipitated the resignations of the Chancellor and of Enoch Powell and Nigel Birch, junior ministers at the Treasury. This episode has been seen as an early battle between 'consensus' and 'monetarist' Conservative political leaders, with the former winning the battle in the end. This view has been question by Neil Rollings (see chapter 6). Additionally, the problem for Macmillan and his Cabinet was that Thorneycroft's proposals did not address the pressing problems of economic growth and expansion. This was the principal issue at stake for Conservative leaders in the late 1950s and early 1960s. By then the economy was perceived not to be performing well and the Party's frontbenchers believed that only by pursuing strategies promoting economic expansion could the Conservatives remain in power. Thorneycroft's replacement, Heathcoat Amory, reiterated promises for growth when he delivered the April 1958 budget:

as a Government we are convinced that the long-term welfare of this country demands a steady expansion of our national economy. This is the objective of all our policies. We shall not, therefore, keep the brakes on one day longer than we must. We dislike restrictions intensely, and we are eager to resume expansion.[75]

This strategy would ultimately prove to be the undoing of the Conservatives' hold on power. They had unleashed consumerism, but were to find the economic expansion which fuelled it difficult to sustain: Selwyn Lloyd's 'Stop–Go' policies, Maudling's 'dash for growth' and Macmillan's abortive bid to enter Europe were all meant to stimulate British industry and economic expansion.[76]

Party leaders' commitment to welfare and employment were always in the context of fairly traditional Conservative principles. For instance, in *The Right Road for Britain*, published in 1950, the system of social services under the Conservatives was envisaged as 'a co-operative system of mutual aid and self-help provided by the whole Nation and designed to give the basic minimum of security ... below which our duty to one another forbids us to permit anyone to fall'. Such sentiments may be found in many Conservative documents written at different points during this and the previous century.[77] Conservative leaders' commitment to full employment was certainly genuine, but it was not a commitment which was at any point seriously challenged during this period: the world in which they operated was one of tight domestic labour markets and world-wide economic expansion. The relatively mild domestic recession during the late 1950s did not have a significant impact upon the rate of employment. The Conservative government actively pursued policies which attempted to promote capitalistic values, like encouraging home ownership and personal savings, and Conservative Chancellors consistently sought to cut taxes after 1951. These strategies were all intended, deliberately, to discriminate in favour of the middle classes, as were proposals put forward by the Conservative Research Department to encourage private health care and education through tax concessions.[78] Conservative leaders were concerned that the middle classes, the Party's bedrock supporters, had been seduced by Labour's welfare state – it has been noted by a commentator that they were 'main gainers from the 1944–8 reforms'.[79] Party strategists thought that a Conservative government in power should aim 'to do something for the middle classes which would be out of the general run of social welfare and would enable these people to get something out their own thrift'.[80] This almost always was to mean tax cuts to the middle classes' benefit.[81] In 1958 when the Treasury had counselled the government to consider tax increases to dampen down the economy, Macmillan rejected the advice, because he thought policies which annoyed 'what remains of the possessing classes are not attractive to our Party and are better left to a Socialist Chancellor'.[82] Finally, when in government Conservative leaders hoped to create, as Iain Macleod put it, 'an Opportunity State'.[83] It was in this general context that welfare spending was deliberated and such measures as expansion of the health service under Enoch Powell in the late 1950s occurred.

The Party did not 'change' in the postwar period[84] – it certainly had not learnt 'to mend its ways' in the aftermath of defeat, as has been suggested by one proponent of consensus.[85] Implicit to the consensus approach is the focus on final outcomes rather on the reasons for and situations behind those result, and this line of analysis has concealed more than it has revealed. Paul Addison has suggested in the most recent edition of *The Road to 1945* that 'consensus is a relative term: it implies only that areas of agreement were more important, historically, than areas of dispute.'[86] However, in the British system of parliamentary democracy it is precisely those 'areas of dispute' between political parties – particularly between the party leaders – that are definitive and fundamental. During the period under consideration superficial 'agreement on policy goals' obscured profound disagreements between Conservatives and Labour leaders on policy solutions and over the details of how goals should be achieved: the purpose of the 'agreed' goals for each of the Parties was distinct; and the concept of the society to be preserved or created was entirely different. Moreover, Conservative leaders did not share the assumptions which underpinned Labour's vision of postwar Britain; they were determined to construct and then maintain Conservatism as a distinct and viable alternative to Labour's socialism, and they wished to preserve and promote capitalism and maintain limited social welfare programmes within the context of increasing economic growth. During this period the Conservative leaders attempted to accommodate to political realities and attempted, as John Turner has put it, to create 'a land fit for Tories to live in'.[87]

NOTES

1.   I would like to thank Peter Catterall, Harriet Jones, Gillian Staerck and Nicolas Weber for their comments on earlier drafts of this chapter. I would also like to thank Kathleen Burk, Rodney Lowe and Jim Tomlinson for their generous help and advice.
2.   Dennis Kavanagh, 'The Postwar Consensus', *Twentieth Century British History*, 2, 2 (1992), p. 175.
3.   Andrew Gamble and S.A. Walkland, *The British Party System and Economic Policy 1945–1983: Studies in Adversary Politics*, 1985, Oxford, Clarendon, pp. 38, 177.

4. Viscount Hinchingbrooke, *Full Speed Ahead: Essays in Tory Reform*, 1944, London, Simpkin, p. 21: 'True Conservative opinion is horrified at the damage done to this country since the last war by "individualist" business-men, financiers, and speculators ranging freely in a laissez-faire economy and creeping unnoticed into the fold of Conservatism to insult the Party with their votes at elections ... and to injure the character of our people.'

5. M.D. Kandiah, 'The Conservative Party and the 1945 General Election', *Contemporary Record*, 9, 1 (1995).

6. Nicholas Deakin, *The Politics of Welfare*, 1987, London, Macmillan, p. 48.

7. *The Industrial Charter*, 1947, London, Conservative and Unionist Central Office, p. 10.

8. Nick Tiratsoo and Jim Tomlinson, *Industrial Efficiency and State Intervention*, 1993, London, Routledge, p. 6. Alan Booth, 'Britain in the 1930s: A Managed Economy?', *Economic History Review*, 40, 3 (1987). R.I. McKibbin, 'Class and Conventional Politics: The Conservative Party and the "Public" in Inter-war Britain', in *Ideologies of Class*, 1991, Oxford, Oxford University Press. Scott Newton, 'Appeasement as an Industrial Strategy, 1938–41', *Contemporary Record*, 9, 3 (1995).

9. Lord Butler, *The Art of the Possible. The Memoirs of Lord Butler*, 1971, London, Hamish Hamilton, pp. 146–7.

10. *The Industrial Charter*, 1947, p. 1.

11. Papers of Lord Woolton, Bodleian Library, Oxford. MS WLTN.20/folios 17–18. (I thank the 3rd Earl of Woolton for the use of these papers.) And see Papers of Lord Butler, Trinity College, Cambridge. MS RAB.G17, 'Reflections on the Recent Election', dated July 1945. (I thank the Master and Fellows of Trinity College, Cambridge for the use of these papers.)

12. Butler, *Memoirs*, 1971, p. 146.

13. Public Record Office, Kew [henceforward PRO], PREM 11/4952 and PREM 11/4955. For instance, the Douglas-Home administration hesitated over, respectively, proposed economies to the NHS and reform of national insurance and pensions.

14. *Daily Mirror*, 25 October 1951, and on the Conservative campaign see David Butler, *The British General Election of 1951*, 1952, London, Macmillan, pp. 55–6. And see John Ramsden, *The Making of Conservative Party Policy. The Conservative Research Department since 1929*, 1980, London, Longman, p. 155.

15. Conservative Party Archives, Bodleian Library, Oxford [henceforward CPA], CRD2/51/3, Liaison Committee.

16. D. Butler and G. Butler, *British Political Facts, 1900–1994*, 1994, London, Macmillan, pp. 248–9.

17. CPA CRD2/12/5, 'Conservative Propaganda as Regards Trade Unions', Mark Chapman-Walker to David Clarke, 4 April 1950. CPA CCO4/4/3, general circular to all Party Agents from Lord Woolton, 9 November 1950, and 'The Industrial and Agricultural Worker', November 1950. CPA CCO4/4/28, Mark Chapman-Walker to Woolton, 27 April 1950, was explicit about the connection they believed existed between a conciliatory stance towards the trade unions and winning working-class votes.

18. Ramsden, *The Making of Conservative Party Policy*, 1980, p. 141; and Andrew Taylor, 'The Party and the Trade Unions', in Anthony Seldon and Stuart Ball, eds., *Conservative Century: The Conservative Party since 1900*,

1994, Oxford, Oxford University Press, p. 514. CPA CRD2/53/31, minutes of the Conservative Steering Committee, 23 July 1958.

19. See article in *The Sunday Times*, 10 June 1956 and letters to *The Times*, 12 June 1956. Also see Alistair Horne, *Macmillan, 1957–1986, Volume II of the Official Biography*, 1989, London, Macmillan, p. 62; and Keith Middlemas, *Power, Competition and the State: Vol. I: Britain in Search of Balance 1940–61*, 1986, London, Macmillan, p. 263.

20. Cmd. 9725 (March 1956). 'Wage–price spiral', see Robert Taylor, *The Trade Union Question in British Politics*, 1993, Oxford, Blackwell, p. 385.

21. PRO CAB128/31, 1 August 1957.

22. CPA CRD2/21/6. Conservative Party Public Opinion Group, 'First Report', Autumn 1960.

23. The Woolton–Teviot Pact is generally, but totally erroneously, assumed to have merged the two Parties.

24. Papers of Lord Simon Papers, Bodleian Library. Oxford MS SIMN.98, Woolton to Lord Simon, undated letter (probably late 1949 or early 1950). (I would like to thank the 3rd Viscount Simon for the use of this source.) Effect of the Liberal vote, see CPA CCO500/24/87. 'Public Opinion During the Election Campaign, 1951'.

25. CPA CRD2/21/1, 'The Floating Vote', 6 December 1949.

26. MS WLTN.21/folios 66–7, circular to constituency agents, 8 May 1947.

27. CPA CCO3/2/112, J.P.L. Thomas to Lord Woolton, 28 September 1949.

28. Papers of Lord Samuel, House of Lords Library and Record Office. MS SAML.A 155/XIII/folio 29, Lady Violet Bonham-Carter to Lord Samuel. (I would like to thank the 3rd Viscount Samuel for the use of this source.)

29. MS SAML.A 155/XIII/folio 262, Lord Milverton to Lord Samuel, 9 January 1951. Also see resignation letters of Lord Cozens-Hardy and the Viscount Cowdray in Samuel Papers, AP/130/folios 34 and 40.

30. CPA CCO3/1/63, for instance, see Stephen Pierssené to Colonel Blair, 20 June 1949.

31. CPA CCO500/folios 329–30, Simon to Woolton, 18 October 1948 and Simon to Churchill, 20 October 1948. MS Simon.97/folio 140, Churchill to Simon, 13 November 1948.

32. CPA CCO3/1/12, Woolton to Dorothy Crisp, 3 February 1948.

33. McKibbin, 'Class and Conventional Politics', 1991, pp. 259–93.

34. F.W.S. Craig, ed., *British General Election Manifestos 1900–1974*, 1975, London, Macmillan, pp. 169–73.

35. Lord Woolton, *The Memoirs of the Rt Hon the Earl of Woolton*, 1959, London, Cassell, p. 359.

36. *The Times*, 10 May 1947.

37. Winston Churchill, *The Day Will Come*, 1946, London, Conservative Central Office, pp. 7–8.

38. Craig, *British General Election Manifestos*, 1975, pp. 169–73.

39. Ina Zweiniger-Bargielowska, 'Rationing, Austerity and the Conservative Party Recovery after 1945', *Historical Journal*, 37, 1 (1994), p. 194.

40. CPA Poster collection.

41. *Hansard*, House of Commons Parliamentary Debates, 5th series, vol. 458, cols 218–19, and 227–8.

42. 'Politics and Local Government', in *Conservative Party: The Archives of the Conservative Party, Series 1: Pamphlets and Leaflets of the British Conservative and Unionist Party, 1868–1963*, 1977–81, Hassocks, Harvester, 1949/58, card 485.

43. Ramsden, *The Making of Conservative Party Policy*, 1980, pp. 118–19.

44. CPA CCO4/3/202, various letters, 1949. CPA CCO 20/1/3. Lord De L'Isle and Dudley to Woolton, 15 March 1949.

45. CPA CCO4/2/125, Spencer Summers to Woolton, undated (late 1947). CPA CCO4/3/202, C.J. Alport to Woolton, 9 June 1949.

46. CPA CCO3/1/65, see particularly Woolton's letter to Henry Hopkinson, 30 November 1948.

47. The 3rd Earl of Woolton's private collection, Woolton to Sir Alec Douglas-Home, 10 September 1964. (I would like to thank the 3rd Earl of Woolton for the use of this source.)

48. MS SIMN.99, memorandum to Woolton, entitled 'Election Expenses' details Tate and Lyle's position. CPA CCO4/3/202. Aims of Industry campaign coordination, Chapman-Walker to Stokes, 2 February 1950.

49. Peter Shore, 'Big Business Invades Politics', *Socialist Commentary*, XVI (1952), p. 15.

50. Quoted in A.A. Rogow and P. Shore, *The Labour Government and British Industry*, 1955, Oxford, Blackwell, p. 149.

51. David Dutton, *British Politics Since 1945: The Rise and Fall of Consensus*, 1991, Oxford, Basil Blackwell, p. 8.

52. PRO PREM11/1824. 'Some thoughts which have occurred to me during my short holiday', C(57)195, 1 September 1957. For the Party's standing in the opinion polls, see Butler and Butler, *British Political Facts*, 1994, pp. 248–9.

53. Malcolm Smith, 'The Changing Nature of the British State, 1929–1959', in Brian Brivati and Harriet Jones, eds., *What Difference Did the War Make?*, 1992, London, Pinter.

54. PRO CAB129/48. C(51)1, Cabinet Memorandum on the Economic Situation, 31 October 1951.

55. PRO CAB128/40, CC(52)23rd, 24th and 25th conclusions. 'Economic situation: Balance of Payments'.

56. *Hansard*, House of Commons Debates, 5th series, vol. 414, 17 October 1947, cols. 1222–3.

57. CPA CRD2/23/1–6, housing policy files.

58. Butler and Butler, *British Political Facts*, 1994, p. 332.

59. *The Economist*, 17 November 1951, quoted in Kathleen Burk, *The First Privatisation: The Politicians, the City and the Denationalisation of Steel*, 1988, London, Historians Press, p. 43.

60. *Challenge to Britain*, 1953, London, Labour Party.

61. Burk, *The First Privatisation*, 1988, p. 43. For the arguments developed, see also Keith Ovenden, *The Politics of Steel*, 1970, London, Macmillan.

62. Burk, *The First Privatisation*, 1988, p. 139.

63. PRO T228/487, letter (signature indecipherable) to Reginald Maudling (Economic Secretary to the Treasury), 2 October 1954.

64. PRO PREM11/711, Woolton to Churchill, 23 March 1954 and Crookshank to Churchill, 24 May 1954.

65.   PRO PREM11/711, Butler to Churchill, May 1954.
66.   Woolton's interview with the *Evening Standard*, in *Harvester Archives of the Conservative Party*, 1977–81, card 464.
67.   Cmd. 1581. Committee on National Expenditure, First Interim Report, 1922.
68.   Craig, *British General Election Manifestos 1900–1974*, 1975, pp. 169–73.
69.   PRO CAB134/856, the cabinet sub-committee on the economic situation, 31 October 1951.
70.   Woolton to Churchill, 28 December 1951, quoted in Harriet Jones, 'New Tricks for an Old Dog?: The Conservatives and Social Policy, 1951–5', in A. Gorst, L. Johnman and W. Scott Lucas, eds., *Contemporary British History 1931–1961. Politics and the Limits of Policy*, 1991, London, Pinter, pp. 38–9.
71.   PRO PREM11/3930, for example, see transcript of Macmillan's remarks to the cabinet on 28 May 1962.
72.   PRO PREM11/1805, Iain Macleod to Macmillan, 31 January 1957.
73.   PRO PREM11/1138, Memorandum, 28 December 1956.
74.   PRO PREM11/4956, Memorandum, 22 June 1964.
75.   *Hansard*, House of Commons Parliamentary Debates, 1957–8, vol. 586, 15 April 1958, col. 55.
76.   Kevin Jeffreys, 'British Politics and the Road to 1964', *Contemporary Record*, 9, 1 (1995).
77.   Quoted by John Barnes, 'Ideology and Factions' in Seldon and Ball, eds., *Conservative Century*, 1994, p.33. It is not surprising that Butler said he had Peel's Tamworth manifesto in mind when constructing *The Industrial Charter*. Ramsden, *The Making of Conservative Party Policy*, 1980, p. 112.
78.   CPA CRD 2/49/30, study group minutes. 13 October 1954.
79.   Howard Glennerster, *British Social Policy since 1945*, 1995, Oxford, Blackwell, p. 12.
80.   CPA CRD2/49/30, Study group minutes. Peter Goldman's comments, 17 November 1954.
81.   PRO PREM11/1805, Macmillan's memorandum, 'Economies of Expenditure'. PREM11/1816. Macmillan to Michael Fraser (Chairman, CRD), 17 February 1957 and Fraser to Macmillan, 25 February 1957. PREM11/2305. Macmillan to Heathcote-Amory (Chancellor), 5 March 1958, which is about the 1958 budget and tax cuts.
82.   PRO PREM11/2305, Macmillan to Heathcote Amory, 2 April 1958.
83.   PRO PREM11/1805, Iain Macleod (Minister of Labour and National Service) to Macmillan, 31 September 1957.
84.   John Ramsden, '"A Party for owners or a Party for earners"? How far did the British Conservative Party really change after 1945?', *Transaction of the Royal Historical Society*, vol. 27 (1987).
85.   Kavanagh, 'The Postwar Consensus', 1992, p. 181.
86.   Paul Addison, *The Road to 1945. British Politics and the Second World War*, 2nd edition, 1993, London, Pimlico, p. 279.
87.   John Turner, 'A Land Fit for Tories to Live in: The Ecology of the Conservative Party, 1945–1994', *Contemporary European History*, 4:2, July 1995.

5 Consensus and Consumption: Rationing, Austerity and Controls after the War

Ina Zweiniger-Bargielowska

There was little common ground on the issue of consumption and living standards between Labour and the Conservatives during the late 1940s. The debate about rationing, austerity and controls strikes at the heart of respective party ideologies and was discussed in terms of competing philosophies, namely socialism versus capitalism and positive versus negative notions of freedom. Labour endeavoured to rebuild Britain as 'a socialist nation. To this end we seek freedom from the enslaving material bonds of capitalism.' 'Justice demands that fair shares should be the national rule' and 'Full employment is essential if men are to be free from fear. Full employment has been achieved and will be maintained only by asserting control over economic forces. Economic power must be responsible to the people [rather than subject to free market] if security and a rising standard of life are to be ensured.'[1] According to the Conservatives, Britain was faced with a choice between two roads: 'One leads downward to the socialist state, and inevitably on to Communism, with all individual freedom suppressed, and living standards lowered.' Only the Conservative road would 'restore to our citizens their full personal freedom and power of initiative'. 'Socialism thrives on scarcity', but Conservatism 'flourishes in conditions of abundance' by freeing 'the productive energies of the nation from the trammels of overbearing state control and bureaucratic management'.[2]

Prior to explaining this argument in detail, it is necessary to sketch briefly what happened to consumption during the middle decades of the twentieth century. The trend of consumer expenditure per capita is summed up well in Figure 5.1, which shows a rapid rise during the inter-war years. This expansion of consumer spending was based on an increase in average income by about one third in real terms. However, it is import-ant to stress that these improvements in average living standards coincided

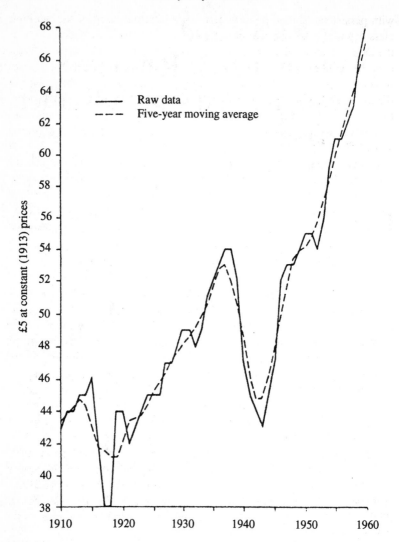

Figure 5.1   Consumers' expenditure per capita at constant (1913) prices, 1910–60.

Source: R.C. Floud, K.W. Wachter and A. Gregory, *Height, Health and History: Nutritional Status in the United Kingdom, 1750–1980* (Cambridge, Cambridge University Press, 1990), p. 321, fig. 7.5; based on C.H. Feinstein, *National Income, Expenditure and Output of the United Kingdom 1855–1965* (Cambridge, Cambridge University Press, 1972), table 17.

with persistent relative poverty affecting about one third of the working class or roughly 20 per cent of the population.[3] Even in the worst years of the Depression, when unemployment among insured workers stood at just over 20 per cent in 1931–2, the majority of the workforce were, of course, in work. Therefore, Labour's focus on poverty and unemployment during the interwar years reflects a minority experience, although a high proportion of manual workers experienced at least a brief spell of unemployment and traditional middle-class humanitarian concern about poverty acquired a new sense of urgency.

During the 1940s the civilian population had to cope with extensive rationing of food and clothing as well as severe shortages of most other consumer goods. In 1942, consumer spending had fallen by about 15 per cent and expenditure on food had been reduced by the same amount. Expenditure on clothing stood at less than two-thirds of the prewar level and expenditure on household and miscellaneous goods had been cut by between one quarter and three-quarters.[4] As a result of rationing and subsidies, coupled with full employment, consumption became more equal in contrast with intense inequalities during the interwar years, and quality as well as variety of most foodstuffs and other goods tended to decline. This reduction in consumption, which is illustrated well in Figure 5.1, was achieved by means of rigid controls on imports, production, distribution and prices. This reduction in consumer expenditure was unprecedented in British history in terms of magnitude and duration.

This austerity policy was generally accepted by the public as a necessary sacrifice for the war effort, but its continuation after the war was controversial and increasingly difficult to justify. In the face of high expectations after a victorious war, shortages actually intensified in the early postwar years; for example, many food rations were lower and more volatile than during war.[5] Despite full employment and high consumer demand, total prewar consumption levels were not reached again until 1950 and for many foodstuffs such as meat or sugar not surpassed until the mid-1950s.[6] Therefore, it is not surprising that Gallup polls and social surveys show that shortages of consumer goods, and particularly of food, were the most important issue on the public mind between 1946 and 1948 (see Figures 5.2 and 5.3). Subsequently, concern about shortages was replaced by worry about rising prices. The figures illustrate the salience of consumption and living standards, as opposed to other areas of economic policy such as nationalisation, in the public mind and political discourse during the late 1940s. As will be seen shortly, the debate about food in particular was important, because it facilitated the translation of party politics into everyday experience.

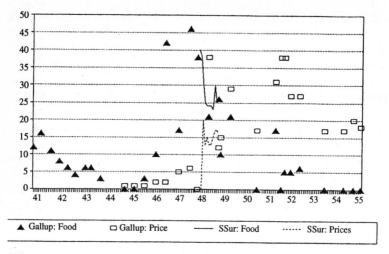

Figure 5.2   Main National Problem, 1940–1955: Gallup poll and social survey (%)

Notes: Main government or national problem, November 1940–January 1955.
Food – Food supplies, food rationing, food shortages.
Prices – Cost of living, rising prices.
From April 1951 fuel is included under 'food' in the Gallup polls.
In the Gallup polls, food scored the highest percentage in November 1940, June 1946, July 1947 and November 1947; other important war problems were shipping losses, the second fron and war production; between 1945–50 housing was the third major concern; in the 1950s foreign policy was second most important problem.
In the social surveys, food scored the highest percentage in December 1947 and January 1948.

Sources: G.H. Gallup (ed.), *The Gallup International Public Opinion Polls: Great Britain, 1937–1975*, vol. 1 1937–1964 (New York, Random House, 1976); PRO, RG 23/92, 94–6, 98–102, 105, Survey of knowledge and opinion about economic situation .

There was no consensus on postwar austerity, and following the end of the war and the termination of Coalition government domestic con-sumption became a subject of intense party political debate. Of course, postwar economic dislocation provided the general background but there were genuine policy choices. Labour's decision to retain wartime controls and restrictions on consumption was not inevitable and was partly motivated by Labour's commitment to establish a socialist society rather than return to the capitalism of the interwar years, which

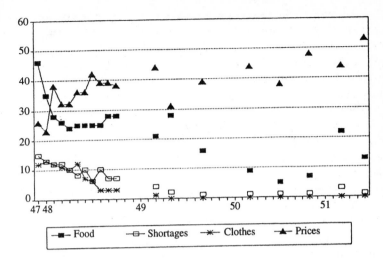

Figure 5.3 Main Personal Problem, 1947–51: social survey (%)

Notes: Main personal and general problem, December 1947–June 1951.
        Food – Food shortages and ration cuts.
        Shortages – Other shortages and queueing.
        Clothes – Clothing difficulties.
        Prices – Cost of living, rising prices.
        Housing, which became more important after 1949, was the other major
        personal problem during the period.

Sources: PRO, RG 23.92, 94–6, 98–102, 105–6, 108, 110, 112, 114, 116–17,
Survey of knowledge and opinion about the economic situation.

was held to have been responsible for working-class poverty and mass
unemployment. Despite the so-called bonfire of controls of 1948 and
some decontrol in the late 1940s, as Neil Rollings has argued convinc-
ingly, Labour planned to make some wartime controls permanent as
part of its full employment policy during the last years of the Attlee
government.[7]

    Disagreement between the major parties focused on the causes of per-
sistent shortages as well as on the most appropriate policies to increase
consumption and living standards. Labour propaganda held that the government was doing a good job in difficult circumstances. Austerity was an
inevitable consequence of postwar dislocation in general, and the world
food and dollar shortage in particular. In view of the balance of payments
deficit, the first priority of economic policy was to raise exports and
reduce imports. On the domestic front, the emphasis was on investment

and social reform rather than on personal consumption. The maintenance of fair shares in the context of full employment and the welfare state were hailed as a major success and a great improvement in working-class living standards in contrast with the bad old days of the interwar years. The Conservatives did not deny that there was postwar economic dislocation, but argued that austerity was largely due to Labour's incompetence, mismanagement and socialist-inspired policies, which were making matters much worse than they need be. Controls were imposed for controls' sake, while excessive bureaucracy stifled the economy and hampered recovery. The Conservatives claimed that for the majority of the population living standards under Labour were worse than during the 1930s, and that only a return to the free market and the abolition of wartime controls would restore living standards.

These arguments, which were repeated over and over again, were based on very different perceptions of interwar years. Labour's theme of 'never again' contrasted unemployment, poverty and hardship with great improvements especially among the poorest sections of the working class during the 1940s. Conversely, the Conservatives emphasised declining levels of personal consumption suffered by the majority of the population, which compared unfavourably with low prices and wide choice in consumer goods during the 1930s. The question is, which argument was more persuasive in the battle for votes during the late 1940s? Despite the popularity of Labour's achievements in maintaining full employment and establishing the welfare state, the Conservatives held the better cards among doubtful voters. The persistence of austerity was hard to bear and popular discontent was fuelled by constant Conservative criticism which was widely reported in the right-wing press.

The use of wartime emergency legislation to control consumption in peacetime entailed many problems for the Labour government. On the one hand, the vast apparatus of controls which was administered by a large bureaucracy was fraught with contradictions and petty restrictions. These were easily criticised and provided the Conservatives with ammunition in their claims that controls amounted to an erosion of civil liberties which was not justifiable in peacetime. On the other, the fuel crisis of spring 1947 and the convertibility crisis of the summer undermined the credibility of Labour's faith in the efficacy of socialist planning. An intense export drive under the menacing slogan of 'We work or want' largely backfired.[8] Import cuts in the autumn resulting in reduced rations proved deeply unpopular. This is illustrated by Conservative gains in the local elections of November 1947, which were the first clear sign of a swing in public opinion away from the Labour Party.[9]

During the war, controls had a positive role in allocating resources between competing claims within the war economy as well as the negative function of reducing resources available to civilian consumers. In wartime, government requirements necessarily took precedence, 'leaving the minimum to be shared out in meeting civilian requirements, [but] there was no such compelling need in peacetime when the whole purpose of production was to meet those very requirements'.[10] Hence, only the negative function of controls remained and government precedence over the private sector with regard to claims on economic resources was now controversial. The question arises, how long can personal consumption be restricted in peacetime in a capitalist democracy? Or, to put it another way, did the election of the first Labour government with a majority in the House of Commons imply a general acceptance among the population that the free market was to be replaced by a planned socialist economy? Of course, socialist economic policy did not restrict consumer spending for dogmatic reasons and, indeed, Labour aimed to raise personal consumption in the long run, once the debts were paid off and the external balance was restored. This was stressed by one party publication:

> [the] only cure for shortages is to abolish them. The way to do this and to raise the standard of living is to increase production. This is the main aim of the Labour Government's economic policy ... . But capital investment can only take place at the immediate cost of the consumer. If electrical equipment factories turn out more electric motors for cotton mills there will be less radio sets than would otherwise be available ... . But if we are prepared to do without some of the frills in the next years, Britain's reward will be a higher standard of living in the future. Soviet Russia demonstrated this truth between the wars; only by sacrificing immediate consumption was that country's colossal industrialisation made possible.[11]

Labour demanded sacrifice now and promised jam tomorrow, but especially after 1947 the goalposts were shifting all the time and tomorrow never came. This gives rise to the question, how long were people prepared to wait or, to be more specific, how many Labour converts in 1945, especially in seats which had returned a Labour MP for the first time, were prepared to accept the continuation of a command-style economy after the initial postwar problems were overcome? The remainder of this chapter illustrates this argument by focusing on two episodes. First, the controversy about food policy and the adequacy of the diet during 1946 and 1947; and second, the debate in the party literature about consumption and controls during the 1950 and 1951 general election campaigns is analysed.

Figures 5.2 and 5.3 show that food was the most important single issue on the public mind during the late 1940s as a result of unprecedented shortages. Bread was rationed for the first time from July 1946.[12] The policy was controversial because the entire system of food control depended on ample supplies of bread and potatoes as well as restaurant and canteen meals. Labour justified bread rationing as a necessary step to guarantee the bread supply and ensure fair shares in the context of the world food shortage, which required sacrifice in Britain to prevent famine in continental Europe and elsewhere. During the spring and summer of 1946 intense opposition to bread rationing was led by the Conservative Party, which doubted that the policy was really necessary and that substantial savings in wheat could be made. The Party leadership deplored the added burden placed on consumers and alleged that the government had mismanaged the supply situation. The Conservatives were backed by the right-wing press, which highlighted opposition to bread rationing among bakers as well as the British Housewives' League. This episode was the first concerted campaign against the Labour government on a major policy issue and marked the beginning of the debate about postwar food policy.

The dollar economy measures introduced during the summer and autumn of 1947, in the wake of the fuel and convertibility crises, included substantial cuts in food imports which had important dietary and political consequences. Many rations, especially of popular items such as meat, bacon and ham as well as fats, now fell to their lowest ever level (that is, below wartime levels) and calorie consumption also declined. These cuts were supplemented by other restrictions such as the abolition of the basic petrol ration and the suspension of foreign currency for pleasure travel.

According to the Labour government, this crisis was caused by postwar economic dislocation and the cuts were necessary to restore Britain's external balance. Indeed, the government actually highlighted the severity of the crisis invoking the danger of national collapse if export targets were not achieved with slogans such as 'We're up against it. We work or want. A challenge to British grit.'[13] Despite present hardships, Labour stressed the government's achievements in contrast with the bad old days of unemployment and inequality under the Tories and called for loyalty and national unity to help Britain pull through in this battle for the peace.[14] The government was defended vigorously in the *Daily Herald*:

> the reason for the cuts, as the country well understands, is that they are unavoidable. They must be made because we have not yet had time to build up our production sufficiently to pay our way in the world … . Obviously it is impossible to expect that the government should have

been able to forecast the whole world food situation and our ability to buy following the end of convertibility of £ ... . Immediately this harsh news should act as a fresh summons to hard work and patriotic action ... . That appeal ... has been met with great response in defiance of the dirges preached in the Tory press.[15]

The Conservative perspective on the crisis was very different. The Party alleged that the crisis was largely the result of Labour mismanagement and incompetence. The right-wing press responded to cuts with anger and dismay. The *Daily Express*, under the headline 'Less – Less – Less: The Reckoning', lamented, 'The nation that used to be proud and strong ... suffers a new humiliation from its rulers. For do not doubt it – the cuts and restrictions ... are not to be counted some natural disaster ... They are the result of wrong thinking and wrong policy on the part of the group of men in power.'[16] Similarly, the *Daily Telegraph* noted 'a grim irony in the reflection that in the third year of peace a victorious country is condemned to revert to a war-time footing in respect alike of the necessities and amenities of life'.[17] The Conservative case against the government was summed up by Churchill, for whom the government was not merely incompetent but fundamentally mistaken. Under the slogan 'Set the people free' he declared in his reply to the King's Speech:

No long-term scheme for keeping a community alive can be based on an export scheme alone.... The conception that any community could make its living without a healthy and vigorous home market and strong domestic consuming power [is] a fallacy.... I do not believe in the capacity of the state to plan and enforce...economic productivity upon its members.... No matter how numerous are the committees...or the hordes of officials...they cannot approach the high level of internal economic production which, under free enterprise, personal initiative, competitive selection and the profit motive...constitute the life of a free society.

He concluded, 'I am sure that this policy of equalising misery and organising scarcity, instead of allowing diligent self-interest and ingenuity to produce abundance, has only to be prolonged to kill this British island stone dead.'[18]

The Labour government took pride in the maintenance of fair shares, full employment and improvements in social services, which meant that the nation was better fed and healthier than ever before. This was evident particularly in vital statistics which registered rapid improvements and much was made of the healthy, rosy-cheeked and well-clad children of the late 1940s compared with the poverty and deprivation, especially among large families, during the interwar years. *Proud Heritage* which featured happy, healthy children on the front cover, contrasts the poverty, unemployment and general hopelessness of the interwar years with the fact that, in spite of the shortages, 'children are rosy-cheeked, well-clothed ... taller, heavier and healthier than before the war.'[19] The continuation of rationing and food subsidies prevented the return of the large income differentials in food consumption observed by Boyd Orr during the interwar years.[20] In contrast with food shortages and rationing by price in continental Europe, the British people were guaranteed their fair share of basic necessities at subsidised prices.[21]

In an Opposition debate about food policy in July 1947, John Strachey, the Minister of Food, denied that there was a food crisis and defended government policy since housewives had the assurance that they would be able to afford the basics which 'for the poorer housewives was a new assurance'. He admitted that there was little surplus but maintained that the diet was nutritionally adequate and well balanced. Strachey categorically dismissed claims by so-called 'calorie-mongers' that the diet had deteriorated drastically since the war and that Britain was 'starving to death', and stressed that in contrast with the interwar years, calorie intake 'today is very largely according to need instead of according to class'. Michael Foot took on the charge that 'there has been a disastrous fall in the standard of life of the people of this country.... That is the charge of Dr Franklin Bicknell, who...says that we are dying of starvation'. However, on the test of infant and maternal mortality there was, in fact, considerable improvement compared with the 1930s. Despite wartime dislocation today's children are 'healthier, tougher, stronger than any breed of children we have ever bred in this country before. This is a fact of which we ought to be proud, and we are proud.'[22]

This optimistic assessment of the postwar diet was rejected by Conservative politicians, who frequently voiced concern about the perceived inadequacy of the diet. In the debate of July 1947, James Reid, the Conservative spokesman, accused the government of 'bad housekeeping, lack of foresight and a failure to face the facts'. He denied that Britain was a well-fed nation and rejected the notion of fair shares since some people had access to ample canteen foods whereas others had to make do with meagre rations. While some people were 'better off today than they were prewar ... the great majority of people who were not in the lowest income class before the war ... are very much worse off than they were prewar.' Calories 'tell only half the story' since 'weight for weight, there are more calories in bread than in stewing steak' but there had been a 'falling off in the quality of our diet'. According to Lady Grant, 'there are a great number of people in this country who cannot understand why the standard of our living is falling now in the open seas of peace. We know perfectly well that since 1945 there have been cuts in several of our vital rations', which meant that 'while we may not be dying of starvation, we are undergoing a famine in quality'. This 'lack of quality ... is having a grave effect upon our people's will to work' and 'a very great number of the people of this country consider not only that we are worse fed than before the war, but that our standard of living is declining and, therefore, that they lack confidence in ... the present administration'.[23]

At this time both features and correspondence in the *British Medical Journal* and the *Lancet* frequently expressed concern about food shortages which might lead to malnutrition. There was a general agreement among GPs that the postwar diet was monotonous and unappetising. Ration cuts and especially the low fats ration were thought to cause fatigue and irritability, with negative repercussions for morale. Not all correspondents were equally pessimistic since vital statistics were improving and there was no hard evidence that public health was deteriorating. Nevertheless, the nutritional situation was perceived to be precarious.[24] In view of this concern, the Hunterian Society debated the motion that 'Our present diet is undermining the nation's health' in November 1947.[25] Dr Franklin Bicknell defended the motion in view of ration cuts and the decline in calorie consumption. Nutritionists such as Sir Jack Drummond and Magnus Pyke stressed that limited malnutrition was extremely difficult to detect, acknowledged that the situation was tight, but defended the postwar diet and particularly the fact that sacrifice was now equally shared compared with the inequalities in food consumption during the interwar years. Despite the fact that little, if any, concrete evidence was produced to indicate that health was deteriorating, doctors were concerned about recent ration cuts resulting in a decline in calorie consumption as well as signs of fatigue and weariness among the adult population. The motion was carried by a majority of three to one. Whatever doctors' motives in supporting the motion, it provides further evidence of low food morale and lack of faith in government policy during the late 1940s.[26]

Social surveys suggest that food morale was indeed low. Regardless of government claims, in 1948 a small majority of the population felt that their diet was inadequate to maintain good health.[27] This disparity between government claims and popular perceptions of the postwar diet, which were highlighted and exploited by government opponents, can be resolved by distinguishing between objective evidence and subjective attitudes. It is necessary to take account of the psychological aspects of the diet. The

Labour government could rightly argue that the postwar diet was nutritionally adequate, public health was maintained and vital statistics improved, but people did not *feel* that they were better fed than ever before. The postwar diet was healthier but it was not popular since people missed fats, dairy products and especially meat. Consumption of these foodstuffs, with the exception of milk, actually deteriorated compared with prewar and even wartime levels.[28] Hence, there was no undernourishment but *perceived deprivation* was intense as illustrated by a social survey of March 1949 – when the worst shortages were over – but 75 per cent thought that their present diet was worse than before the war and another 9 per cent were doubtful.[29]

It is impossible to say which Party was winning this debate and public opinion was above all divided. Nevertheless, the controversy about bread rationing in the summer of 1946 shows that Labour's honeymoon was already over during Dalton's *annus mirabilis*, and the beginning of the Conservatives' recovery can be traced back to the local elections of November 1947 in the wake of austerity cuts. Reversing the losses of 1945 and 1946[30] the Conservatives made sweeping gains in what Morgan Phillips described as a 'food and basic petrol' election. He rejected suggestions that the results implied a political landslide since Labour had consolidated a high proportion of recent gains 'in the face of a high-pressure Tory attack, which was deliberately aimed at exploiting popular discontent over inevitable shortages and restrictions'. By contrast, Churchill rejoiced at this 'splendid victory over the inept and wrong-headed forces which have already led us far along the road to ruin. ... The result deprives the Socialist government of any mandate they obtained at the general election.'[31] Bolstered by this result the *Daily Express* claimed that the 'Socialist government does not command the confidence of the people' and endorsed Conservative calls for a general election under the slogan 'Set the people free'.[32] For the *Daily Herald* the elections were the 'climax of a campaign of misrepresentation unparalleled in British political history'. Highlighting continuous criticism of the government, the editorial continued, 'Such an incessant and indefatigable barrage of slanders was bound to make some impression, especially when fullest opportunity was taken to exploit for political ends the sacrifices made necessary by the economic crisis.'[33] The political temperature remained high until Labour's success in holding the Gravesend by-election at the end of the month. This victory was hailed as a triumph for Labour and was clearly a bitter blow for the Conservatives. Gravesend indicated the limits of the Conservative recovery but also showed how much the government was now on the defensive and how vulnerable Labour had become during Dalton's *annus horrendous*.

The debate in the party literature during the 1950 and 1951 general election campaigns similarly illustrates a lack of consensus on the issue of consumption. With deeply held opinions on both sides of the divide, the forthcoming general elections were vital for each party as well as the county's future. According to Morrison a second victory was

> of the greatest importance ... to develop and consolidate our policy and achievements. ... a second defeat for the Tories would be a great blow to them and should seriously shake their political morale ... but a defeat for Labour would have a very bad effect not only on the morale of the British Labour Party but on the cause of democratic progress throughout the world ... . If we win the next election ... there is a likelihood of winning the one after that... . If we lose ... we could not rule out the possibility of more than one Tory parliament.

Morrison acknowledged that it would be a lot more difficult to put forward Labour's case than it had been in 1945 and expected that the result might very well be close.[34] Similarly, for Churchill, 'Never ... have the British people been called upon by their votes to take so momentous a decision as that which lies before them.' At the general election the 'choice was between two ways of life; between individual liberty and state domination ... between a policy of increasing restraint and a policy of liberating energy and ingenuity; between a policy of levelling down and a policy of finding opportunity for all to rise up.'[35]

Labour propaganda took pride in the Attlee government's successes in contrast with the broken promises after the Great War and unemployment and hardship of the interwar years. Labour's central achievement was the maintenance of full employment which, coupled with rationing, food subsidies and social reform, had transformed working-class living standards. Thus, according to the 1951 election manifesto, 'To-day, after six years of Labour rule and in spite of post-war difficulties, the standard of living of the vast majority of our people is higher than ever it was in the days of Tory rule. Never have the old folk been better cared for. Never had we so happy and healthy a young generation.'[36] In order to contain inflation under full employment as well as to maintain fair shares, permanent controls were a central feature of Labour's economic policy. 'Only by price control and rationing can fair shares of scarce goods be ensured.' 'Food subsidies, rationing, price control of essentials, rent control ... these are all helping to keep down the cost of living' and Tory cries to scrap controls would be disastrous since cuts in subsidies would mean dearer food. The fundamental question was whether Britain should 'continue along the road of ordered progress' or should 'reaction, the protectors of privilege and the apostles of scarcity economics ... take us back to the bleak years of poverty and unemployment.'[37] Labour's policy directed at consumers aimed to make distribution more efficient as a means of lowering prices. This was to be achieved by nationalising some areas of the wholesale trade and retaining bulk buying along with government purchasing which kept down the cost of imports. By contrast, 'Tory policy would cause a catastrophic rise in the cost of living. They are for high profits and against controls. They demand the abandonment of bulk purchase.'[38]

For the Conservatives the economic crisis itself was due to the failure of socialist planning and mismanagement as well as excessive controls and bureaucracy rather than the war. Government policy was the prime cause of persistent shortages which could be eased by returning to the free market, which would result in wider choice and lower prices of consumer goods. There were four main arguments in Conservative propaganda.[39] In the first place, the Party criticised the meagre rations and other shortages, which compared unfavourably with prewar and even wartime consumption standards. This was the main reason for allegations that living standards had declined under Labour. The Conservatives made much of the lowest-ever meat ration in 1951[40] which was a consequence of the near breakdown of negotiations with Argentina, a major British supplier. The episode provided ammunition for the Conservative opposition to bulk purchasing. Second, the high number of controls were depicted as an erosion of traditional civil liberties and, third, the Conservatives opposed the large bureaucracy administering the controls apparatus along with the 'crushing burden of taxation' which was an integral part of the socialist state. Finally, the Conservatives highlighted examples of mismanagement such as the fuel and convertibility crises of 1947 along with projects such as the groundnuts scheme, which were said to have cost £500 million and ridiculed unconventional foods such as snoek or whale meat.

The Conservatives vigorously opposed Labour plans to make the wartime emergency powers permanent as proposed in the King's Speech of October 1950: 'In order to defend full employment, to ensure that the resources of the community are used to best advantage and to avoid inflation, legislation will be introduced to make available ... on a permanent basis ... powers to regulate production, distribution and consumption and to control prices.'[41] In Churchill's words, 'war-time controls in time of peace [are] a definite evil in themselves' and permanent controls amounted to a 'blank cheque for totalitarian government'. As Butler put it, the policy amounted to the 'Reichstag method of government'. The Conservatives demanded an annual renewal of emergency legislation and held that useful controls should be transferred to statute book. The remainder should be reduced to a minimum and abolished as soon as possible:

> To make such powers permanent ... is a confession by the Government that they believe the emergency itself will be permanent: that supplies will always be scarce; that ration-books and identity cards will never disappear ... Conservatives hold that a perpetual emergency is a contradiction in terms, and that, if the liberty of the subject is to be preserved ... the State cannot be granted, as a normal and everlasting part of its authority, powers of government by decree originally conceived at a time of impending military peril.[42]

Following the Conservative election victory of 1951 – in the context of more favourable international economic conditions – wartime controls on consumption were gradually abolished, culminating in the termination of food rationing in the summer of 1954. In the run-up to the 1955 general election, Conservative propaganda celebrated rising living standards and the return to freedom of choice: 'Austerity had gone the way of shortages, black markets, controls, power cuts ... and ration books.' While the economy had been stifled under Labour and controls and rationing had been accepted as inevitable, the Conservatives had freed the economy, abolished rationing, removed controls and lowered taxes. With the help of stable prices and improved economic circumstances the postwar consumer boom was well under way, resulting in more choice, greater variety and better quality of goods and food consumption finally returned to prewar levels. The Conservative government now presided over the restoration of 'general prosperity' since 'To-day the British people are earning, eating, producing, buying, building, growing and saving more than they ever did under the Socialists.'[43]

There is little evidence of a consensus on postwar austerity between the major political parties and these divisions are reflected in popular attitudes. Of course, the general economic background was important, the immediate postwar period was difficult and the Conservatives were fortunate to come to power when the worst of the crisis was over. Nevertheless, there were genuine policy choices to be made and both parties, influenced by their respective ideologies, had very different priorities with regard to rationing, controls and consumption. The issue was central to political debate during the period and the electorate was deeply divided as indicated by the close result of both the 1950 and 1951 general elections. Turnout at over 80 per cent reached an all-time high since 1918, and the early postwar years also mark a high point of party membership. This evidence is not a sign of an enhanced sense of citizenship. Rather, it indicates powerful disagreement between the Parties and in the press as well as among the electorate, not least on the issue of consumption and controls. There was no general repudiation of Labour's policies and the Party remained strong, especially in its heartlands, with Labour polling a slight majority and its highest vote ever in 1951. And yet, the Conservative Party was the main beneficiary in the battle for votes during the late 1940s. The party recovered from their apparent 'Waterloo'[44] in 1945, when it obtained a poor second place, to a neck and neck position during the height of postwar austerity. Victory in 1951 was based on establishing a broad coalition of consumer interests as southeastern suburbia and women voters in particular became disillusioned with the privations and restrictions of Labour Britain.

NOTES

1.   Labour Party, *Labour Believes in Britain*, 1949, London, Labour Party, p. 3; Labour Party, *Labour and the New Society*, 1950, London, Labour Party, p. 4.
2.   Conservative and Unionist Central Office (hereafter CUCO), *The Right Road for Britain*, popular edn, 1949, London, CUCO; CUCO, *This is the Road*, 1950, London, CUCO, pp. 3, 22, 23; CUCO, *The Industrial Charter*, 1947, London, CUCO, p. 14.
3.   H. Perkin, *The Rise of Professional Society: England since 1880*, 1989, London, Routledge, pp. 276–80.
4.   E.L. Hargreaves and M.M. Gowing, *Civil Industry and Trade*, 1952, London, HMSO, p. 648, table 10; G.D.N. Worswick and P.H. Ady, eds., *The British Economy 1945–1950*, 1952, Oxford, Oxford University Press, p. 47, table 7.
5.   I. Zweiniger-Bargielowska, 'Rationing, Austerity and the Conservative Party Recovery after 1945', *Historical Journal* 37, 1994, p. 177 and app. 1.
6.   See Figure 5.1; Worswick and Ady, 1952, p. 47, table; B.R. Mitchell, *British Historical Statistics*, 1988, Cambridge, Cambridge University Press, p. 713.
7.   N. Rollings, '"The Reichstag Method of Governing"? The Attlee Governments and Permanent Economic Controls', in H. Mercer, N. Rollings and J.D. Tomlinson, eds., *Labour Governments and Private Industry: the Experience of 1945–1951*, 1992, Edinburgh, Edinburgh University Press, pp. 15–36.
8.   PRO: INF 2/110; W. Crofts, *Coercion or Persuasion? Propaganda in Britain after 1945*, 1989, London, Routledge, pp. 40–7.
9.   Zweiniger-Bargielowska, 1994, p. 184 and table 3.
10.   A. Cairncross, *Years of Recovery: British Economic Policy, 1945–51*, 1985, London, Methuen, p. 343.
11.   Labour Party, *Fair Shares of Scarce Consumer Goods*, Labour discussion series no. 2, 1946, London, Labour Party, pp. 7, 4.

12. I. Zweiniger-Bargielowska, 'Bread rationing in Britain, July 1946–July 1948', *Twentieth Century British History*, 4, 1993, pp. 57–85.

13. Crofts, 1989, p. 45.

14. See e.g., Labour Party, *ABC of the Crisis*, 1947, London, Labour Party.

15. *Daily Herald*, 28 August 1947.

16. *Daily Express*, 28 August 1947.

17. *Daily Telegraph*, 28 August 1947.

18. *Ibid.*, 29 October 1947.

19. Labour Party, *Proud Heritage*, 1949, London, Labour Party; see also Central Office of Information, *Something Done: British Achievement 1945–47*, London, HMSO, 1948, showing a picture of well-fed and well-dressed children and stressing the decline in mortality rates as well as advances in welfare policy.

20. J. Boyd Orr, *Food, Health and Income*, London, Macmillan, 1936.

21. See e.g., Labour Party pamphlets, *Two Queues: Britain and Europe*, London, Labour Party,1947; *Food: What Happens When You Lift Controls*, London, Labour Party, 1947; *Housewives' Choice: Labour is Better*, London, Labour Party,1949.

22. *Hansard*, 5th series, 1 July 1947, 439:1174–6, 1183, 1190–1, 1193.

23. *Ibid.*, 1155–6, 1160, 1208–9.

24. See *British Medical Journal*, 1, 1947, pp. 235, 525, 863; 2, 1947, pp. 422, 696–7, 882–4, 926, 1011–12; 1, 1948, pp. 27, 73–4, 476, 619; 2, 1948, pp. 231–2, 397. *The Lancet*, 1, 1947, p. 196; 2, 1947, pp. 41, 60, 67, 72, 391, 407–8, 660, 768–70, 775–6, 848. From 1949 onwards, when the worst shortages were over, discussion on food issues was less prominent and more favourable to the Government's point of view.

25. *British Medical Journal*, 2, 1947, pp. 882–4.

26. It is, of course, only possible to speculate about GPs' motives and whether opposition to government policy on the National Health Service may have prejudiced GPs' attitudes towards nutritional policy.

27. PRO: RG 23/96, 98, 100, 102, Survey of knowledge and opinion about the economic situation. A representative sample of the population were asked whether they felt that they were getting enough food to keep in good health. In April, June, August and October 1948, 55 per cent, 53 per cent, 48 per cent and 51 per cent respectively replied 'no', with another 7 per cent, 9 per cent, 10 per cent and 9 per cent doubtful.

28. See Zweiniger-Bargielowska, 1994, appendix II; Ministry of Food, *The Urban Working Class Household Diet 1940–1949*, London, HMSO, 1951; Ministry of Agriculture, Fisheries and Food, *Studies in Urban Household Diets, 1944–49*, London, HMSO, 1956.

29. PRO: RG 23/105, Survey of knowledge and opinion about the economic situation.

30. See Zweiniger-Bargielowska, 1994, p. 185, table 3.

31. *Daily Herald*, 3 November 1947.

32. *Daily Express*, 3 November 1947.

33. *Daily Herald*, 3 November 1947.

34. Labour Party Archives, Research Department, RD 175, memorandum by H. Morrison, October, 1948.

35. CUCO, *The Right Road for Britain*, Foreword, p. 5; Nuffield College, Oxford, Conservative Party Pamphlets, PP Cons 2, Churchill speech, launching *The Right Road for Britain*, 23 July 1949.

36. F.W.S. Craig, ed., *British General Election Manifestos, 1918–1966*, 1970, Chichester, Political Reference Publications, p. 150.

37. Labour Party, *Let Us Win Through Together* (1950 Manifesto), 1950, London, Labour Party, pp. 4, 7.

38. Craig, 1970, p. 149.

39. See Zweiniger-Bargielowska, 1994, pp. 186–8.

40. Note the resurgence of the food issue in Figures 5.2 and 5.3 which coincides with this reduction in the meat ration.

41. F.W.S. Craig, ed., *The Most Gracious Speeches to Parliament 1900–1974: Statements of Government Policy and Achievements*, 1975, London, Macmillan, p. 134.

42. CUCO, *The Campaign Guide*, 1951, London, CUCO, pp. 97–102.

43. Conservative Research Department, *Three Years' Work: Achievements of the Conservative Government*, December 1954, London, Conservative Party, pp. 39, 7; see also pp. 9–11, 36–41.

44. R.B. McCallum and A. Readman, *The British General Election of 1945*, 1947, Oxford, Oxford University Press, p. 243.

6 Butskellism, the Postwar Consensus and the Managed Economy
Neil Rollings

Recently there has been a trend in the literature on the postwar consensus to broaden the area of perceived consensus to incorporate foreign and defence policy.[1] None the less even these accounts still place great weight on those areas in which the postwar consensus has traditionally been located: the welfare state, the mixed economy and the use of demand management to ensure full employment. With regard to the last of these, it has been conventional to argue that both Conservative and Labour governments during the 1940s and 1950s were committed to the maintenance of full employment and used Keynesian demand management to ensure this occurred.[2] Frequently, the term 'Butskellism' has been used as a shorthand expression of this consensus.[3] Whether Butskellism existed is open to debate, but to equate the term with the postwar consensus is a dubious practice. This raises the fundamental issue of definition, a great bone of contention amongst historians of the postwar consensus. Even if Butskellism can be applied to the period 1945–55, its use to describe the period after then, when neither Gaitskell nor Butler was Chancellor of the Exchequer, must be seen as unwise. How then do the three concepts of Butskellism, the postwar consensus and the managed economy relate to each other? This question will form the basis of the chapter. It begins with a section on Butskellism. This is followed by a section on economic policy in the 1950s, in which the focus will be on three issues: the impact of changing personnel within the Treasury, Peter Thorneycroft's resignation as Chancellor of the Exchequer in January 1958, and the government's response to the 1958–9 recession. A concluding section comments on the relationship between Butskellism, the postwar consensus and the managed economy, and more generally, what this tells us about the debate on the postwar consensus.

BUTSKELLISM

One of the main problems confronting historians looking at the postwar consensus is that of definition. There is disagreement on such fundamentals as to whether the postwar consensus was one form of a more long-standing consensus in British politics or an historically unique consensus, which is either confined to Britain or is seen to be common to other European states or even to the industrialised nations of the Western hemisphere.[4] One is based on the nature of British politics while the other focuses on a particular period in history. Efforts have been made to define the term, but the most outstanding features of these has been their lack of consensus and the tendency to adopt rather broad definitions. This may reflect the character of consensus but makes it extremely hard to pin down.[5] As such there is no agreed precise working definition. Perhaps a typical definition would be Anthony Seldon's recent suggestion: consensus represents 'a broad parameter of agreement on many key areas of policy'.[6] Such a definition leaves many issues open to debate and individual interpretation. For example, what policies are key areas, what constitutes a broad level of agreement and what brings this broad level of agreement about? An extra complication comes with Rodney Lowe's argument that while a postwar consensus existed, 'its nature was constantly evolving'.[7] One is left with an amorphous concept, which is perceived in different ways by different people and which was constantly changing in any case. It is hardly surprising that the debate amongst historians of the postwar consensus seems to be making little progress.

Anthony Seldon adds the further condition to his definition of consensus that it is 'between the leaderships of both main parties when they are in office'. Thus he sees little to distinguish between the concepts of the postwar consensus and Butskellism, but this addition would not be accepted by all. Peter Clarke and Rodney Lowe both support the notion of a postwar consensus but reject Butskellism. I reached a similar conclusion in an earlier article about Butskellism, as I believed it was something more specific and definable than postwar consensus.[8] This proved too optimistic in terms of definition yet, even broadly defined, Butskellism remained distinct from the much wider notion of a postwar consensus because of its historical specificity and focus on the policy and attitudes of only two Chancellors of the Exchequer, Hugh Gaitskell and R.A. Butler. This does not, however, mean that the conclusions of that article are of no relevance to the debate on postwar consensus; rather, that it is dangerous to transpose the conclusions about Butskellism on to the postwar consensus. In brief, the article suggested that the traditional picture of the development of postwar macroeconomic policy is flawed.

This picture highlights continuity in policy and in attitudes between Labour and Conservative governments around the 1951 election. The policy of both parties when in power was characterised by indirect demand management, in which budgetary policy was seen as the dominant tool. Moreover, both governments were committed equally to the maintenance of full employment. Central to this picture was the rejection of planning and controls by the Labour governments following the 1948 'bonfire of controls', in favour of demand management based on the budget, and the Conservative government's rejection of 'Operation Robot' in 1952, which, had it been introduced, would have threatened the commitment to full employment. These events are conventionally seen to confirm the existence of both Butskellism and the postwar consensus in the area of demand management.

This picture, it is argued, is flawed in certain fundamental ways with regard to both Labour and Conservative administrations. Under Labour there was a move away from planning, decontrol did occur and budgetary policy did become more important. However, direct controls were seen to have a continuing role in economic policy by Labour ministers, including Gaitskell. As he put it, 'It is the use by the government of direct controls...which has been the distinguishing feature of British socialist policy.'[9] To this end, during 1950 and the first two months of 1951 the government was involved in the drafting of legislation to take powers to allow the use of direct economic controls on a permanent basis. Significantly, ministers rejected the original draft drawn up by civil servants because it dealt only with negative controls, that is, controls which prevented or limited actions. Ministers insisted that positive powers, dealing, for example, with powers to manufacture, should also be included in the draft legislation. Although the legislation was never brought before Parliament this was not because of any decision that these powers were unnecessary, but because of the Korean War, which required the introduction of rather different temporary controls. The intention to introduce such legislation remained. It should, however, be noted that the purpose of the legislation was not to plan the economy but to ensure full employment. This was most definitely Gaitskell's view.[10] In other words, the Labour government by 1951 was attempting to manage the economy but in a way very different from how it has been customary to perceive it.

A very similar argument can be made with regard to Conservative economic policy after the 1951 election. The rejection of 'Operation Robot' has been presented as confirmation of the Conservatives' commitment to full employment and to the use of budgetary and monetary policy to manage the economy. However, this, it is argued, makes too much of the significance of this episode. To view it as a simple choice between international and domestic considerations ignores other factors, such as personalities, which played a role in the decision. Rejection of a radical crisis measure put forward in unusual circumstances does not necessarily mean a rejection of the principles underlying that measure. Certainly, international considerations, such as the maintenance of confidence in sterling and the desire for convertibility, continued to play a central role in policy formulation. More specifically, budgetary and monetary policy were used to stimulate the economy but always with these considerations in mind. In both 1953 and 1954 a budget deficit was avoided when, on the basis of Keynesian economic calculations, one was felt necessary. Similarly, monetary policy under Butler tended to follow the recommendations of the Bank of England rather than the Economic Section, the Keynesian economists in the government. As Jim Tomlinson has put it, there does not appear to have been 'an overwhelming willingness to sacrifice other policies to employment' in the period of Butler's chancellorship.[11] The Conservatives were managing the economy and were concerned about the maintenance of full employment but this was constrained by the extent to which this policy fitted in with other objectives. In other words, there was neither continuity in policy between Labour and Conservative governments nor did either government's policies fit the conventional Butskellite image. Both governments did adopt a form of managed economy but these differed in fundamental ways from each other, both in terms of the balance of priorities and the tools used. In many ways this leaves a very ambiguous and ambivalent picture with regard to the debate on consensus, in which the definition of consensus adopted will determine whether consensus is perceived or not.

AFTER 1955

This rather unsatisfactory conclusion suggested that it was necessary to extend the analysis into the later 1950s to see if a clearer picture emerged at that time. Perhaps by the later 1950s macroeconomic policy was being formulated on the lines conventionally depicted. There were three reasons to suggest that this might be the case: there was a change in the top Treasury personnel in the mid-1950s; there was the resignation of Peter Thorneycroft and the rest of the Treasury ministerial team in January 1958 over the Cabinet's rejection of their proposal that inflation should be the

main objective of economic policy; and 1958–9 saw the emergence of the
deepest recession since the war, which would give clearer evidence of the
Conservative government's response to unemployment. These three
aspects will now be considered in more detail.

Treasury Officials

The mid- to late 1950s did see the end of an era in the Treasury.
Sir Edward Bridges, the Permanent Secretary since 1945, who had first
joined the Treasury in 1919, retired in 1956.[12] Almost as significant in this
context was the retirement in the same year of Sir Bernard Gilbert, the
Joint Second Secretary. Gilbert was renowned for his traditional views on
public expenditure and the budget, and had been a fierce critic of
Keynesian techniques. From 1953 he had also been in charge of the
Central Economic Planning Staff, his outlook contrasting sharply with that
of his predecessor, Sir Edwin Plowden.[13] Sir Herbert Brittain, a Third
Secretary, departed a year later. By the summer of 1958 further departures
included that of Leslie Rowan, described by Robert Hall, the Chief
Economic Adviser and a Keynesian economist, as 'a great thorn in my
flesh at various times'.[14] On the overall situation Hall commented, 'the
whole face of the Treasury has now changed since, let us say, five years
ago... It is an astonishing change.' He added, 'It is a most sriking fact that
there have been or are going to be these very widespread changes: and at
the end of them there will be no one in a top position who was there five
years ago, except myself.'[15]

Obviously, it would be wrong to assume that these changes of personnel
would lead to overnight shifts in the attitudes of the Treasury as these
officials were replaced, but it would seem that continuity in the views of
leading Treasury officials is more apparent than change at this time. For
example, the form of government accounts had been a long-standing bone
of contention between the Economic Section, consisting largely of
Keynesian economists, and Treasury officials. The traditional form of
accounts presented to Parliament with the budget speech was vastly different from the national income accounts used by economists to measure the
economic impact of the budget. As early as 1947 the Economic Section
was proposing the revision of the accounts to a more economic basis.[16]
However, Treasury officials resisted and opposed any change throughout
the late 1940s and early 1950s: while government accounts were drawn up
on a national income basis the Treasury ensured that they remained
unpublished and an uneasy relationship existed between the two sets of
accounts.

This opposition to reform from within the Treasury appears to have continued after 1955. In 1957 members of the Economic Section tried once more to get the economic classification of the budget accounts published. A major justification for this was that it was felt that previous objections were no longer felt to be so powerful.[17] In response Edmund Compton, while not being averse to putting the subject to ministers, was against the proposal. The subject did go to the Budget Committee but no changes occurred until 1962 and it was not until a year later that the government published its White Paper, *Reform of the Exchequer Accounts* (Cmnd. 2014).[18] In other words, progress towards reform remained slow, with Treasury officials dragging their heels, a situation paralleling that before 1955.

More concrete evidence of the resilience of traditional Treasury views amongst its officials can be seen in their continued dislike and avoidance of measures of general reflation. This has at times been presented as the ultimate test of the acceptance of Keynesian principles.[19] When discussing responses to the 1958–9 recession, the deepest recession since before the Second World War, Treasury officials consistently tried to avoid the implementation of measures of general reflation to ease the problem of rising unemployment. They and officials from the Board of Trade recommended a reactivated regional policy to deal with 'soft spots' rather than the use of general reflation.[20] In part this was because it was felt that general reflation would not solve the problem of rising local unemployment. Such a view had been held by the Treasury when the 1944 White Paper on *Employment Policy* (Cmd. 6527) was being drafted.[21]

However, a second argument was the need to be seen to be doing something to solve the problem of unemployment, in this case a more active regional policy, precisely because this 'was probably the best means of preventing pressure for the relaxation of the Government's general economic policy'.[22] In this sense 'flag-waving' measures were seen as a way of averting the build-up of public pressure for general action to stimulate the economy.[23] It was also hoped that such 'flag-waving' measures would maintain business confidence and prevent the emergence of a 'recession mentality', thereby making unnecessary any growth in public investment to ease unemployment.[24] On one level Treasury officials argued that the way to move out of the recession was through increased private investment rather than by means of greater public investment. Their preference for private investment was based on the belief that, unlike public investment, it 'would increase the basic strength of the country and enable us to emerge from a recession with bigger and better industrial capacity'.[25] A Treasury report to the Subcommittee on Local Unemployment of the

Economic Policy Committee set out these views for ministers: 'Most private investment...is more useful than nearly all public investment, in as much as private investment in industrial and commercial enterprises can provide continuing employment.'[26]

This did not mean that public investment was seen to have no role: a 1959 Treasury paper, 'Public Investment as an Instrument of Reflation', looked back on the lessons to be learnt from 'the first postwar attempt to use public investment as an instrument of reflation in this country'.[27] Six lessons, it was argued, needed to be learnt. First, time-lags meant that it was impossible to increase public investment in the short term to any significant extent and that the rise could come on stream when it was no longer required.[28] Secondly, this was not an effective way of helping high unemployment areas. Thirdly, it was easier to alter investment pro-grammes in the direction in which they were already moving rather than against that tide. Next, automatic reflation would occur and this would ease the extent of reflation necessary. There was also a need for flexibility and a wider range of projects, and finally, much better statistics were required. Whilst these lessons all pointed to problems with the use of public investment as a reflationary tool, they were presented as lessons for the future rather than as obstacles to any future use.

However, at the time of the recession Treasury officials were not so open-minded and positive about the use of public investment as a reflationary tool: it was 'very low in the "reflation" batting order'.[29] Some of the arguments used to sustain this position were similar to those con-tained in the 1959 paper, for example, that public investment should not be used for short-term stimulation of the economy, nor that it could be turned on and off like a tap.[30] Similarly, it was suggested that the public works schemes proposed in the 1944 White Paper were outmoded.[31]

None the less, a more immediate factor in determining Treasury officials' opposition to the reflationary use of public investment in 1958 was a practical concern with the control of public investment. Significantly, this concern about using public investment to reflate the economy went beyond general reflation. Thus while Treasury officials argued that regional policy measures were more appropriate to the problem of unemployment at that time, the use of public investment in any reflationary sense was criticised.[32] Otto Clarke in particular was greatly worried about the long-term consequences for public expenditure of increasing public investment to ease unemployment:

We have striven for years to get control over public sector investment, and to get it properly phased on a long-term basis.... This structure of control and regular review would be irrevocably prejudiced if the Government were suddenly to change direction, and tell us to press Departments to forget about cutting, abandon their ceilings, and go in for expansion. Control of investment is not maintainable in such conditions.[33]

Accordingly, Treasury officials resisted any increase in public investment and, where it did occur, attempted to keep it to a minimum and to once-and-for-all expenditures rather than continuing commitments.[34]

This illustrates that Treasury officials were not willing supporters of the use of public investment to ease the problem of unemployment and over-come the recession in 1958. In fact, many of the arguments used will be familiar to historians of the 1930s and 1940s: the arguments were very similar to those which earlier Treasury officials had used when discussing this subject.[35] The 1959 paper 'Public Investment as an Instrument of Reflation' highlights the point that Treasury officials did not reject out of hand the principle of using of public investment as a reflationary tool, simply that there were limits to its usefulness. However, concerns about controlling public expenditure meant that the 1958 recession was not seen as a suitable occasion on which to use this tool. It must be wondered whether such immediate considerations would ever have meant that Treasury officials would be in favour of going down the path of reflation by means of increased public investment.

Thorneycroft's Resignation

However, Treasury officials did not formulate economic policy alone and, even if their views appear to have remained relatively constant over the 1940s and 1950s, it is also necessary to consider ministerial views and the actual economic policies that were implemented.[36] After all, despite Treasury concerns, public investment was increased to deal with the recession. Equally significant was Harold Macmillan's reaction as Prime Minister to a Treasury paper which Heathcoat Amory believed to show 'the limitations on the use of public investment as an instrument either for fostering reflation or checking inflation'.[37] Macmillan responded, 'This is a *very bad paper*. Indeed a disgraceful paper. It might have been written by Mr Neville Chamberlain's Government' (original emphasis).[38]

The resignation of Peter Thorneycroft, the Chancellor of the Exchequer, and his two junior ministers, Enoch Powell and Nigel Birch, in January 1958, are, in this context, seen as crucial. This is commonly presented as a victory for Macmillan, the commitment to full employment and to the welfare state and defeat for the Treasury and the objective of price stability.[39] As Kenneth Morgan has put it, 'The battle fought over "Robot" in 1952 was again won by the consensus, one-nation party.'[40] This episode has certainly been endowed with symbolic significance for the Conservative Party, particularly since the late 1970s, with Thorneycroft presented as 'an early martyr' for the cause of monetarism.[41]

There were very clearly divisions between ministers at this time, well illustrated by the Cabinet minutes, which normally give little indication of dissent.[42] However, it must be wondered whether the differences were so great as is commonly portrayed and whether with hindsight the episode has been given undue significance. Macmillan is always presented as the consummate politician, in the sense of always being concerned with the presentation as well as the content of policy. Morgan thus notes that Macmillan's letter to Thorneycroft accepting his resignation made it appear that this had been on a very narrow point, later making one of his famous quotes that these were 'little local difficulties'.[43] Against this it must be remembered that Thorneycroft was out to emphasise the differences between them if only to justify his resignation, which was completely unexpected by the general public. He suggested that 'he alone in the Cabinet stood against inflation'.[44] Thorneycroft, rather than Macmillan, may have won the propaganda war and become the basis of accounts of this episode.

Were the differences as clear-cut as Thorneycroft suggested? Newton and Porter hint implicitly that the episode was not as fundamental as Thorneycroft and others have presented it. To them, 'the liberal Keynesian synthesis...survived' the resignation, but 'the priority which Thorneycroft had given to sterling was not questioned'.[45] In other words, an underlying ambiguity between domestic and international considerations remained just as had been the case in the early 1950s. A related question is whether Macmillan and his colleagues had given up on the objective of controlling inflation. In July 1957 it is clear that Cabinet ministers were becoming increasingly worried by the ever-rising trend of prices and its impact on the economy, society and their own political fortunes.[46] Significantly, Macmillan concluded one discussion by emphasising that the government 'should not relax its pressures as soon as some signs of disinflation began to appear'.[47] Following this discussion, Macmillan did accede to Thorneycroft's request for a circular calling for restraint on public expenditure, although with some reluctance.[48] It was this circular that called for the 1958/9 estimates not to exceed the level of 1957/8 and which became the resignation issue.

Similarly, Macmillan and the rest of the Cabinet did accept Thorneycroft's September measures, with their focus on maintaining confidence in sterling and controlling inflation, even though some commentators see this as a turning point in policy.[49] When establishing the committee of ministers to redraft the Chancellor's proposed statement, Macmillan noted:

> There appeared to be general agreement that the Chancellor of the Exchequer...should be fortified by some expression of the government's determination to maintain the present sterling–dollar exchange rate and to adopt measures which...would secure a better balance between the demand for and supply of the resources of the economy. It remained to be decided, however, how this general agreement in principle should be defined in a public statement...how the government's action could be so presented to public opinion, both at home and abroad, as to be seen to be neither inconsistent with their previous economic policy nor prompted by fundamental doubts about the strength of the currency; and how the adjustment of emphasis which it was the government's purpose to achieve would best be translated into practical measures which would be adequate to this objective.[50]

Ministers might have disagreed over the combination of measures required, for example, Macmillan was apparently doubtful about increasing Bank Rate to 7 per cent, but there was agreement over the general principles underpinning the measures.[51]

Likewise, one author has called the Cabinet paper, 'The Economic Situation' of 1 September 1957, 'Macmillan's riposte to Thorneycroft'.[52] While there were some differences in their theoretical approaches, both Macmillan and Thorneycroft were rather confused and inconsistent in their use of these approaches.[53] Moreover, the paper cannot be seen as a rejection of the objective of controlling inflation:

> We are trying to keep full employment, high rates of investment and expenditure and a fixed value of the £... Short therefore of going on to a floating exchange rate...the only method is to reduce the pressure...
>
> But there is a great prize to be politically gained, apart from the economic or social aspects. If we can steady prices by reducing the pressure we shall gain enormously, and if we can do it in such a way as to make unemployment still negligible – 2 to 3 per cent. – we shall lose no votes and injure nobody.[54]

Macmillan was concerned about the level of unemployment but was willing to see unemployment rise in order to bring about price stability.

These views were very similar to those of Thorneycroft, who thanked Macmillan for his support and urged the paper's circulation amongst fellow ministers.[55] He also circulated a paper to accompany Macmillan's at Cabinet.[56] He ended the paper:

> The above paragraphs describe the policies which I regard as necessary if we are to have any chance of maintaining the value of our currency. They are not easy. Thier success would probably be reflected in an increase in the level of unemployment to around 3 per cent. This would be forgiven us. A collapse of the pound would not.[57]

Equally, both Macmillan and Thorneycroft emphasised the detrimental impact of inflation on the Party's likely political fortunes and the high possibility of defeat at the next election. As Thorneycroft put it:

> A continued rapid rise in the cost of living, even if there is no devaluation, will have most serious electoral consequences...
>
> What is certain is that a great number of those who are suffering from inflation are just the people who form the hard core of the Tory Party.... To enter a difficult electoral battle with the 'old guard' disaffected is to risk a smashing defeat.[58]

If it can be said, as has been suggested, that in September 1957, both Macmillan and Thorneycroft agreed that the control of inflation was the priority, even if this meant some increase in unemployment, and that differences were limited to the specific measures required to bring this about, it suggests that either their positions changed radically between September and January 1958, when Thorneycroft resigned, or the differences were not as great as has been believed.

While positions did harden, it would be argued here that in terms of economic policy there has been a tendency to exaggerate the differences between Thorneycroft and Macmillan. Thorneycroft's resignation was more to do with bad judgement on his part than a fundamental disagreement of principle. By December 1957 Thorneycroft was getting the first indications that the Estimates for 1958/9 represented 'the largest increase in Estimates ever recorded in peace time'.[59] Civil Estimates were £275 million higher than the original Estimates and £175 million above the total Estimates for 1957/8, which included £100 million of Supplementary Estimates. It was this £175 million which Thorneycroft wished to eliminate.[60] By 3 January this figure had been reduced to £153 million and it was around savings of this figure which the Cabinet debated.[61] When Thorneycroft resigned, the gap was down to about £50 million. Clearly, there were major policy decisions required to make that £50 million reduction, for example over family allowances, but Macmillan was right to play down the inflationary impact of such a sum. He was misleading to say that this represented only 1 per cent of total government expenditure since this was a meaningless comparison.[62] Put in a more meaningful way, it was 1.8 per cent of the total civil estimates of 1957/8. This would have had an inflationary effect, but Macmillan believed that making those cuts would also have inflationary effect on wages. This would be 'a pyrrhic victory': 'We might win a few millions for the Exchequer and lose immensely on the wages front by appearing to take the offensive against the working class.'[63]

Macmillan and other Cabinet ministers did not give up on the objective of controlling inflation, nor of achieving this by means of reducing public expenditure. On 1 January 1958 Macmillan had circulated a note to ministers calling for measures, however undesirable, to close the gap.[64] Similarly, during the heated Cabinet discussions the point was made on more than one occasion that there was unanimity on the importance of curtailing public expenditure by all possible means.[65] The split with Thorneycroft was over whether to hold the Estimates to 'a precise arithmetical equilibrium', not the principle of holding down public expenditure.[66] This was particularly so when some of the increase in expenditure was determined by factors beyond the government's control.

In any case, Thorneycroft seems to have made a stand on the financial sum required to bring about his desired equilibrium, that is the £153 million, at a time when the figures for the 1958/9 Estimates were still in some flux and were altered by his successor.[67] This was a further element of a unnecessary rigidity in his stance. As Robert Hall put it:

I was getting uncomfortable about his rigidity on things like social services and aid to underdeveloped countries where he seemed to be making principles of tactical points and thus in fact making bad errors of judgment....

It was P.T. [Thorneycroft]'s extreme rigidity which succeeded in the end in turning a Cabinet which had begun on his side unanimously against him....

Although I can see P.T.'s point of view, it was all his fault that he had erected a symbol based on faulty economics and sworn allegiance to it so regularly and publicly that he felt he could not now disown it in public.[68]

After Thorneycroft's resignation ministers remained committed to controlling inflation and curtailing public expenditure. As Macmillan told Eccles, 'It is of the greatest importance that the change at the Treasury should be represented in its true light, not in any way as a weakening of the main policies of the government to fight inflation by every possible means.'[69] This message was repeated by others, who stressed that the resignation was over an issue of method, not of principle, and that the government was still earnest in its determination to restrain inflation.[70] Nor was this simply rhetoric. At the ensuing Cabinet meetings ministers continued to discuss and agree further cuts in public expenditure.[71] Indeed, if anything ministers were forced into the same trap as Thorneycroft in their determination to illustrate their continued commitment to controlling inflation and public expenditure after his resignation. This was because it was believed that the figure of £50 million had become established in public as the maximum amount by which the Estimates for 1958/9 could exceed expenditure in the previous year.[72] Given all of this, it would seem wrong to see Thorneycroft's resignation as marking a major turning point in the government's economic policy. At this point the government remained committed to controlling inflation and to keeping public expenditure down, and that the criterion which Thorneycroft imposed was an arbitrary one with regard to the fight against inflation.

1958–9 Recession

This is not to say that there were no changes in the tone of economic policy after January 1958. The 1959 budget, Heathcoat Amory's second, is remembered as one of the most generous peace-time budgets ever introduced and one that is still widely criticised as far too expansionist.[73] Related to this, Macmillan had a far greater influence on economic policy than earlier.[74] For example, he wrote to Heathcoat Amory proposing the contents of the latter's 1958 budget, excusing this highly uncommon practice by ending, 'I apologise for sending you these thoughts, for this is really your affair, but I know how generous you are in accepting suggestions.'[75]

Perhaps even more striking as evidence of a marked shift after Thorneycroft's resignation is the growing concern over rising unemployment and the fear of a recession. Less than one month after his departure from the government ministers, including Heathcoat Amory, were already wondering about the need for expansion.[76] It is hard to imagine the same occurring with Thorneycroft as Chancellor.

Can this apparent shift be explained in terms of the interpretation offered here? First, it should be noted that ministers were concerned about the drafting of plans to deal with unemployment, not their actual implementation at that time. This was in response to the forecast that unemployment would continue to rise at least until January 1959. The discussions were also exploratory, leading only to studies of available measures. Secondly, actual measures in the early months of 1958 concentrated on local unemployment rather than general reflation. Both Heathcoat Amory and Eccles wanted action to reduce unemployment levels in these soft spots in order to avoid public pressure for general reflation.[77] As has been shown, this was exactly what Treasury officials were proposing.

Thirdly, Macmillan was very concerned about the possibility of a slump and did try to persuade Heathcoat Amory that it was closer than the latter thought.[78] However, this was not the only motive behind his interference in the 1958 budget deliberations. Macmillan was already thinking of the next election. He wanted his Chancellor to accept that with an election imminent, 'we are not likely to have more than two [budgets], and that it might be better to make any remission now than in the second budget'.[79] He was looking for 'anything that has to do with encouraging house ownership' and other measures, such as the abolition of the income tax rule on the aggregation of the incomes of husbands and wives, which would have 'great political attraction' and be 'very popular with women and with all the middle and professional classes'.[80] Significantly, these specific expansionary proposals had little to do directly with the alleviation of unemployment. Moreover, Macmillan accepted Heathcoat Amory's advice that little could be done on income tax, despite this meaning that 'once again we have to sacrifice the middle and salaried classes to the needs of the wage battle.... However, since the inflationary battle is obviously not yet won, we must be patient.'[81]

In line with Macmillan's acceptance of the need for caution, Heathcoat Amory's 1958 budget represented a virtual standstill with only a £50 million handout. Given the rising unemployment and level of stocks this was, according to Hall, much less expansion than was required to halt, let alone reverse, the downward trend in the economy.[82] Ministers were worried about rising unemployment but their policies changed little in substance at this time. Indeed, while Hall became increasing concerned about the general state of the economy, ministers took little action beyond minor specific and limited measures.[83] By June it was estimated that unemployment was likely to have risen to 750 000 by the following January and ministers did finally take some steps to ease the situation. However, the removal of the restriction on the level of bank advances, the relaxation of hire purchase control and an increase in public investment of £30 million cannot be seen as wildly expansionist and were changes which it was believed could be made 'without impairing the fundamental objectives of strengthening sterling and checking the wage–price spiral'.[84] In other words, while policy did shift from what it had been under Thorneycroft, this was gradual and, initially at least, ministers 'showed little alarm' with the deflation of the economy.[85]

However, by October ministers were much more edgy, even panicky, about the economic situation and a rush of measures ensued. Hire purchase was eased further and public investment was increased again. Schemes that could be brought on stream quickly, were short term and offered the maximum employment benefit were to be given priority.[86] Behind this lay ministerial concern that the recession was continuing to deepen and unemployment was by then over the politically embarrassing level of 500 000 and looked likely to stay there.[87] Macmillan was very much of this mind and personally chaired a new ministerial Employment Committee. Throughout the rest of 1958 and at least for the first half of 1959 Macmillan remained anxious about the economic situation, constantly worried at the slow pace of recovery and wondered whether further expansionary measures were required.[88]

Nevertheless, in the October 1958 discussions and thereafter, Heathcoat Amory argued very much along the lines of his officials, as already discussed. In October he played up the measures already introduced and recommended delay to give them a chance to work. Ministers rejected his advice, believing that the economic situation was worse than he set out and that steps had to be taken to expand the economy.[89] However, on fundamental principles they still agreed with the Chancellor. Thus there was general agreement at the Economic Policy Committee with his statement: 'the main strategic objectives were to secure and maintain a strong currency, to stabilise prices, and to achieve as high a level of employment as was consistent with the first two aims.'[90] In other words, the desire for a high level of employment had not replaced the objectives of controlling inflation and maintaining confidence in sterling. The level of reserves had risen rapidly in 1958 and inflation was virtually non-existent, meaning that there was no conflict between them and the measures taken to improve the level of employment. Just as under Butler's chancellorship, there was no need to sacrifice other policies to employment. Moreover, while Hall criticised ministers for panicking in October, this was because:

I warned them in June that there was likely to be a good deal of unemployment (700,000) by January, that in my experience this was a very sensitive point politically, and that if they wanted to do anything they ought to start fairly soon. However they were all very bold then and it was all I could do to get the Chancellor to agree to the steps we actually took.[91]

While Conservatives did take positive action to bring about general reflation to alleviate unemployment in 1958, it should not be assumed that all other policy objectives were forgotten or relinquished. Nor should it be assumed that ministers embarked upon this route with wild abandon once Thorneycroft had resigned.

CONCLUSIONS

What picture has emerged of economic policy in the late 1950s and how does this relate to the themes of the managed economy, Butskellism and postwar consensus? First, while Treasury officials did accept the need for some reflationary measures in 1958, they were determined to keep these to a minimum and specific rather than general. They also continued to fight the use of public investment as a tool of demand management. Secondly, at a ministerial level the Thorneycroft resignation did not signify the rejection of the control of inflation as the primary objective of economic policy in favour of full employment. Thirdly, despite this, a Conservative government did respond in 1958 to the threat of unemployment rising to 3 per cent with reflationary measures. However, they did not embark on this course of action as quickly as they might have.

In other words, the picture that emerges is more complex and ambiguous than that often presented, where implicitly all are reconstructed Keynesians and the maintenance of high or full employment was fundamental. The confused picture which emerged from looking at Butskellism in the early 1950s has been replicated here. The economy was certainly being managed by the government, but it was being done in not quite such a simple and consensual way as is sometimes suggested. Treasury officials do not seem to have altered their views much since the 1940s and possibly even earlier. They were anxious not to damage the control of public expenditure and preferred to reflate the economy via private investment. They continually played down the need and desirability of measures of general reflation, in particular increased public investment. In contrast, Macmillan came out with some archetypal Keynesian statements. For example, he told Heathcoat Amory:

> You should I think indicate that these figures [for public investment] will be increased, or, if necessary, decreased; that it is right that this sector of the economy should be used for the purpose of steering a middle course between inflation and deflation; and that there is no need for an apology for a change of policy since last year. If we find that the

economy runs too fast ahead, then we shall slow it down again; surely government expenditure on the best modern theory should be used as one of the regulators. Of course, there are problems of the time lag in public investment, but if plans are got on with and sometimes even initial work done, it should be possible to select projects which can be started or stopped fairly quickly.[92]

However, even here one must be careful of not caricaturing Macmillan. His view of the role of the budget and the use of budget surpluses and deficits was far from that of an archetypal Keynesian: he was critical of the view that the budget was 'an instrument of economic policy'.[93] Equally, it has been shown that he and Thorneycroft were not as fundamentally divided over policy as is commonly presented. He even told Cabinet that Thorneycroft's September measures 'are the only real protection of full employment' as a way of presenting them to the public.[94]

The existing historiography oversimplifies or misses these complexities and as a result presents an interpretation that lacks subtlety and sophistication. This has a number of consequences, which this chapter has attempted to illustrate and which were also apparent in looking at Butskellism. It has tended to over-dramatise the development of policy and the significance of perceived turning points, for example the notion of Macmillan's 'victory' over Thorneycroft. Policy-making occurs as an amalgam of different forces which come together and from which policy emerges. On the level of personalities this means policy is not decided by one person, that is Macmillan or Thorneycroft, but by the interaction of a whole range of groups and individuals. Macmillan and the Treasury officials did not see eye to eye but both were major forces in policy formulation. In other words, it is the balance of these forces which shifts.

Related to this, the old adage that policy is a seamless web needs to be repeated. To ask the question whether or not the Conservative government was committed to maintaining high employment levels is the wrong question, because it implies a positive or negative response in isolation to all other considerations. The appropriate question to ask is how this objective related to the government's other objectives, in particular those that are likely to conflict with it, notably the desire to maintain confidence in sterling and to control inflation. Again it is a question of the balance between these objectives. As has been shown, it is a caricature to depict the Thorneycroft resignation and the reflationary action of 1958 as the abandonment of the objectives of controlling inflation and maintaining confidence in sterling and their replacement by the aim of maintaining high employment levels. Given that there was only £50 million difference between ministers and that there was a justified fear that enforcing these extra cuts would release other inflationary forces through increased wage demands, it is hard to see how the resignation had anything to do with the control of inflation. Moreover, during the period of reflation neither confidence in sterling nor inflation were pressing concerns, and hence did not impinge on the government's freedom to act against unemployment.

This is relevant to the debate on the postwar consensus. One response to the argument that the situation was more complex and ambiguous than traditionally presented has been to suggest that an unduly micro-level approach has been adopted: a focus on the trees rather than the wood.[95] However, the point being made here is rather different. Some elements do seem to fit the notion of consensus, but others do not. Yet one is left with a clear choice of either supporting the notion of consensus or of rejecting it. Generalisation and simplification are inevitable, but in this case are too arbitrary and perhaps help to explain why the debate has produced more heat than substance. Moreover, while this element of the debate is far too rigid, that of definition of the term postwar consensus seems infinitely flexible. It seems highly unlikely that an agreed working definition of the term will ever exist.

In this sense Anthony Seldon is right to entitle his recent article 'Consensus: A Debate Too Long?', but he then presents his own definition in the hope that this will become generally accepted. A different reaction to the title would be to suggest that contemporary historians should be aware of the extent to which this issue has dominated the study of the postwar period, and, important as the subject is, there are unhealthy consequences that also ensue. This domination means that by choice or necessity historians angle their work to relate to this debate. There is a grave risk here of not only diminishing returns but also of a partial and incomplete history of the postwar period. For example, awareness of the Economic Powers Bill and its contents does alter our perception of the economic policy of the Attlee governments. Evidence illustrating the significance of the Bill was readily available from the 1950s to historians, yet this evidence was ignored, presumably because it did not fit into the generally accepted account of the development of economic policy.[96] The issue of a postwar consensus is a valid one to study, but it is only one of a whole range of possible questions which contemporary historians should be asking of the postwar period. Given the current state of the debate on the postwar consensus, with its focus on semantics, its tendency to pigeon-hole contributors in one camp or the other, and its resulting failure to cope with the subtlety with which economic policy developed, contemporary historians might be advised to focus their attention on these other possible questions.

NOTES

1. For example, A. Seldon, 'Consensus: A Debate too Long?', *Parliamentary Affairs*, 47, 1994, pp. 501–14; and D. Kavanagh and P. Morris, *Consensus Politics from Attlee to Major*, 2nd edn, 1994, Oxford, Blackwell.

2. D. Dutton, *British Politics since 1945: The Rise and Fall of Consensus*, 1991, Oxford, Blackwell, p. 7; Kavanagh and Morris, 1994, pp. 4–5.

3. Dutton, 1991, p. 43. The term was coined in 'Mr Butskell's Dilemma', *The Economist*, 13 February 1954, pp. 439–41 and was made up by conflating the names of the last Labour Chancellor of the Exchequer, Hugh Gaitskell, with his Conservative successor, R.A. Butler.

4. Seldon, 1994, p. 513; J. Harris, 'Enterprise and Welfare States: A Comparative Perspective', *Transactions of the Royal Historical Society*, 5th ser., 40, 1990, pp. 175–95.

5. B. Pimlott, 'The Myth of Consensus', in L.M. Smith, ed., *The Making of Britain: Echoes of Greatness*, 1988, Basingstoke, Macmillan.

6. Seldon, 1994, p. 508. See also R. Lowe, 'The Second World War, Consensus, and the Foundation of the Welfare State', *Twentieth Century British History*, 1, 1990, p. 157.

7. Lowe, 1990, p. 180.

8. N. Rollings, '"Poor Mr Butskell: A Short Life Wrecked by Schizophrenia"?', *Twentieth Century British History*, 5, 1994, pp. 183–205.

9. PRO CAB134/225, EPC(50)9, 7 January 1950.

10. PRO CAB21/3701, note by Gaitskell, 8 February 1951.

11. J. Tomlinson, *Employment Policy: The Crucial Years, 1939–1955*, 1987, Oxford, Oxford University Press, p. 156.

12. R.A. Chapman, *Ethics in the British Civil Service*, 1988, London, Routledge.

13. K. Jones, *An Economist among Mandarins*, 1994, Cambridge, Cambridge University Press, p. 134.

14. A.K. Cairncross, ed., *The Robert Hall Diaries, 1954–1961*, 1991, London, Unwin Hyman, p. 166.

15. *Ibid.*, pp. 165, 166.

16. For an explanation of the differences, see N. Rollings, 'British Budgetary Policy, 1945–1954: a "Keynesian Revolution"?', *Economic History Review*, 2nd ser., XLI, 1988, pp. 292–3; and N. Rollings, 'The Control of Inflation in the Managed Economy: Britain 1945–53', 1990, University of Bristol, unpublished doctoral thesis, pp. 179–94. See also J.R. Hicks, *The Problem of Budgetary Reform*, 1948, London, Oxford University Press, and the *Report of the Committee on the Form of Government Accounts*, 1963, Cmnd. 7969.

17. PRO: T230/376, F. Atkinson to Hall, 21 February 1957.

18. See various Budget Committee minutes and memoranda in PRO: T230/377, T171/506, T171/515, and T171/592–3.

19. J. Tomlinson, 'Why Was There Never a "Keynesian Revolution" in Economic Policy?', *Economy and Society*, 10, 1981, pp. 72–87.

20. PRO: T234/372, note of a meeting, 18 March 1958, and EA(58)24, 'Local Unemployment' by Heathcoat Amory, 24 March 1958. This point is

expanded upon in Susan Richards's postgraduate research on 'The Scottish Office and Regional Policy, 1939–1962'.

21. G.C. Peden, 'Sir Richard Hopkins and the "Keynesian Revolution" in Employment Policy, 1929–45', *Economic History Review*, 2nd ser., XXXVI, 1983, pp. 281–96.
22. PRO: T234/372, note of a meeting, 18 March 1958.
23. *Ibid.,* M. Stevenson to R.W.B. Clarke, 'Reflation', 8 October 1958.
24. PRO: T234/320, note of a meeting, 28 April 1958.
25. *Ibid.,* Stevenson to M. Flett, 30 April 1958, and T234/372, Clarke to Makins, 'Gradual Expansion', 21 February 1958.
26. PRO: T234/372, EA(LU)(58)5, 'The Possibilities of Selective Encouragement of Capital Investment in Areas with Relatively High Unemployment', by J. Simon, attached Annex A by the Treasury, 25 July 1958.
27. *Ibid.,* 'Public Investment as an Instrument of Reflation', by the Treasury, October 1959.
28. This is one of the main arguments in the standard work on demand management in this period, J.C.R. Dow, *The Management of the British Economy, 1945–60,* 1964, Cambridge, Cambridge University Press.
29. PRO: T234/320, Clarke to T. Padmore, '"Reflation Plans"', 11 April 1958.
30. *Ibid.,* unsigned to Padmore, 'Gradual Expansion', 26 February 1958, and Clarke to Padmore, '"Reflation Plans"', 11 April 1958.
31. PRO: T234/320, Stevenson, 'Note of a Meeting', 24 July 1958.
32. PRO: T234/372, EA(LU)(58)5, Annex A.
33. *Ibid.,* Clarke to Makins, 'Gradual Expansion', 21 February 1958. See also PRO: T234/372, Clarke at a meeting, 'Reflation', 15 April 1958; and T234/320, Clarke to Padmore, '"Reflation Plans"', 11 April 1958.
34. PRO: T234/320, Clarke to B.D. Fraser, 'Fuel Efficiency', 10 June 1958.
35. A. Booth, 'The "Keynesian Revolution" in Economic Policy-making', *Economic History Review*, 2nd ser., XXXVI, 1983, pp. 103–23; G.C. Peden, 'The "Treasury View" on Public Works and Employment in the Interwar Period', *Economic History Review*, 2nd ser., XXXVII, 1984, pp. 167–81; R. Middleton, 'The Treasury and Public Investment: A Perspective on Interwar Economic Management', *Public Administration*, LXI, 1983, pp. 351–70.
36. See Rollings, 1988, 1988, for the distinction between the attitudes of Treasury officials and the implementation of policy.
37. PRO: PREM11/2311, Derick Heathcoat Amory to Macmillan, 'Public Investment and Reflation', 27 October 1958.
38. *Ibid.,* added by Macmillan.
39. For example, K. Morgan, *The People's Peace*, 1990, Oxford, Oxford University Press, pp. 171, 175; James Foreman-Peck, 'Trade and the Balance of Payments', in N. Crafts and N. Woodward, eds., *The British Economy since 1945*, 1991, Oxford, Oxford University Press, p. 168; S. Brittan, *Steering the Economy*, 1971, Harmondsworth, Penguin, p. 218.
40. Morgan, 1990, p. 175.
41. *Ibid.* See also A. Seldon, 'Conservative Century', in A. Seldon and S. Ball, eds., *Conservative Century: The Conservative Party since 1900*, 1994, Oxford, Oxford University Press, p. 49.

42. See PRO: CAB128/32 part 1.
43. A. Horne, *Macmillan 1957–1986: Volume II of the Official Biography*, 1989, London, Macmillan.
44. *Ibid.*, p. 73, quoting Macmillan's diary, 7 January 1958; PRO: PREM11/2306, Thorneycroft to Macmillan, 6 January 1958; and *Hansard*, 5th series, 23 January 1958, 580:1294–7.
45. C.S. Newton and D. Porter, *Modernization Frustrated: The Politics of Industrial Decline in Britain since 1900*, 1988, London, Unwin Hyman, p. 132.
46. PRO: CAB128/31 part 2, CC(57)55th, minute 1, 19 July 1955. See also correspondence with Macmillan from Eccles and Thorneycroft in this month in PRO: PREM11/2306.
47. PRO: CAB128/31 part 2, CC(57)55th, minute 1, 19 July 1955.
48. PRO: PREM11/2306, correpondence between Thorneycroft and Macmillan, 19 July 1957 to 6 August 1957 and circular to ministers, 10 August 1957.
49. A.K. Cairncross, *The British Economy since 1945*, 1992, Oxford, Blackwell, p. 110.
50. PRO: CAB128/31 part 2, CC(57)67th, minute 2, 12 September 1957. For records of the comittee see CAB130/131, GEN.611.
51. Thorneycroft was himself not keen on increasing Bank Rate to 7 per cent, see Cairncross, 1991, p. 127. For illustration of other concerns see PRO: CAB128/31 part 2, CC(57)66th, minute 2, 10 September 1957, Butler, Macleod and Henry Brooke. Eccles did want a more fundamental change by adjusting the exchange rate.
52. A. Taylor, 'The Party and the Trade Unions', in Seldon and Ball, 1994, p. 520. See PRO: CAB129/88, C(57)194.
53. Both Macmillan and Thorneycroft point to disagreements amongst economists over the nature of inflation but then say that whatever the cause they have to do something and then conflate the two theories in PRO: CAB128/88, C(57)194 and C(57)195 respectively. See also Cairncross, 1992, p. 109, and R. Lowe, 'Resignation at the Treasury: The Social Services Committee and the Failure to Reform the Welfare State, 1955–57', *Journal of Social Policy*, 18, 1989, p. 519.
54. PRO: CAB129/88, C(57)194.
55. PRO: T172/2137, Thorneycroft to Macmillan, 3 September 1957.
56. PRO: CAB129/88, C(57)195, 'The Economic Situation', by Thorneycroft, 7 September 1957, pp. 2–3.
57. *Ibid.*, p. 6.
58. *Ibid.*, p. 1, and C(57)194, p. 2.
59. PRO: PREM11/2306, Thorneycroft to Macmillan, 8 December 1957. These were also the views of Birch, see Cairncross, 1991, p. 124.
60. PRO: CAB129/90, C(57)295, 'The 1958/59 Civil Estimates', by Thorneycroft, 27 December 1957.
61. PRO: CAB129/91, C(58)2, 'Government Expenditure 1958/59', by Thorneycroft, 3 January 1958. For the Cabinet discussions see CAB128/32 part 1.
62. PRO: PREM11/2306, Macmillan to Thorneycroft, 6 January 1958. This comparison was also used in Cabinet, see PRO: CAB128/32 part 1, CC(58)1st, 3 January 1958, and CC(58)3rd, 5 January 1958. See PRO:

CAB129/91, C(58)6, 'Government Expenditure', by Heathcoat Amory, the new Chancellor, 10 January 1958, for the reasons why this comparison had to be taken with a pinch of salt.

63. PRO: PREM11/2306, Macmillan to Eccles, 6 January 1958. Thorneycroft was aware of the problems that his policy was likely to cause, see Cairncross, 1991, p. 136.

64. *Ibid.*, M2/58, '1958/59 Civil Estimates', by Macmillan, 1 January 1958.

65. PRO: CAB128/32 part 1, C(58)1st, 3 January 1958, and CC(58)3rd, 5 January 1958.

66. *Ibid.*, C(58)3rd, Macmillan's summing up. It should be noted that some care must be taken in the use of these minutes. Cabinet minutes are always of ambiguous accuracy but there was a longer delay than normal in the writing up of these meetings. See PRO: T172/2138, Thorneycroft to Butler, 3 January 1958.

67. *Ibid.*, C(58)5th, minute 10. See also Cairncross, 1991, p. 140.

68. Cairncross, 1991, p. 144.

69. PRO: PREM11/2306, Macmillan to Eccles, 6 January 1958.

70. *Ibid.*, unsigned, Commonwealth Relations Office to U.K. High Commisioner in Canada, 6 January 1958; and Selwyn Lloyd to UK Ambassador to the USA, 6 January 1958.

71. For example PRO: CAB128/32 part 1, CC(58)4th, 5th, 6th, 7th and 8th.

72. *Ibid.*, CC(58)6th.

73. See Brittan, 1971, pp. 224–5; and Horne, 1989, p. 143.

74. Horne, 1989, p. 141; Cairncross, 1991, 1991, pp. 153–4.

75. PRO: PREM11/2305, M42/58, Macmillan to Heathcoat Amory, 5 March 1958.

76. Cairncross, 1991, 1991, p. 145; PRO: T234/372, M21/58, Macmillan to Heathcoat Amory, undated; and Eccles to Heathcoat Amory, 'Plans to Deal with Unemployment', reporting on a meeting of ministers, 25 February 1958.

77. PRO: T234/372, EA(58)24, 'Local Unemployment', by Heathcoat Amory, 24 March 1958; and EA(58)7th, minute 2, 26 March 1958.

78. PRO: PREM11/2305, Macmillan to F.A. Bishop, 16 March 1958.

79. *Ibid.*

80. *Ibid.*, M42/58, Macmillan to Heathcoat Amory, 5 March 1958, and M60/58, Macmillan to Thorneycroft, 17 March 1958.

81. PRO: M107/58, Macmillan to Heathcoat Amory, 5 April 1958.

82. Cairncross, 1991, 1991, p. 154.

83. *Ibid.*, p. 158. See PRO: CAB128/32 part 1, CC(58)40th, Macmillan, 12 May 1958.

84. PRO: CAB128/32 part 2, CC(58)52nd, minute 5, Heathcoat Amory, 3 July 1958; and CC(58)66th, minute 5, 31 July 1958.

85. Cairncross, 1991, p. 164.

86. PRO: PREM11/2311, M375/58, Macmillan to Heathcoat Amory, 31 October 1858; and CAB129/95, C(58)227, 'Employment-Directive by the Prime Minister', by Macmillan, 28 October 1957.

87. PRO: T234/372, CC(58)78th, 27 October 1958.

88. *Ibid.*, ED(59)10, 'Public Investment', by Macmillan, 23 January 1959; and M149/59, Macmillan to Heathcoat Amory, 4 May 1959.

89. PRO: PREM11/2311, Heathcoat Amory to Macmillan, 5 October 1958; T234/372: EA(58)71, 'Economic Prospects', by Heathcoat Amory, 13 October 1958; EA(58)22nd, minute 2, 16 October 1958; CC(58)77th, minute 9, 24 October 1958; CC(58) 78th, 27 October 1958; and CAB129/95, C(58)211, 'Economic Situation', by Heathcoat Amory, 21 October 1958.

90. PRO: T234/372, EA(58)22nd, minute 2, 16 October 1958.

91. Cairncross, 1991, p. 178. Brittan argues a similar point, 1971, pp. 225–6, in stating that the error of the expansionary 1959 budget was not that it gave away too much but that it came too late.

92. PRO: PREM11/2311, M375/58, Macmillan to Heathcoat Amory, 31 October 1958.

93. PRO: CAB129/88, C(57)194, 1 September 1957.

94. PRO: CAB129/89, C(57)225, 'Explaining the Economic Situation', by Macmillan, 5 October 1957.

95. Seldon, 1994, p. 503; and Dutton, 1991, p. 2.

96. H. Morrison, *Government and Parliament*, 1954, London, Oxford University Press; and J. Eaves, *Emergency Powers and the Parliamentary Watchdog: Parliament and the Executive in Great Britain 1939–1951*, 1957, London, Hansard Society.

7 The Politics of the 'Social' and the 'Industrial' Wage, 1945–60[1]

Noel Whiteside

INTRODUCTION

At first glance, the case for a political consensus in industrial relations policy in the postwar years seems a strong one. Both parties maintained a commitment to full employment and both supported free collective bargaining as the basic system for negotiating wages and conditions of work. When faced with the problem of inflation, both sought to develop controls on prices and wages: promoting productivity bargaining as the means to contain the wage–price spiral which was commonly assumed to threaten Britain's industrial performance. Although the Conservative governments of the 1950s were more reluctant to adopt such strategies, there still appears to be a degree of continuity in industrial relations policy in the immediate postwar decades.

Appearances can, however, be deceptive. While the approach of both Conservatives and Labour to industrial relations appears remarkably similar, each Party set their agenda within very different political contexts. Wartime controls were not abolished overnight; the central state remained the chief architect of industrial reconstruction. How far state regulation of the economy should continue in peacetime was, however, a contentious issue – between (and within) the two major political parties. Further, both Parties – under the reconstruction plans drawn up by the wartime Coalition – committed themselves to full employment; there was, however, no automatic political consensus about how this might be achieved. Finally, with the election of a Labour administration in 1946, the state also emerged as (indirectly and directly) a major employer in its own right – thanks to the programme of nationalisation and the expansion of a welfare state. Conservative commitment to these policies remained uncertain.

State welfare had implications for wage bargaining. The growth of state-funded social support rendered the industrial wage less significant in the maintenance of working class living standards than had been the case in the interwar years. Universal – not residual – provision of health care, child allowances, secondary education, comprehensive social insurance (including retirement pensions), subsidised council housing – all helped alleviate the social obligation and financial burden which, at the turn of the century, had been borne by the wage-earner alone. To such well-known state benefits we can add others, namely food subsidies and rent controls, which had been introduced during the war and were subsequently rendered permanent by the postwar Labour government as part of their commitment to 'fair shares for all'. Consumer subsidies like these were openly supported by the TUC, becoming the central component in negotiations on informal and formal systems of wage regulation, which entered the political arena for the first time in the immediate postwar period. The scope of the 'welfare state', as conceived by the Labour Party, was thus broader than is sometimes supposed, reflecting an ideological commitment to state planning and regulation much stronger than that propagated by the Conservatives. The Conservative Party, by contrast, viewed universal state welfare as a waste of resources and sought to reduce public expenditure (in the name of 'sound finance') on subsidised welfare for the whole community. This restored wages as the central means of support for the average household. For the Conservatives, universal welfare was rooted in full employment, which allowed everyone to earn the means to secure the subsistence of themselves and their dependants, while permitting the easy identification of the incompetent and the work-shy. This allowed state-funded welfare to return to its traditional, residual role.

When viewed from this angle, we can see that the industrial relations policy of each Party operated within very different sets of assumptions. Both, however, had to deal with common economic problems. The expansion of the welfare state was expensive and other demands on the national income were equally pressing. In the postwar years, central governments were repeatedly faced with the problem of how national resources should be allocated. In the immediate aftermath of the war, some Labour ministers argued that a properly planned economy was impossible as long as wages were permitted to run free. This line of argument was unacceptable to both sides of industry, who were severally opposed to political intervention in matters deemed to be the province of industrial management or free collective bargaining. Rightly or otherwise, however, union demands for higher wages in the ensuing decades continued to be seen as damaging to Britain's economy. Higher wages meant higher industrial costs. Higher costs meant inflation: stimulating further wage demands, undermining the competitiveness of exports, threatening the external account and the value of sterling. It was the repeated sterling crises of the late 1950s that forced the Conservative government to change tack, to address the question of voluntary wage restraint and eventually moved them to more positive forms of intervention early in the following decade.

Initially at least, both Labour and Conservative governments were reluctant to intervene permanently in collective bargaining. The former – although committed to the idea of state planning – could not tackle the question without facing accusations of bad faith from the unions, who formed the backbone of Labour Party support. The latter, the party of free enterprise, championed a private sector eager to keep state intervention at arm's length. Political difficulties aside, the rising costs of the 'social' and the 'industrial' wage did not allow the issue to be ignored. Discussion of statutory incomes policies were eventually to take place alongside proposals for public expenditure cuts and the 'targeting' of welfare. After the fall of the Labour government in 1951, however, there is remarkably little evidence of attempts to reconcile the two policy areas: the exception being Part 1 of the Social Contract, a short-lived attempt by the Labour Party and the TUC leadership in the early 1970s to secure respect for official wage guidelines in return for compensatory, upward adjustments in the 'social wage'. The failure of this initiative – and the preference demonstrated by the union rank and file for tax cuts – gives an insight into the appeal of Mrs Thatcher's 1979 election campaign, which promised to reduce the role of the state in regulating people's lives.

Social policy and industrial relations are rarely studied together, in spite of the way the both issues affect living standards and questions of state economic management. This is not altogether surprising as the two areas rarely came together in the policy-making world. None the less, explicit links were made in the immediate postwar period (by the union leadership at least) between the willingness of government to offer protection against a rising cost of living and the willingness of the unions to exercise wage restraint. These links were premised on notions of universalism in welfare provision, which had been recognised and implemented by the Attlee government, and on a degree of central state planning, which had been accepted by the Labour Party. It was not recognised – because unrecognisable – by the Conservative administrations of the 1950s, which aimed to restore market forces in determining prices. The following analysis will draw out implicit assumptions about the ways in which social expenditure redefined the sphere of collective bargaining and will establish the implications of these redefinitions for industrial relations in this period. The aim is to highlight the changed context of postwar free collective bargaining and to indicate why bargaining systems, developed in a period pre-dating state management of the economy, proved so ill-suited to the postwar environment. For the delimitation between public policy and private responsibility continues to be a focal issue in political debates which has yet to be satisfactorily resolved.

BALANCING WAGES AND WELFARE: THE ATTLEE GOVERNMENTS, 1946–51

Trade union attitudes towards state welfare reflected the experience of the slump years, which had exposed the limitations of industrial bargaining and trade union benefits in the protection of working-class lives.[2] The advent of a Labour government after the war, committed to full employment and universal welfare, won the whole-hearted support of a TUC leadership able to recall sharply earlier hardships. Such recollections of the relatively recent past played a powerful part in sustaining the support of the TUC leadership for the Attlee administration, including some of its more unpopular policies: wage restraint being a case in point. The legacy of the war was also significant. During the war, the TUC had negotiated voluntary wage restraint with the Coalition government in exchange for compulsory price controls on essential foods, clothing and household goods, together with the extension of state support for those in need. The object of wartime incomes policies had been to limit inflation and to encourage labour mobility to essential industries. Although the strategy stimulated complaints from union members – that the system protected the unskilled but not the skilled, that it allowed some industries to make fat profits in which the workforce could not share and that the official cost of living index (against which wage claims were judged) failed to reflect real prices – the system managed to survive. For this, credit must be given to Ernest Bevin who, as Minister of Labour and National Service in the Coalition government, was chiefly responsible for wartime wage restraint. Time and again, the Attlee administration used the (now) Foreign Secretary's influence with union leaders to foster TUC support for Labour's economic strategies. Bevin appeared as the TUC's ally and could appeal for union loyalty:

> The last thing in the world I want to see is a conflict between the Government and Trade Unionists of this country.... As the Prime Minister knows, if anybody talks to me of state regulation of wages, my hair bristles. I am ready to fight it in any circumstances because I do not like it, I hate it. I think it took one hundred years to win our freedom. I

hate to see anything clamped down on the unions by state regulation if I can help it. I am one of your greatest protagonists on that score....[3]

The restoration of prewar practices was progressively delayed when peace returned. In the postwar context of full employment, pent-up domestic demand and the desperate need to raise exports (requiring the control of domestic consumption), inflation was a primary economic threat. The Labour government tried to reconcile full employment with low (or no) inflation and a system of 'fair shares for all' through the continuation of wartime controls, including cost of living subsidies to shield consumers from rising import prices. By 1948–9, state intervention on prices and profits, initially introduced to secure short-term wage restraint in 1948, were viewed by Labour ministers as permanent features in the managed economy.[4] The corollary of this was the continuation of 'responsible' collective bargaining, to be achieved through cooperation with the union movement, which would stabilise production costs, promote exports and contain domestic consumption. The only alternative – floating the exchange rate – was dismissed by both Treasury and Bank of England as politically and economically unviable.

Hence the inflationary threat was tackled by the Attlee government with a mixture of voluntary wage restraint and direct controls on consumption. This was not easy. Although, in the 1940s, the TUC was closely involved with the policy-making process and willing to negotiate on the question, wage restraint was still seen as essentially an emergency measure, to be applied on an *ad hoc* basis. Notions of manpower planning and the development of a full-blooded wages policy, which divided the Cabinet in 1947,[5] were less acceptable. For trade unionists, permanent wage guidelines were only remotely conceivable if the state intervened on prices and profits. This strategy could claim limited political support within the Cabinet, but considerably less outside it. Private industry chafed at Labour's attempts to 'modernise' production or at any intervention in what employers conceived as their private business.[6] State regulation was unacceptable to American investors who, in the context of the Cold War, sought to foster free market economies in Western Europe, not to extend 'socialism'. Finally, within Whitehall, senior civil servants cavilled at the cost and consequences of extensive state subsidies, whose merits in containing wage demands were easily outweighed, in official eyes, by the burden they imposed on the public purse, their distortion of the price mechanism and the damage they inflicted on the balance of payments by raising demand for imported foodstuffs.[7]

Cooperation between TUC leadership and the Labour government was rooted in a common agreement on the provision of social welfare and cost of living controls. The creation of a National Health Service, the extension of school meals and council housing, the introduction of factory canteens, cheap milk, universal social security and, above all, the commitment to full employment, all helped foster 'responsible' attitudes in collective bargaining.[8] Even before formal agreements on wage restraint were negotiated, the TUC was responding to the government's efforts to keep wage claims in check, to help secure postwar reconstruction. When a balance of payments crisis developed in 1947–8 (the consequence of escalating costs of primary products on world markets), the TUC leadership supported the Labour government's attempts to restore financial stability. In October 1947, formal discussions started between the TUC and the Chancellor of the Exchequer, culminating in agreement to confine wage rises to higher productivity and undermanned industries. The eventual outcome was voluntary wage restraint which, in varying degrees of severity, lasted from March 1948 to the autumn of 1950. Following devaluation in May 1949, Congress narrowly accepted the need for a wage freeze at the TUC conference at Bridlington in September. The long-term preservation of free collective bargaining, the continuation of price stability and a commitment by the government to protect the social services were the main conditions exacted in return for full cooperation. In general, however, little conflict existed between the Treasury and the TUC leadership over the policy to be pursued.[9] Instead, the TUC became responsible for extracting conformity from the rank and file.

Conflict over wage restraint was thus internalised within the union movement. TUC leaders argued that the extension of state welfare, in its widest sense, was the best way of optimising the living standards for all. Unions should not confine their attentions to wages alone. While, in the United States, trade unions had to bargain with employers for a range of social benefits (principally superannuation and health care),[10] in Britain the Labour government's welfare measures covered all workers; this offered better protection than had ever been possible under sectional, penny-pinching bargaining strategies which had characterised the interwar years. Thanks to Labour, progress since the Second World War could be consolidated:

> The general level of wages has been considerably improved; prices have been kept stable; the cost of living has been kept in close approximation to the means of the average wage earner; expenditure on social services repays in real benefits to the bulk of the population and especially to the

wage earner; the number of people in employment has never been so high; the number of unemployed has never been so low.[11]

In similar vein, rank-and-file protests about the impact of income tax on earnings were countered by TUC propaganda stressing new areas of public expenditure which benefited the working class:

> the money you pay in taxes goes to provide subsidies for food to keep down the cost of living, provide higher old age pensions, educational services and social service benefits, and more will be needed if the new schemes which the government is pressing through Parliament come into operation.[12]

Cost of living subsidies were a central part of state welfare; TUC spokesmen stressed how public expenditure in this area was raising the real value of the wage packet. Following the introduction of voluntary wage restraint in 1941, subsidies ensured the cost of living rose only 1 per cent in 1941–6;[13] this was a major prop to wage stability. Subsidies prevented sliding-scale wage agreements pushing wages up during the war; they protected those on fixed incomes. They were, however, very expensive: rising from a total cost of £72 million in 1940 to £526 million in 1948.[14] In spite of pressure from Treasury officials, Dalton refused to cut food subsidies in the 1947 budget; although Cripps contained expenditure in this area, Gaitskell also rejected Treasury demands for further reductions in 1951.[15] At their zenith, subsidies represented an estimated addition of 12s 6d (£0.62) weekly income per head.[16] While the costs of the National Health Service in the financial year 1950–1 were predicted to rise to £351.54 million (leading the Treasury to conclude that the scheme was out of financial control) the estimates for food subsidies alone that year still stood at £410 million.[17] and the government was preparing a Bill to make price controls a permanent part of economic policy.[18]

The Economic Advisory Section wished to replace food subsidies with higher children's allowances, but the TUC would have none of this.[19] To remove subsidies in the absence of union agreement was to release a spate of wage claims; as it was, Cripps' ceiling on subsidy expenditure made for difficulties, allowing critics to claim that wages were failing to keep up with rising prices in 1949–50. The TUC remained resolute that price stability was the primary condition for wage restraint. In unofficial discussions with the Treasury in April 1950, George Woodcock even claimed that the TUC was considering asking member unions to fight for price reductions rather than wage rises.[20] This commitment to price controls accurately reflected working-class preoccupations. In a Gallup survey in

May 1948, asking respondents to identify the chief problems for government action, the cost of living came top of the list (38 per cent of respondents naming it as the principal issue), followed by housing (31 per cent) and the food situation (21 per cent).[21]

Hence, from its first mooting through to the final collapse of the policy late in 1950, the TUC leadership fought an uphill battle to convince member unions of the need for pay restraint-and those unions' general secretaries fought equally hard to enforce rank and-file cooperation. Rising prices aside, many problems stemmed from prewar pay anomalies, frozen in place during the war, which affected members expected to see rectified. The disappearance of manpower controls also saw a revival in the traditional methods of attracting labour to essential industries – through raising wages. Workers also demanded a share in the record profits being made by industry, as delegates from Scotland, South Wales and Lancashire pointed out to a NUM conference in 1949.[22] Finally, those on the political left opposed pay restraint because it was precisely that – it was not a proper pay policy, set within the context of a socialist planned economy. This ideological objection was voiced increasingly towards the end of Labour's period in office. The wage freeze of 1949, opponents argued, forced the workers to bear the cost of increasing the competitiveness of British industry. The Labour government was not tackling the issue of industrial planning; in its absence, Labour policy was identical to that of any capitalist government – to cut costs as the means to promote growth. Although these criticisms seem a little harsh (Labour had developed a policy of state direction of industry – albeit with limited success)[23] such arguments were well received on the shop floor. The block card vote at a conference in January 1950 supported the TUC line by the narrowest of margins (4.2 million in favour and 3.6 million against).[24] By June, the Chancellor concluded that the wage freeze was no longer tenable. At Congress that autumn, the TUC was faced with a mass of resolutions deploring rising prices and calling for an end to all official restraint on wages.[25]

Even so, while it lasted, wage restraint worked. As a senior Treasury official minuted:

> illogical though it may be, the present system has been brilliantly successful. Between June 1947 and March 1948 the wages index rose by 5 points. It rose only 3 points in the following 12 months and one point in the 12 months from June 1949 to June 1950. I do not believe for a moment that any machinery whatever which would have been acceptable to the workers would have produced such small changes as this.[26]

At the same time, the cost of the social services rose by £300 million between 1948 and 1950.[27] Extended social expenditure facilitated voluntary curbs on wages. There were even signs that the Chancellor was willing to extend concessions in the 1950 budget, in return for a further period of wage restraint, but union members, the General Secretary of the TUC informed Cripps, would not respond to the idea of a 'social wage'. In the final months of the Attlee government, the Economic Section tried to develop a Wages Advisory Council, to draw up official guidelines on pay and productivity. In February 1951, the idea was put to the TUC – which rejected it because it did not promise price controls.[28] However, attempts to replace temporary emergency measures with permanent mechanisms for regulating wages were well under way before Labour lost the general election in the autumn of that year.

Taken the TUC's interest in price controls and the moves of Labour towards their permanent application, there is every reason to think that a Labour government in the 1950s would have tried to balance wages, welfare and price controls in a permanent fashion. Whether this would have been successful is another question. For the price the union movement paid for the close involvement of its leadership in policy-making was considerable; the centralisation of authority generated strain between the TUC officials and the shop floor. This period witnessed the appearance of shop stewards in the car industry and extensive unofficial action on the docks: indications of general rank-and-file disillusion with the official union machine.[29] Whether or not such difficulties could have been overcome remains a conjectural question, for the following thirteen years changed totally the environment within which the question of an official wages policy came to be discussed.

ABANDONING CONSENSUS: THE CONSERVATIVE GOVERNMENTS, 1951–64

The Conservative administration elected in 1951 held different views on the role of a welfare state. It was, however, aware of the popularity of Labour's welfare measures and of the association in the public mind between Conservative government and the mass unemployment of the 1930s. Sensitivity to the messages conveyed by public opinion polls in the early 1950s (indicating apprehension over education cuts and NHS charges) and a slim Parliamentary majority prevented any serious consideration of reductions in the social services.[30] Albeit that the Conservatives were committed to cut public expenditure, they were aware of the constraints surrounding this pledge. In the event, public opinion proved persuasive; in their first five years in office, Conservative expenditure on social welfare rose by 28 per cent.[31] Harold Macmillan's housing programme extended public provision in that area well beyond anything achieved by Labour and was largely responsible for this growth. This was, however, a temporary expedient to reinforce electoral support and to cope with the chronic housing shortage. From 1953–4, the Conservative government viewed all subsidies in the same light – as undesirable and unnecessary distortions in the market mechanism. Although opposed by Labour-controlled local authorities, attempts were made to reduce council building, to remove rent controls and generally to restore incentives towards home ownership.[32]

Other efforts to reduce welfare expenditure – particularly on the NHS – met with less success. The Chancellor, R.A. Butler, turned his attentions elsewhere. In 1952, food subsidies, which had formed the mainstay of wage restraint in the late 1940s, were cut by £160 million. At the same time, Butler raised pensions, family allowances and other benefits to help the poor to cope;[33] and the blow to the average wage-earner was fortunately cushioned by falling world prices. The same year, the first plans were made to remove rent controls on private accommodation, a policy brought to fruition in the Housing Repairs and Rent Acts in 1954 and the Rent Act of 1957. From 1953 onwards, public subsidies for council housing were directed increasingly towards slum clearance (residual housing) programmes and support for 'general needs' council housing was progressively reduced.[34] Food subsidies were cut again in 1956. Although family allowances were raised marginally that year,[35] union leaders claimed that the majority of their members had gained no protection against the impact of Conservative policy on the cost of living.[36] The TUC, under no political obligation to a Conservative administration, made common cause with their rank and file, using industrial muscle to safeguard real earnings. Throughout the 1950s, the union movement remained united in defence of free collective bargaining and resistant to all official attempts to regulate wages.

Initially at least, the Conservatives left the wages question well alone. In spite of the exhortations of their senior civil servants, ministers proved dilatory about developing any public policy in this area.[37] It was only when Macmillan became Chancellor in 1955 that a much delayed White Paper was published on the subject and this went no further than extolling the virtues of voluntary restraint.[38] This initiative cut little ice with the TUC, as Macmillan was withdrawing subsidies on bread and milk at the time. By 1956, however, official concern over rising domestic costs was growing. Increasing competition for overseas markets politicised the question of industrial costs; rising wage rates threatened the balance of payments, the value of sterling and the continuation of full employment. The Permanent Secretary to the Treasury set up a Group on Wages and Prices[39] to examine the issue. In July, the Treasury sought a voluntary stabilisation of prices in the private sector as a prelude to negotiations on wage restraint. The nationalised industries were willing to cooperate, but the Federation of British Industry (FBI) would not; inflated prices reflected rising import costs which the private sector could not control. The Conservatives backed away from mandatory central controls and the talks came to nothing. In the summer of 1957, the Labour Party's idea of a Wages Advisory Council was revived in the form of a Council on Prices, Productivity and Incomes, designed to create independent official guidelines on wage rates, salaries and profits. Its first report in 1958 made a fundamental political error by arguing that inflation could only be checked by controlling monetary growth and letting unemployment rise, recommendations that led to the withdrawal of TUC cooperation.[40]

Other means of securing wage restraint met with no more success. The Ministry of Labour refused to countenance the use of its arbitration service to enforce such a policy; this risked compromising its impartiality, alienating referrals of industrial disputes and aggravating unrest, without necessarily reducing the wages agreed under a final settlement.[41] Attempts to shore up employer resistance to wage demands also failed. In July 1957, when sterling was under severe pressure on the foreign exchanges, the Chancellor met representatives of the FBI and the British Employers' Confederation (BEC). As the employers' representatives pointed out, previous efforts by the Ministry of Labour to maintain production and avoid confrontation had undermined resistance to expensive concessions; early conciliation kept production going, but at the price of higher costs.[42] Unions knew that any claim would meet with some reward; employers knew that the employer who refused higher wages was liable to see his workforce move elsewhere. Trade-based, centralised bargaining allowed well-organised unions to play employers in one sector off against another – to force laggards to meet rates and conditions already conceded elsewhere. Thus the wages round had become an institutionalised practice in British industrial relations.

In the event, it was only the advent of another severe sterling crisis in the summer of 1961 that moved the Conservative government to force the issue. An indefinite pay pause for government employees, extended to workers covered by wages councils, signalled the final conversion of the Conservative government to the need for a wages policy – albeit one that excited hostility within the union movement and, initially at least, loaded the burden largely on public sector workers.[43] In its final years, the Conservative administration sought to establish some central advisory body to provide guidance on wage settlements, a move that eventually resulted in the establishment of the National Economic Development Council which led the way in establishing pay guidelines in 1963–4. This did not meet with any great success. On the one hand, the government was openly interested in controlling wages, not prices; on the other, as union representatives negotiated with the employers and the Chancellor, the TUC Conference voted to oppose wage restraint in any form. In the context of full employment – and the Macmillan government refused to countenance abandoning it – there were no avenues available to a Conservative government to negotiate, or enforce, a pay policy. Free collective bargaining proceeded unchecked, reinforcing the commitment of the trade union membership to traditional pay negotiating procedures. They worked.

The economic crises that provoked official interest in wage restraint also led the Treasury's Social Services Committee to recommend economies in state welfare in 1956. While extending the Conservative attack on general housing and food subsidies, the Committee also aimed to reduce expenditure on welfare foods, including school meals and milk.[44] Again, in accordance with Conservative preferences for selective rather than universal benefits, family allowances for the second child also became a candidate for official cuts in 1957/8; money saved would be used to raise children's allowances under the national insurance and national assistance schemes, to keep social security benefits in line with inflation.[45] Those who could afford to pay should be made to pay, the Treasury Committee argued. Universal services, introduced after the war, were outdated – a necessary response to the problems of mass unemployment and widespread poverty in the 1930s, which had now disappeared. The very success of free collective bargaining thus strengthened the Treasury's case against universal welfare and in favour of allowing state provision to return to its traditional, residual role.[46]

Paradoxically enough, the industrial situation undermined the political feasibility of cutting state benefits. In a tight labour market, attacking the welfare state stimulated demands for compensatory higher wages. The withdrawal of cost of living subsidies – with the consequent rise in prices for basic essentials – had had this effect. For a prime minister seeking ways of keeping wages in check, cutting social welfare proved resistable. The threat of further industrial action kept the remaining welfare state intact. Hence the trade union rank and file came to understand industrial bargaining power as primary to the protection of their social benefits as well as wages. Thirteen years of Conservative government reinforced this perspective; rising standards of living were not attributed to the welfare state, but to successful collective bargaining. The process of centralisation within the union movement – perceptible in the interwar years and reinforced by both the war itself and the politics of the postwar Labour government – was thrown into reverse, reflecting rising organisational power on the shop floor. Plant bargaining became central to union strategy: a shift in authority reflected in the rise of the shop stewards in the following decade.

As a result, Conservative policy on industrial relations and social welfare became internally inconsistent. By the mid-1950s, the Treasury was supporting the activities of two committees, one examining controls over industrial wages, the other looking for cuts in welfare expenditure, which appear to have operated in ignorance of each other's existence. Rising wages were used to justify the removal of universal welfare, and universal social welfare was used to justify appeals for wage restraint. Conservative economic ideology demanded the restoration of market forces in determining prices, residualising welfare. In executing this policy, no attention seems to have been paid to the likely industrial consequences of unravelling the system of protection built up by the previous Labour government; nor to how industrial militancy might be contained. While remaining committed to full employment, none of the Conservative Cabinets managed to develop a strategy for dealing with its consequences. The result was a mess. Industrial relations policy developed hand to mouth; employers were told to resist wage claims by one government department while being encouraged to pay up by another, to avoid strikes and disruption. This experience encouraged the union movement in general to see political strategies as a supplement, not a replacement, for industrial ones: a conclusion that proved particularly hard to shift in the ensuing years.

CONCLUSIONS

This paper has argued against the case for political consensus in industrial relations in the immediate postwar decade; while we might argue that such a consensus developed in the 1960s, it would be wrong to superimpose this on the earlier years. Wage restraint was only feasible in the context of consensus between unions and government. The TUC remained adamant that price stability was a primary condition for cooperation and only the

Attlee governments were willing to construct policy along these lines. Here, the record of the late 1940s seems to have been more successful than most, albeit that the (very late) attempt to create the framework within which a permanent wages policy could be negotiated did not come to fruition.

The extension of social welfare incorporating state controls over the cost of living provided one of the few ways through which central government could foster cooperation with official wage guidelines: albeit only on a temporary basis. Here, the Attlee governments established a framework for state intervention that was quite different from that adopted by their successors. The 'welfare state' of the late 1940s did not merely cover the provision of full employment and the recommendations of the Beveridge Report. The ideology of universal protection and 'fair shares for all' encouraged economic interventions that were much broader in scope. Social expenditure was also directed at controlling the prices of household essentials, to reconcile economic efficiency and social justice. The collapse of union endorsement for government policy can be directly attributed to the decision to restrict – even reduce – the scope of price controls in 1949. The rising cost of living was foremost among the reasons for resisting further restrictions on free collective bargaining in 1950–1. And subsequent efforts to introduce incomes policies saw the TUC impose precisely the same condition: that government take responsibility for protecting working-class families against the indiscriminate effects of market forces. This was how the union movement constructed state welfare – but only the postwar Attlee government shared this perspective.

At the Conservative government's insistence, market forces played a more dominant role in determining food prices and housing costs. This reduction in the scope of state welfare had several important consequences. First, it allowed the TUC leadership to make common cause with their members in promoting free collective bargaining. While full employment lasted, it was much easier to raise wages than safeguard welfare; this reversed the political priorities observed by the trade unions in the interwar years. Second, the shrinking area covered by the 'welfare state' demonstrated that it was not a fixed entity, but was subject to ideological reconstruction as well as economic pressures. Third, following from this, there is no self-evident demarcation between the proper province of collective bargaining and that of public policy – although it has frequently suited politicians to state otherwise. Under the Conservative governments of the 1950s, the 'industrial' and 'political' spheres were redefined, and union leaders lost their automatic involvement in economic policy-making which they had enjoyed in the previous decade. The reintroduction of what purported to be a free market allowed trade unions to behave in a manner appropriate to free market conditions. There was little compunction on them to heed political pressure on wages – which only became really strong towards the end of the Conservative period in office. The thirteen years of Conservative government destroyed the previous, tenuous relationship between wages and state welfare; questions of wages were now discussed in the contexts of productivity and economic growth alone.

It does not follow that, given another term of office, the approach of the Attlee administration would have been successful in securing a framework for wage bargaining within the context of economic planning. We have to remember that the Attlee government inherited a number of advantages, whose value diminished over time. Memories of mass unemployment were still fresh and trade union leaders were peculiarly eager to support a Labour government which, they were convinced, would safeguard union interests. Union men had been involved in the planning of Labour policy in the 1930s; union leaders had taken responsibility for the implementation of policy in the war years. All this served to render opposition within the ranks as the equivalent of treachery to the British labour movement. It was a political legacy that served the Attlee government well.

At the same time, the administrative machine that had emerged from the war – and which the government sought to adapt for peacetime purposes – was showing signs of strain. Wartime administration and postwar planning fostered an unprecedented degree of centralisation in government policy-making and, as a result, in the trade union movement. By the late 1940s, this structure was beginning to crack. These years were characterised by the appearance of unofficial strikes, the emergence of shop stewards, the development of more informal systems of plant negotiation, thinly disguised as productivity bargaining, which reasserted the authority of the shop floor. Such developments were indirectly encouraged by official promotion of productivity bargaining which permitted higher wages in return for higher output. Local bargaining recognised and rewarded work requiring special skills, or performed under difficult circumstances, or within specific time schedules; it accommodated variance in local working practices. It formed a 'second tier' to formal, centralised systems of negotiating wages and proved far more difficult to control. The TUC itself had no powers to enforce formal agreements; within unions, the executive that took a hard line could stimulate opposition – even break-away movements – in old strongholds.[47] Equally, employers' organisations could not police their members. Resentment at the intrusion of heavy-handed bureaucracy into managerial affairs, visible in other areas of policy, was also evident here. We can assume that, all round the country, individual employers connived with their workers to get round restrictions imposed from the centre – and that the inequalities so created helped feed more general discontent. Government in 'austerity Britain' was necessarily authoritarian: the aim of raising prosperity with 'fair shares for all' did not guarantee the popularity of the means adopted to achieve this end. By the early 1950s, with the remnant of wartime regulation finally removed, national wage agreements did little more than establish a framework of minimum rates and established conditions, within which local arrangements might be agreed.

The problem of central control over such questions remained highly significant; postwar industrial relations continued to reflect a distrust of state intervention or direction of any sort. We need to explain the continuing affinity shown by working people for protecting their autonomy and their continuing hostility to central control. Some of the reasons for this have already been touched on: the difficulty of influencing remote bureaucracies in Whitehall being one case in point, the growing emphasis on plant bargaining being another. Underpinning both lies the wide variety of forms of employment, working agreements, conventions of labour management as well as types of production that continued to characterise labour markets in Britain in the postwar years, but which remained unrecognised in policy-making circles. While higher wages earned by higher productivity were exempt from official restrictions, for example, there was no compensation for the vast army of newly created public service workers, whose 'productivity' could not be assessed – far less raised – and whose earnings therefore tended to drift downwards in periods of wage restraint. A single model of industrial production was imposed, willy-nilly, on all forms of employment. Union members preferred to stay clear of official regulations which assumed uniformity where little existed and, under the guise of productivity bargaining, fought to keep their 'freedom' to bargain over wages in their own hands. The preference for wages over state welfare – which emerged in this period – stems from the way that the former was capable of adaptation to local conditions while the latter was not. Had the Attlee government proved capable, not of dismantling state controls, but of decentralising them; had it allowed more industrial participation in the process of regulating wages; had it, in other words, proved a little more sensitive to the processes of industrial democracy, then possibly opposition to an official wages policy would not have been so strong.

Such speculation is arguably beside the point. By 1951, support for an unregulated market economy was evident on both sides of industry. Most trade union members were eager to take advantage of a labour market operating strongly in their favour and to throw off the obligations that had been imposed in the name of loyalty to the Labour government. Certainly, the 'hands off' approach adopted by the succeeding Conservative government suited trade unionists well. In the name of productivity bargaining, higher wages were exacted for the renegotiation of manning levels, or of job demarcation and the removal of other 'restrictive' practices. The industrial coordination that had begun to emerge in the previous decade disappeared; the potential causes for industrial disagreement and dispute multiplied. How far these developments should be held responsible for Britain's economic decline is the subject for another paper. The point to be established here is that this *laissez-faire* strategy was quite different from the policy that preceded it, and proved equally untenable in the longer term.

NOTES

1. The author would like to thank Harriet Jones, Neil Rollings, Nick Tiratsoo, Jim Tomlinson and Jonathan Zeitlin for their comments on an earlier draft of this paper. I remain solely responsible for the shortcomings of the argument presented here.
2. N. Whiteside, 'Social Welfare and Industrial Relations, 1914–39', in C.J. Wrigley, ed., *History of British Industrial Relations, 1914–1939*, 1987, Brighton, Harvester.
3. PRO: T172/2033, Minutes of deputation from TUC, November 1947, p. 10 (Ernest Bevin speaking).
4. N. Rollings, '"The Reichstag Method of Governing"? The Attlee Governments and Permanent Economic Controls', in H. Mercer, N. Rollings and J. Tomlinson, eds., *Labour Governments and Private Industry*, 1992, Edinburgh, Edinburgh University Press.
5. J. Tomlinson, 'The Labour Government and the Trade Unions, 1940–45', in N. Tiratsoo, ed., *The Attlee Years*, 1991, London, Pinter, p. 100. Also PRO: T172/2033.
6. See, for example, N. Tiratsoo, 'The Motor Car Industry', in Mercer, Rollings and Tomlinson, 1992.
7. PRO: T229/280, National Food Policy Review.
8. R. Jones, *Wages and Employment Policy*, 1987, London, Allen and Unwin, pp. 18–19.
9. See PRO: T230/293; also Modern Record Centre [MRC], Warwick, MSS 292/110.44/1a–2b.
10. MRC MSS 292/110.44/2b, 'Trade Unions and Wages Policy'; Conference of Trade Union Executive Committees, 12 January 1950, pp. 25–6.
11. MRC MSS 292/110.44/2b, TUC, Council's Supplementary Report to Congress at Bridlington: Research and Economic Supplementary Report C, September 1949, p. 6.

12. MRC MSS 292/577/1, A probable reference to the NHS. Draft Production Quiz, 28 Oct. 1946, p. 3.
13. MRC MSS 292/557/1, Ministry of Labour, 'Statement on the Economic Considerations affecting the Relations between Employers and Workers' (n.d. [?] early 1947), p. 4.
14. MRC MSS 292/110.44/1b, TUC figures.
15. N. Rollings, 'Controls and Butskellism'; unpublished paper presented to the Economic History Conference, Hull, April 1993, p. 4.
16. PRO: T172/2033, Ernest Bevin, minutes of TUC delegation meeting with Prime Minister, 17 November 1947, p. 5. The TUC estimated subsidy value dropped to 14 shillings [£0.70] per week for a family of four by 1949: see TUC at Bridlington: Research and Economic Supplementary Report C, p. 3.
17. PRO: T172/400, Treasury paper 'The National Health Service' (n.d. but probably March 1950).
18. This was the Full Employment Bill; it was dropped after the first General Election 1951 as too controversial for a government with a majority of six. Rollings, 1993, p. 5.
19. See PRO: T230/111.
20. See PRO: T172/2033.
21. Cited in N. Tiratsoo and J. Tomlinson, *Industrial Efficiency and State Regulation: Labour, 1939–1951*, 1993, London, Routledge, p. 165.
22. MRC MSS 292/110.44/2b, minutes of NUM conference 29 December 1949.
23. Tiratsoo and Tomlinson, 1993, chs. 4–8.
24. 'Trade Unions and Wages Policy', 1950.
25. See MRC MSS 292/110.44/1a.
26. PRO: T230/294, Hall to Bridges, 20 September 1950.
27. See PRO: T172/2033.
28. R. Jones, 1987, pp. 38–40.
29. See essays by S. Tolliday and N. Whiteside, in S. Tolliday and J. Zeitlin, eds., *Shop Floor Bargaining and the State*, 1985, Cambridge, Cambridge University Press. Also essay by R. Hyman, in J. Fyrth, ed., *Labour's High Noon*, 1993, London, Lawrence and Wishart.
30. H. Jones, 'The Conservative Party and the Welfare State, 1942–55', 1992, unpublished doctoral thesis, London School of Economics, ch. 4.
31. Excluding National Insurance expenditure; PRO: T227/413, Treasury memorandum (Hall), May 1955.
32. H. Jones, 1992, ch. 5.
33. See PRO: T227/119.
34. H. Jones, 1992, ch. 5.
35. See PRO: T227/968.
36. *The Times*, 26 April 1956.
37. R. Jones, 1987, pp. 50–3.
38. *The Economic Implications of Full Employment*, Cmd. 9725/1956.
39. See PRO: T234/670.
40. R. Jones, 1987, pp. 55–6.
41. PRO: T234/670, report to Permanent Secretary, 5 October 1956.
42. *Loc. cit.*, minutes of meeting, 18 July 1957.
43. R. Jones, 1987, pp. 57–8.
44. PRO: T227/413, memoranda by Clarke, May and October 1955.

45.   See PRO: T227/968.
46.   See PRO: T227/ 413–5.
47.   For the example of the docks, see G. Phillips and N. Whiteside, *Casual Labour*, 1985, Oxford, Oxford University Press, ch. 8.

8 Industrial Organisation and Ownership, and a New Definition of the Postwar 'Consensus'

Helen Mercer

Paul Addison has defined his notion of consensus quite specifically. First, he defines it as an 'elite' consensus: the shape of events of the postwar years were defined by an elite consisting of 'the old governing class', the trade union oligarchy and intellectual mandarins. By 1939, he argues, 'the trade union movement and the Labour Party, were controlled...by a generation of leaders who were essentially moderate social patriots'. Hence:

> The 1940s were the decade when the Conservatives were obliged to integrate some of Labour's most important demands into their own philosophy. They were able to do so without too much pain because Labour's demands had largely been cast in a mould of thought provided by the non-socialist intelligentsia between the wars and during World War II.[1]

Secondly, Addison is quite specific on the issues on which there was consensus: a managed economy, including limited nationalisation, and the welfare state.

This chapter concentrates on Addison's very precise and clear definition. It argues that Addison was correct to speak of a consensus in the sense of a meeting of minds among this 'elite' group, but that the issue around which this consensus was formed was a far more basic one: it was to secure the future of capitalism, and specifically, the future of private ownership of the means of production, both as a principle and in practice. Those issues which Addison sees as embodying a 'consensus' – the welfare state and the managed economy – were, as several papers in this volume point out, issues of intense debate and little approaching consensus. Events, legislation on specific issues, in the case of industrial organisation and ownership as elsewhere, were the outcome not of consensus but of compromise. In the case of industrial

139

organisation the choices made represented one route to an agreed goal – the preservation of the status quo. Furthermore, Addison fails to take sufficient account of international pressures which conditioned British decisions. This point also will be examined in greater detail in this chapter.

INDUSTRIAL ORGANISATION AND OWNERSHIP: THE NATURE OF THE POSTWAR CONSENSUS

This paper looks first at the problems of industrial organisation which confronted Britain by the 1940s and illustrates how their solution necessarily involved challenging existing patterns of ownership.

Since the interwar years the view that Britain's future prosperity lay in rationalised integrated production has been almost universally held. Then and since British governments have displayed a great zeal for the large industrial concern, promoting integration, consolidation and merger, through the rationalisation policies of the 1920s and 1930s, and many postwar policies like the Industrial Reorganisation Commission. The eagerness to join Europe in the late 1950s and 1960s owed much to the belief that the elimination of tariffs between Britain and Europe would stimulate industrial 'efficiency' and large-scale integration.

However, while large-scale integrated production has had widespread approval, controversy has dogged two further issues: how the process is to be achieved and how large firms are to be controlled.

In 1929 the Balfour Committee on Industry and Trade put forward arguments and recommendations typical of the interwar years. It saw Britain's relative slowness in developing trusts and cartels of German or American types as a major factor in her lagging industrial competitiveness. It outlined two possible agencies to achieve integrated production methods. In common with many economists and businessmen of the time, the report derided 'the operation of free competition' as 'a slow and costly method' to ensure the elimination of the inefficient firm, recommending instead the 'rational' planning of industrial organisation:

> The tenacity of life shown by businesses working at a loss is sometimes extraordinary...the results of the prolonged competition of inefficient undertakings react on the more efficient and tend to depress the whole industry; and an operation of cutting out the dead wood may be essential for the speedy restoration of prosperity and the resumption of growth of the vigorous branches. It seems unquestionable that this oper-

ation can often be performed more speedily and 'rationally' and with less suffering through the mechanism of consolidation or agreement than by the unaided play of competition'.[2]

Clearly, such an operation to cut out dead wood, either by competition or rationalisation, would eliminate not only machines but also their owners. Hence the two methods of reorganisation outlined here – competition and rationalisation – implied rearrangements of ownership patterns also. It was on this point that both methods foundered by the 1930s. While the belief in market forces at this time to achieve restructuring was a minority interest, schemes to amalgamate and regulate key sectors, such as coal, cotton, iron and steel, floundered against the opposition of existing owners, and became instead state-sponsored cartels. The government came to promote cartelisation partly because schemes for integration and concentration met resistance, but partly because, together with a new tariff system, they offered a means to raise profits and prices, maintain wages and mitigate unemployment.[3] The government also experimented with a system of 'industrial diplomacy': informal contact between government officials and businessmen, outside the terms of specific legislative proposals, to discuss and implement schemes for reorganisation. In 1930, Sir Horace Wilson was appointed Chief Industrial Adviser and his team attempted to discuss common problems of rationalisation, but moves to examine these issues in more detail failed.[4]

Moreover, whether modern production methods were to be achieved using competition or rationalisation to force out obsolete machinery and owners, there remained the problem of control of large firms and of the cartels fostered by government policies: this was the essence of the 'trust problem' as analysed since the late nineteenth century. A leading Fabian put the question in a nutshell:

> Private monopoly is a public danger, and yet it cannot be undone by law; nor if it could would any economist recommend that the community should abandon the most efficient method of production for a worse. The problem is, how to secure the benefits of combination without its disadvantages...[5]

These disadvantages have been variously seen as the potential for monopoly abuse: raising prices and 'profiteering', failing to implement technical advance, conspiring against trade union demands. Moreover concentration of ownership raised the potential for market-fixing by agreement and hence restricting new entrants. For many neoclassical economists one of the greatest dangers was the threat to the spirit of entrepreneurship.[6]

However, any control over large firms and cartels also involved intervention with the rights of private property, especially the right to manage. Hence even mild forms of control were conceded very unwillingly by businessmen, even where their own interests as consumers of products affected by monopoly conditions were concerned. According to the Balfour Committee again, businessmen 'preferred to rely on trade negotiation rather than government action as a remedy for their grievances'.[7] In 1918 the Committee on Trusts, while generally sanguine about the trend, had proposed a permanent tribunal to inquire into the development of trusts and cases of complaint. For two years after 1918 the government implemented Profiteering Acts, but after that initiative lapsed nothing more along these lines was attempted.[8] Interwar experience of regulation of industries such as coal and the railways was also unhappy, and hence by the 1930s:

> The unsatisfactory experience with regulation had prompted a long-term drift into public ownership, while the obscurantist opposition of private owners in the coal industry in particular during the 1930s suggested to many that only nationalisation was likely to break the power of such vested interests.[9]

Nationalisation not only promised to achieve large-scale production, but also to provide public safeguards against the abuse of monopoly positions. Increasingly the solution to the problem of improving industrial efficiency and removing the disadvantages of economic concentration in some basic industries came to be seen as removing private ownership entirely. On this point, there was by the 1930s an emerging 'elite consensus' that certain basic industries be nationalised, and this consensus was at the heart of the 'Middle Way'. The 'Conservative planners' of the 1930s proposed not only statutory cartelisation of many sectors, but also limited nationalisation. The best-known interpretation of this viewpoint was made by Harold Macmillan, who outlined a lifecycle for industries, in the third and senile stage of which certain industries could no longer be directed simply by the profit motive for this stood in the way of integration and planning of industries vital to the economy. He therefore proposed nationalisation of coal, greater control of other forms of energy allowing an integrated energy policy, and statutory control and supervision of transport. Harold Macmillan was President of the Industrial Reorganisation League, a group of industrialists in large-scale industries such as ICI, and supported by another grouping, Political and Economic Planning, also financed by some leading sectors of British industry.[10] The Liberal Industrial Enquiry had similarly seen a widening sphere for the public board, viewing the development of public concerns not as a question of principle 'but only one of degree, expediency and of method'.[11]

Meanwhile, of course, by the 1930s and 1940s the Labour Party and the TUC were developing more precise plans for nationalisation. Although enthusiasm for nationalisation waxed and waned, by 1945 it was a path which would not only secure efficient basic industries 'without enthroning private monopoly', but would also give a Labour government general leverage over economic activity.[12] It should also be added, that some of the Labour Party's commitment to nationalisation sprang from problems of regulation in the 1930s, specifically, the problem of acquiring the information necessary to secure regulation.[13]

This discussion illustrates that whichever of the three routes used to promote efficiency through the development of large-scale firms existing owners would be forced out: this was as much the case for selection of the fittest via market forces as for state takeover. However, while competition and rationalisation would have changed the pattern of private ownership it did not lay down a challenge to its efficacy and legitimacy. Nationalisation did.

Indeed, another approach to the question of industrial organisation and ownership threatened the very future of the system of private property and private enterprise: this was the Marxist approach, calling for expropriation.

Since the late nineteenth century European Marxists had argued that the contradiction between the social nature of productive forces and private ownership of them identified by Engels became acute in the era of 'monopoly capitalism'. This view was central to the British Communist Party's critique of 1930s Britain, expressed for instance in *Britain without Capitalists*, its main economic manifesto of the period. As a result of this contradiction monopoly capitalism now imposed fetters on the forces of production, creating redundancy of plant and men in the search to maintain profits. The book dismissed plans to control or curb 'this or that monopoly interest' or to introduce a measure of public control, because, 'the problem of monopoly is ... something woven into the very texture of monopoly capitalism'. The problems could only be tackled if, as a prerequisite, the 'problem of class power be solved': ' While the vested interests of Finance-Capital remain entrenched across the path, he who devises "plans" and "development schemes" is condemned to be either an academic trifler or else a maker of tools for others to distort to different and nefarious purposes.'[14] Such an approach threatened widespread expropriation, not piecemeal nationalisation. Hence, although after the war the sectors targeted for immediate nationalisation by the Communist Party were not that different from those of the Labour Party, the accompanying political measures, such as control of building and engineering industries, increased taxation of profits and a reorientation of foreign policy towards cooperation with the Soviet Union gave a different flavour to their overall approach.[15]

THE POSTWAR THREAT TO PRIVATE PROPERTY AND A CONSENSUAL RESPONSE

There was indeed a popular resonance in Marxist attacks on modern capitalism as parasitic, failing to provide the public benefits from the pursuit of private profit. Cartelisation in Britain inspired many comments along these lines. One civil servant defined cartels as 'the unwilling tribute that capitalism pays to socialism' or 'social security for shareholders'.[16] The war saw a significant increase in political consciousness among working people in Britain. This may not have led to majority feeling in favour of socialism or even nationalisation,[17] but represented a radical change among certain sectors of the working class of immense momentary political significance.

In 1918, surveying the revolutionary movements in Europe, J.A. Hobson declared that 'For the first time property is seriously afraid'. Can the same be said for 1945? Eldon Barry has argued that within Britain there was nothing approaching the 'revolutionary' feeling of 1918: profiteering at retail level was prevented by controls and rationing and there was greater political unity around the anti-fascist aims of the war, reducing pacifist opposition and industrial disputes.[18] However, industrial performance during the war was poor to the extent of being alarming. There was a major production crisis in 1941–2 and the official historian blames the 'independent status of engine firms' as a chief cause of shortages of supplies for bomber aircraft in 1941.[19] Hence the war showed up long-standing deficiencies in strategic industries, incompetence by management in planning expanded production and distribution. American evidence was also to demonstrate that some prewar cartels, in which British firms had been involved, had jeopardised supplies of vital materials such as magnesium.[20] During the war the system of controls, which both encouraged further cartelisation and made businessmen controllers of their own industries, was widely criticised. Although profiteering at the retail level was controlled, there remained several publicised cases of profiteering on government contracts.[21] Meanwhile, intervention to direct the economy was seen to have been highly successful, indeed indispensable to the war effort. Again the official historian asserts how 'surprisingly efficient' Royal Ordinance factories were compared with private munitions firms.[22] British industrialists emerged with little glory in the fight on the home front. This compared most unfavourably with the success of Soviet socialism under war conditions. As Minkin argues:

> The Government itself took the lead in encouraging hundreds of pro-Soviet committees and societies and as the war progressed and the Germans were turned around at Stalingrad, it became difficult to separate the virtues of heroic defence and patriotic resilience from the advantages of the Soviet economic planning system.[23]

Moreover, many leading British businessmen were known to have admired the Nazi regime and to have favoured appeasement, while European businessmen in the occupied countries had collaborated. Meanwhile, Communists had been in the leadership of resistance movements in Europe and of anti-fascist movements in 1930s Britain. Hence the world situation looked exceptionally threatening for the future of private property in 1945. In general, the spirit in Britain was enought to warrant a remark by Quintin Hogg to the effect that: 'If you do not give the people social reform, they are going to give you social revolution.'[24]

The response was an 'elite consensus' that the need of the day was a vigorous reassertion of the validity of private enterprise. A greater sense of urgency prevailed in 1945, as compared with 1918, to rework and reassert arguments for the legitimacy of private enterprise. At the international level, the counterattack was led by the USA. The Americans explicitly framed their foreign policy in terms of the defence of a system of private property. The enunciation of the Truman Doctrine on 12 March 1947 is well known, but a few days earlier Truman had made a speech at Baylor University, in which he had outlined his opposition to all restrictions on free enterprise. He declared that freedom was more important than peace, that the defence of freedom involved 'something deeper than a desire to protect the profits of ownership', for freedom of worship and speech was dependent on freedom of enterprise. The speech caused concern in Europe, for it not only attacked Soviet planning but government control of trade, which operated in Labour Britain and other European countries. State trading and planning restricted free enterprise, and the USA would not go this way or the government would soon be 'telling every trader what he could buy and sell, and how much, and when, and where'.[25]

The Pope was to add his voice to the rising tide of opposition to state intervention. Addressing Catholic employers present in Rome in May 1949 for the annual meeting of the Conference of Directors of European

Industrial Federations, Pope Pius XII 'says socialism can't solve troubles'. He argued that: 'For the moment the favour goes in preference of statism and the nationalisation of enterprises. The Church accepted that some properties could be reserved to public powers', but:

> to make of this statism the normal rule of the public economy would be to reverse the order of things. The mission of public law is, in effect, to serve private right not to absorb it...the economy is not by nature an institution of the state; it is, to the contrary, the living product of the free initiative of individuals and groups freely constituted.[26]

This revulsion against state intervention had already been expressed by Friedrich von Hayek in his famous work, *The Road to Serfdom*, written in 1943. Among the twelve main points on the jacket of the volume were the following:

> In a planned system we cannot confine collective action to the tasks on which we agree, but are forced to produce agreement on everything in order that any action may be taken at all.
> The economic freedom which is the prerequisite of any other freedom cannot be the freedom from economic care which the socialists promise and which can be obtained only be relieving the individual at the same time of the necessity and power of choice: it must be the freedom of economic activity which, with the right of choice, inevitably also carries the risk and the responsibility of that right.
> What our generation has forgotten is that the system of private property is the most important guarantee of freedom, not only for those who own property, but scarcely less for those who do not.[27]

In 1947, he founded an organisation dedicated to research and propaganda in favour of liberal economic thinking – the Mont Pelerin Society – and at its first meeting this endorsed Hayek's main points.[28]

Meanwhile in Britain John Jewkes and Lionel Robbins rehearsed again many of the arguments of Hayek: the former, in his attack on British planning, stressed the cascade of controls involved in planning: 'It is, in particular, vital to recognise, that the economic freedoms cannot be whittled away without destroying social and political freedoms.' A free society, he said, always appeared defenceless because it was open to assault from any angle. 'It can only be defended by a robust defence at every point of the precious minimum circle of individual rights.' The latter added his voice to the legion calls made by members of this group for the construction of a 'competitive order'.[29]

Most significant in Britain at the time, however, were the myriad of groups established to hold back the encroachment of the state on free enterprise. Some of these were organisations primarily of politicians and publicists: the Society of Individualists founded in November 1942 and which merged with the National League for Freedom, or the Progress Trust, founded in November 1943.[30] In addition, businessmen themselves sought to defend their interests, founding groups whose main aim was to raise money from the defence of private enterprise. Among these groups were Aims of Industry, founded in 1942, and British United Industrialists, founded near the end of the war.[31] The Institute of Directors, originally incorporated by Royal Charter in 1906 but moribund for many years, was revived in 1948 and declared its main intention to be 'to fight for free enterprise in no mean way'. In 1951 it launched a 'Free Enterprise Campaign'.[32] An organisation for smaller firms, the National Union of Manufacturers, launched an attack on the FBI for failing to defend the principle of free enterprise strongly enough. Finally, leading figures in the FBI itself considered setting up a research organisation to promote the achievements of free enterprise and to analyse the failings of nationalised industries. It decided in the end that such a move was unfitting for its purpose, but encouraged its members to donate generously to Aims of Industry and the Economic League instead.[33]

Moreover, within the labour movement also we can see a willingness, a concern to declare commitment to capitalism. This eagerness to seek compromise with industrialists has been well documented, but it is worth emphasising here that the leadership of the Labour Party accepted the profit motive 'as the main driving force of industry'. Almost the first thing that Stafford Cripps told his staff at the Board of Trade was that the government's aim was to 'create orderly conditions by which private enterprise can make the most effective contribution to the country's economic welfare'.[34] In 1947 a Labour Party subcommittee on privately-owned industry produced a research paper which threw doubt on the extent to which a cooperative attitude from industrialists was to be expected given 'the short-sighted pursuit of quick and easy personal gains by greedy shareholders or businesses'. Most members of the Party's policy committee roundly criticised the document for failing to highlight the benefits of capitalism. A sentence in the revised report read: 'The aim of Government policy should be to stimulate enterprise on the part of managements.'[35]

There was, therefore, a consensus, a true meeting of minds by the leaders of British industry, and finance, by the Labour leadership, and of course supported by the Americans, and this consensus was that the system of private enterprise itself was to be preserved.

INDUSTRIAL OWNERSHIP AND ORGANISATION: THE
POSTWAR COMPROMISE

Concern among industrialists to redress the propaganda balance in favour
of free enterprise was mitigated by the need for caution and pragmatism,
and by divisions among different business sectors. It was this interaction
of the defence of private enterprise as a whole, with concerns about
specific sectors and rivalries between business groupings, that determined
fundamentally the nature of the postwar settlement on issues of ownership
and organisation. A series of compromises were forged, therefore, through
the mediation of the civil service. The rest of this paper looks briefly at
some of the actions of the Labour governments of 1945–51 to illustrate
this point.

　　Three possible approaches to the achievement and control of industrial
efficiency through modernisation and large-scale production have been
outlined above: the forces of competition, directed 'rationalisation' and
nationalisation. Each method was applied in Britain under the postwar
Labour government. First, there were the well-known cases of nationalisation: enforced state resolution of the organisation and ownership question
together. Secondly, the Labour government sought to harness industrial
self-government – using statutory means where desired – to induce firms
in an industry to cooperate and rationalise, even amalgamate. This was the
purpose of the ill-starred Industrial Organisation and Development Act.
Thirdly, an attempt was made, under American pressure, to overcome
cartels and hence achieve reorganisation through competition and the
market.

　　On the issue of nationalisation two major compromises were worked
out between business and the Labour government and between the Labour
government and the USA. There was, first, a spirit of compromise abroad
with the Labour government itself. The line taken by the FBI was one of
overt cooperation. This tactic was suggested by the need for a long-term
strategy to defend private enterprise. In October 1945 Guy Locock, head
of the FBI's Economic Directorate, wrote a memorandum on 'Private
Enterprise'. In it he argued that the FBI 'must accept the verdict of the
country that steps are to be taken to nationalise certain industries', and
that they should cooperate in making the policy successful, for 'the cause
of private enterprise could be seriously damaged if the Government were
able to claim that the blame for failure lay in obstruction by the employers'. At the same time the FBI believed that 'private enterprise is the only
sound basis for national prosperity'.[36] Moreover, sections of industry were
not opposed to some of the nationalisations which took place, as we know.

This spirit of compromise in the FBI was criticised by other organisations – the National Union of Manufacturers, the Institute of Directors and Aims of Industry; however, other businessmen criticised the FBI for failing to respond sufficiently positively to the policies of the Labour government.[37]

But by 1947 the immediate danger had passed and with it the spirit of compromise. 1947 meant the reining in of demands by the Labour left for further nationalisation. Just as the parameters of state intrusion and of socialist incursions within Britain had been laid down by 1947–8, on the international level the parameters of socialism generally were becoming firmer and consolidationism was also proceeding here. This is evident in many events: the Truman Doctrine, the expulsion of Communists from government in Italy and France, the moves towards more Soviet-style economies in Czechoslovakia and East Germany. The process of containment was taking place both domestically and internationally. Bill Schwarz has argued that the clear commitment to a Cold War, anti-Soviet stance by the British government by 1947 was vital in rallying the Conservatives.[38] This, the avoidance of a postwar slump and expanding domestic markets had put the situation back on 'an even keel'. This produced increasing resistance to much of Labour's programme. The most obvious symbol of this was the vigorous defence of a private iron and steel industry. Not only was this a profitable industry but in April 1949, the Labour Party's new batch of industries for nationalisation put the whole of industry onto the defensive.[39] Interestingly, as an uncooperative attitude by industry became evident on a number of fronts, some Labour ministers began a search by 1950 for greater control over the private sector.[40] The level of compromise, and even possibly of consensus, on the part of business and the Labour leadership, therefore diminished in the course of Labour's time in office.

Secondly, the Labour government was operating under the general terms of the United States' hegemony. We have already noted that Truman's Baylor speech sent warning signals to European governments of America's attitude to state planning and control. The speech effectively argued that, for the American system to survive, 'the whole world must adopt the American way'. The process of 'Americanisation' involved two key policies for industry: productivity policies and anti-monopoly policies, both arguably inconsistent, given that improvements in productivity might well involve the further creation of large firms. It is quite clear that the Labour government did not necessarily agree with the economic policies being pushed from Washington, but nevertheless went along with them either, in the case of anti-cartel policies, to make a good impression, or, in the case of productivity policies, additionally to secure some genuine discussion among British industrialists and trade unions on the issues being raised.[41] Within this general context we can now turn to discussion of the three main methods of industrial reorganisation outlined above.

It was actually around the issue of nationalisation and the specific sectors nationalised that the greatest consensus is to be found. It has been well accepted for some time that the specific nationalisations carried out, with the exception of steel and road haulage, encountered little real opposition from the Opposition and from British business. Minkin disputes the extent to which businessmen complied, arguing that the owners in the case of mines and the railways 'behaved as if they wanted to retain the benefits of ownership'.[42] However, this ignores the differences between businessmen as owners and as consumers: many industrialists and farmers had advocated nationalisation of railways since 1844, and by the 1930s one consumer of coal, ICI, favoured extensive state intervention in the mines. Indeed, the President of the FBI was willing to go on record in support of coal nationalisation.[43] Moreover, owners did exceptionally well out of the actual terms of nationalisation. Compensation levels were very generous for what were often 'a very poor bag of physical assets', as Dalton described the railways.[44] The total bill was £2.6 billion, a sum to be compared in magnitude with that of the Anglo-American loan (of £3.75 billion), although payable not in cash but in government stock.[45] Many former owners also retained an involvement in their industry. Arguably, for many former owners nationalisation was a more profitable and comfortable method of rationalisation than that to be promised by either the forces of competition or statutory rationalisation.

The actual terms of nationalisation also derived from 'a progressive consensus... covering both Liberal and advanced Conservatives'[46] around such issues as compensation, Morrisonian forms of management and a specific regard to determining prices according to the interests of manufacturers. For instance, the Iron and Steel Act abjured the Corporation to

> promote the efficient and economical supply of the products... and to secure that these products are available at such prices as may seem to the Corporation best calculated to satisfy the reasonable demands of the persons who use these products for manufacturing purposes and to further the public interest in all respects.[47]

This echoed the sentiments of Harold Macmillan, who saw coal being a socialised concern 'not making its first objective the securing of a profit on its own operations, but seeking to serve other industries and assist them to become profitable'.[48] Only on the issue of trade union involvement in management could there be said to have been a significant divergence of opinions between the Labour ministers and businessmen. Even here, trade unionists were split on the issue, some fearing trade unionists on the boards of nationalised corporations would be racked by divided loyalties.[49]

The second method to which we have referred to achieve restructuring of industry was through the medium of conscious rationalisation programmes through a partnership of industry and business. It was in fact in this sphere that Labour made its most 'distinctive' contribution to Britain's economic institutions: the Development Councils. The story of the Industrial Organisation and Development Act has now been told many times and it is necessary here only to point out a few key features as they impinge on the issue of postwar consensus. The Act allowed for a statutory Development Council to be set up for industries where a 'substantial' sector of the industry or trade wanted one. The Development Councils were tripartite bodies with trade union representation, and with the power to provide common services to firms in the industry such as research and development, standardisation, marketing, recruitment and training. Their powers stopped short of rationalisation, although that the Councils would encourage such moves was clearly an aim. It was an issue where a certain consensus between the civil service, Labour ministers and the TUC can be seen, especially in wartime discussions on similar proposals by civil servants for measures to promote efficiency through industrial boards. The Labour government expected to get support from industry on the issue, for the scheme bore some resemblance to industrialists' schemes in the 1930s for statutory, legally enforceable trade associations. Indeed, some industries welcomed the opportunity for cooperation. However, the initiative was effectively killed, partly because of the opposition of those industries where the Labour government tried to move ahead with establishment of a Development Council, namely hosiery, wool and clothing, and partly because of the determined resistance of the FBI. Their opposition was based on three main fears. First, Development Councils, although conceived as alternatives to nationalisation, were viewed by the FBI as the thin end of the wedge of nationalisation. Secondly, Development Councils threatened to diminish the importance of existing independent trade associations. And thirdly the employers would not tolerate 'anything which would give workers a statutory right to be brought into the consideration of matters which are regarded as largely the prerogative of management'.[50] Hence this attempt at a consensual, voluntary approach to problems of industrial organisation floundered because of a jealous guarding of the rights of ownership and management: the Labour government had, almost inadvertently, stepped outside the boundaries of the postwar consensus and into an area challenging the rights of private ownership across a very broad spectrum of industry.

The final method of achieving restructuring of industry which we outlined at the beginning was through competition and market forces. The Labour government also implemented the first piece of competition legislation in Britain: the Monopolies and Restrictive Practices Act of 1948. This very mild piece of legislation also carries apparent consensus. It stipulated that instances of monopoly should be investigated to establish whether a monopoly did in fact exist and, if so, if it operated against the public interest. It was no different in practice from Conservative election policy, it was in large part framed by civil servants interpreting policy laid down by the Coalition government on the issue. However, it actually represented a series of compromises. It represented a general compromise with the suspicions of the labour movement of private enterprise and its hostility towards cartels and restrictive practices. Lord Woolton remarked that if British businessmen did not accept some control over these cartels, 'there really was no argument left against wholesale socialisation'.[51] It represented compromise by the Labour Party, which had actually advocated rather stronger legislation in its election manifesto, and Labour ministers attempted to enact this while in power. Ministers were dissuaded, however, by civil servants from rocking the boat of government–industry relations, and the Act was viewed as the most that was politically possible at the time. An idea of the extent to which stronger legislation would have aroused industrial ire can be gained from wartime Reconstruction discussions when businessmen tacitly threatened non-cooperation with the war effort should any inquiry, such as a Royal Commission, on trusts be set up. The Act represented a compromise between business sectors: between those most harmed by restrictive practices and others. Hence an FBI enquiry on the subject accepted the need for some inquiry into monopoly in goods the cost of which enters into the costs of other manufacturers.[52]

But the most important compromise was tacitly reached between British businessmen and the USA. The latter sought anti-cartel provisions across the world, ostensibly because this would be a guarantor of world peace, more probably as a means to break down restrictions on American exports of goods and capital. The former, however, were virulently opposed to any restrictions on the right of industrialists to cartelise, especially on the right to form international cartels. British businessmen were, ironically, concerned to keep this right mainly for fear of the effects of unrestricted American competition on British businesses. The FBI played an important role in Britain's negotiations with the USA on this topic, and Britain maintained a firm stance against American demands, in spite of warnings of a rift between Britain and the USA on the issues. The final formula omitted any specific commitment to ban international cartels, but would, it was felt, be an earnest of the government's good intentions to meet American pressure. The Act had little economic significance, but some political importance. The passage of the 1948 Act represented, therefore, not consensus but compromise. Here the outcome was the result of civil servant mediation between the US government's pressure for radical antitrust moves and almost unanimous business opposition to the disruption or even discussion of the 'trade association system'.[53]

These two other methods of industrial restructuring saw the Labour Party adopting a much more dynamic 'modernising' approach, but they were unable to secure even compromise with industry on the Industrial Organisation and Development Act, and only grudging acquiescence to a limited anit-cartel law.

CONCLUSIONS

I would argue, therefore, that in one way Addison has backed down too far from his line on consensus, and has been looking in the wrong places for signs of it. It is actually very obvious, but still rarely stated, that there was a consensus among the 'old governing class' and the Labour leadership on the future of private ownership. This consensus was helped along by the tough line taken by the US and the emerging lines of the Cold War. At the same time, his view of a settlement, which I would call a series of pragmatic compromises, needs to be better defined. It is incorrect to speak of the 'old governing class, the trade union oligarchy and the intellectual mandarins' as though they were of equal strength and significance. Civil servants certainly had an influential role, as we have seen, in the development of policy on monopolies and Development Councils, but it was essentially a mediating role among conflicting interest groups. In addition, the contribution of the United States to the development of consensus on the big issues and the outcome of negotiations around the compromises needs to be brought fully into our picture of British economic policy in the postwar period.

NOTES

1.   P. Addison, 'The Road from 1945', in P. Hennessy and A. Seldon, eds., *Ruling Performance: British Governments from Attlee to Thatcher*, 1987,

Oxford, Basil Blackwell, pp. 5–27; P. Addison, *The Road to 1945*, 1977, London, Quartet Books, pp. 276, 278.

2. British Parliamentary Papers (hereafter BPP) *Final Report of the Balfour Committee on Industry and Trade*, Cmnd. 3292, 1929, p. 178.

3. A. Booth, 'Britain in the 1930s: a Managed Economy?', *Economic History Review*, 57, 2, November 1987, pp. 237–57.

4. R. Roberts, 'The Administrative Origins of Industrial Diplomacy: an Aspect of Government–Industry Relations, 1929–1935', in J. Turner, ed., *Businessmen and Politics. Studies of Business Activity in British Politics 1900–1945*, 1984, London, Heinemann, pp. 93–104.

5. H.W. Macrosty, *Trusts and the State. A Sketch of Competition*, 1901, London, Grant Richards, p. 283.

6. D.H. MacGregor, *Industrial Combination*, 1906, London, George Bell and Sons.

7. *Balfour Committee*, 1929, p. 89.

8. H. Mercer, *Constructing a Competitive Order. The Hidden History of British Antitrust Policies*, 1995, Cambridge, Cambridge University Press, p. 44.

9. M. Chick, 'Nationalisation, privatisation and regulation', in M.W. Kirby and M.B. Rose, eds., *Business Enterprise in Modern Britain from the Eighteenth to the Twentieth Century*, 1994, London, Routledge, p. 322.

10. H. Macmillan, *The Middle Way*, 1938, London, Macmillan, pp. 230–8; D. Ritschel, 'A Corporatist Economy in Britain? Capitalist Planning for Industrial Self-Government in the 1930s', *English Historical Review*, 106, January 1991, pp. 41–65.

11. Liberal Industrial Enquiry, *Britain's Industrial Future*, 1928, London, Ernest Benn, p. 456.

12. 'Let us Face the Future', in F.W.S. Craig, ed., *British General Election Manifestos 1900–1974*, 1975, London, Macmillan, 2nd edn; TUC, *Interim Report on Postwar Reconstruction*, 1944; J. Tomlinson, *Government and the Enterprise since 1900. The Changing Problem of Efficiency*, 1994, Oxford, Clarendon Press, pp. 89–191.

13. Chick, 1994, p. 319; PRO: BT64/318, 'The Control of Monopoly', Part II by Hugh Gaitskell, 'The Control of Monopoly Prices', July 1943.

14. Anonymous, *Britain without Capitalists*, 1936, London, Lawrence and Wishart, p. 15.

15. H. Pollitt, *For Britain Free and Independent,* report to the 20th Congress of the CPGB, February 1948.

16. Dalton Papers, LSE, 7/6, unsigned memorandum by an official at the Board of Trade, 30 September 1944.

17. S. Fielding, '"Don't Know and Don't Care": Popular political attitudes in Labour's Britain, 1945–51', in N. Tiratsoo, ed., *The Attlee Years*, 1991, London, Pinter, pp. 106–25. Two recent works to dispute an emerging tendency to downplay the extent of radicalism in the British working class and to redefine the quality of that radicalism are L. Minkin, *The Contentious Alliance. Trade Unions and the Labour Party*, 1991, Edinburgh, Edinburgh University Press, pp. 55–8; and J. Fyrth, 'The Mood of Working People', in J. Fyrth, ed., *Labour's High Noon. The Government and the Economy 1945–51*, 1993, London, Lawrence and Wishart, pp. 243–54.

18. E. Barry, *Nationalisation in British Politics*, 1965, London, Cape, p. 370.

19. M.M. Postan, *British War Production*, 1952, London, HMSO, p. 167; see generally, N. Tiratsoo and J. Tomlinson, *Industrial Efficiency and State Intervention. Labour 1939–51*, 1993, London, Routledge, pp. 21–2.

20. PRO: BT64/410 file on the international magnesium cartel; see generally J. Borkin and C.A.Welsh *Germany's Master Plan*, 1943, London, Left Book Club.

21. W.T. Morgan, 'Britain's Election: a debate on nationalisation and cartels', *Political Science Quarterly*, 61, 2, June 1946, p. 233.

22. Postan, 1952, p. 430.

23. Minkin, 1991, p. 56.

24. Addison, 1977, p. 232.

25. D.F. Fleming, *The Cold War and its Origins, 1917–1960*, 1960, London, George Allen and Unwin, Volume I, p. 436.

26. Modern Records Centre (MRC) MSS200/F/3/E1/16/27, CDEIF – 1949 Conference in Rome, extract from newspaper, 10 May 1949, 'Pope Pius XII says socialism can't solve troubles'.

27. Cited in R. Cockett, *Thinking the Unthinkable. Think-tanks and the Economic Counter-Revolution, 1931–1983*, 1994, London, HarperCollins, p. 81.

28. *Ibid.*

29. J. Jewkes, *Ordeal by Planning*, 1947, London, Macmillan, pp. 196, 197; L. Robbins, *The Economic Problem in Peace and War*, 1947, London, Macmillan, pp. 81–4.

30. Cockett, 1994, pp. 67–72.

31. *Ibid.*, pp. 72–3.

32. MRC MSS200/F/3/S2/20/1, extract from *Financial Times*, 21 December 1948.

33. MRC MSS200/F/3/S2/20/1, letter from Sir Norman Kipping, Director-General, to all members, 6 January 1948 and 14 March 1949.

34. PRO BT13/220A M/M/24, 'Draft directive to the Board of Trade' by Stafford Cripps, 28 August 1945.

35. K.O. Morgan, *Labour in Power*, 1984, Oxford, Oxford University Press, p. 121; Labour Party Archive, RD69/October 1947 'Socialism and Private Enterprise' by George Miller; Home Policy Committee minutes, 25 November 1947; RD236/December 1948 'Report to Policy Committee of sub-committee on privately-owned industry'. See also H. Mercer, 'The Labour Governments of 1945–51 and Private Industry', in Tiratsoo, 1991, pp. 71–89.

36. MRC MSS200/F/3/S1/14/16 'Private Enterprise' memo by Guy Locock 22 October 1945.

37. G. Schuster, *Private Work and Public Causes*, 1979, Cambridge, D. Brown, p. 146; MRC MSS200/F/3/S2/10/7, extract from *The Recorder* (a small right-wing paper taken over by William J. Brittain in 1943), 14 May 1949, 'Small Firms Join for Freedom'.

38. B. Schwarz, 'The Tide of History. The Reconstruction of Conservatism 1945–51', in Tiratsoo, 1991, p. 161.

39. Barry, 1965, pp. 378–9.

40. Mercer, 1991, p. 83; N. Rollings '"The Reichstag Method of Governing"? The Attlee Governments and Permanent Economic Controls', in H. Mercer

et al., eds., *Labour Governments and Private Industry. The Experience of 1945–1951*, 1992, Edinburgh, Edinburgh University Press, pp. 15–36.

41. C. Maier, *In Search of Stability: Explorations in Historical Political Economy*, 1987, Cambridge, Cambridge University Press, pp. 133–4; A. Carew, *Labour under the Marshall Plan: The Politics of Productivity and the Marketing of Management Science*, 1987, Manchester, Manchester University Press; Tiratsoo and Tomlinson, 1993, pp. 132–6.

42. L. Minkin, 'Radicalism and Reconstruction: the British Experience', *Europa* 5, 2, 1982, pp. 177–210.

43. MRC MSS200/F/3/S1/14/16 cutting from *Financial Times*, 5 May 1949, address by Sir Robert Sinclair to the Advertising Association.

44. Cited in G. Crompton, 'The Railway Nationalisation Issue 1920–1950', unpublished paper for conference on Industrial Organisation and the road to nationalisation, 1993, Manchester, p. 58.

45. D.N. Chester, *The Nationalisation of British Industry 1945–1951*, 1975, London, HMSO, p. 1017.

46. Tomlinson, 1994, p. 193.

47. Cited in D. McEachern, *A Class against Itself: Power and the Nationalisation of the British Steel Industry*, 1980, Cambridge, Cambridge University Press, 1980, p. 83.

48. Macmillan, 1938, p. 231.

49. Tomlinson, 1994, p. 195.

50. Harold Wilson, cited in Mercer, 1992, which see generally.

51. Dalton Diaries, I, Box 30, 27 June 1944.

52. Mercer, 1995, p. 98.

53. *Ibid.*, chapter 5.

9 Decolonisation and Postwar Consensus
Nicholas Owen

INTRODUCTION

The question of whether (and in what senses) the period after 1940 was characterised by a political consensus has been debated almost exclusively within the framework of domestic policy. Yet the war which spawned commitments to full employment and the welfare state, it should be remembered, was primarily a struggle for Britain's survival as a great power. In the thirty years that followed, Britain shrank from the status of a global leader with far-flung imperial interests to a less certain position on the fringes of Europe. This adjustment occupied much of the energies and resources of Cabinets, officials and political parties. That the 'consensus' debate has made such advances on its home front while neglecting issues such as the Atlantic Alliance, European integration and the end of empire is therefore a serious deficiency.

This historiographical insularity is, of course, not entirely accidental. As both the supporters and opponents of 'consensus' have acknowledged, the debate is almost as much about present concerns as it is about the past.[1] It has become an arena in which contending explanations of Britain's national decline fight. The historical battle is at its fiercest where it concerns issues which resonate in contemporary politics: the economy, health and education.[2] Indeed, perhaps one reason for the renewal of the debate in the last few years has been the sharpness of recent challenges to established notions of the proper limits of the state in the provision of welfare and economic management. While such debates remain unresolved, there are bound to be conflicting assessments of the postwar period.

In marked contrast to the turbulent waters of the debate over consensus in social and economic matters, the end of empire seems a placid stretch of backwater, remote from the urgent demands of Britain's current politics. Partly because so few of the consequences of colonial retreat remain visible enough to haunt British voters and politicians (compare France's persistently troubled relationship with Algeria), judgements of British decolonisation have tended until recently to be uncritical and laudatory.

While it is no longer possible to take seriously Whitehall's conveniently flattering account of readily offered 'transfers of power' in which control passed gracefully and deliberately from statesmanlike imperial politicians to their duly grateful subjects, decolonisation is still all too easily represented as an uncontested and peaceful process, in which (to quote one leading postwar historian) 'the curtain went down in dignity and tranquillity ... without traumas and without tears'.[3]

Partisan consensus over the ending of the empire is an essential component of this view. The 'success' of Britain's decolonisation is held up for approval as a *national* achievement: a vindication of her constitutional arrangements and the good sense of those who worked them. It is frequently compared favourably with the agonies endured by other, supposedly less mature and stable European colonial powers, whose quarrelsome politicians failed to demonstrate the pragmatism and mutual tolerance that characterised their counterparts at Westminster and whose political systems proved too weak to contain their conflicts. The smooth disengagement of the British state from its colonial responsibilities has also been contrasted, once again to its advantage, with its inability to deliver economic prosperity or social improvements. Here at least, it is implied, politicians were able to set aside their factional differences and look to the 'national interest'.

While Paul Addison acknowledges the necessity for including external affairs and defence in any comprehensive account of 'consensus', *The Road to 1945* does not extend its analysis beyond domestic policy.[4] In recent years, however, other authors have been keen to integrate 'ending the empire' into the argument. In 1987, Dennis Kavanagh claimed that decolonisation was one of the 'core issues' of the postwar consensus.[5] In more recent work with Peter Morris, he goes further still in asserting that it was in colonial policy that bipartisanship was 'at its strongest and ... most explicitly asserted'.[6] David Dutton too has suggested that 'the inexorable progress of the colonies towards independence' formed part of the cross-party consensus.[7] In his detailed history of colonial issues in British politics, David Goldsworthy labels the period 1945–51 'the bipartisan years', although he acknowledges that after 1954 the consensus began to break down.[8] The purpose of this paper is to extend the debate beyond its domestic frame and explore how far British responses to colonial nationalism and the policy of decolonisation were genuinely characterised by consensus.

As those acquainted with the literature hardly need reminding, 'consensus' is itself a contested concept. To simplify, we can identify three different meanings: consensus as *policy settlement*, consensus as *partisan convergence* and consensus as *popular contentment*.[9] The first of these corresponds roughly with what Addison terms a 'Whitehall consensus': that is, elite-level agreement among policy-makers. For present purposes, this means a group consisting of the core executive (Cabinet ministers and senior civil servants) which extends through the Colonial Office and other relevant departments to governors and their advisers. Policy settlement is generally indicated by continuity of policy from one administration to the next. Consensus as *partisan convergence* entails harmony among party leaders and activists outside the policy-making elite, and is usually characterised by interpenetration of party programmes and the low intensity of (genuine) party competition. Consensus as *popular contentment* involves the relative absence of divisions in the electorate and those non-party bodies which sought to influence the public (rather than the ministerial, parliamentary or official) debate, and is best indicated (if not by unanimity) by the existence of a broad-based 'middle ground'. Of course, some individuals (Cabinet ministers are the obvious example) participated in more than one arena. But while the definitions overlap, they remain centred in different places, and distinguishing them allows us to capture the tensions that such figures experienced when required to meet the expectations of different constituencies.

CONSENSUS AS POLICY SETTLEMENT

At first sight, as John Darwin has suggested, Whitehall's colonial policy after 1945 seems utterly unplanned and inconsistent. At almost the same time as it transferred power in India, Pakistan, Burma and Ceylon, the Attlee government was also engaged in the construction and forcible imposition of a new federation in Malaya and an intensified penetration into the economies of tropical Africa. In the Middle East, the surrender of the Palestine Mandate in May 1948 was matched by Bevin's determined, if ultimately fruitless, attempt to rebuild Britain's informal empire in the Arab world. Later, as West African politicians anxious for constitutional advances found themselves pushing at an open door, the African populations of Northern Rhodesia and Nyasaland were brusquely bundled into a white-dominated federation which in 1962 Whitehall proceeded to demolish despite vehement settler opposition. All in all, government policy is a puzzling 'jungle of quirks and quiddities', an unpatterned, unpredictable succession of 'leaps and lurches ... riddled with extraordinary and baffling inconsistencies'.[10]

Yet the puzzle is more apparent than real. It would be rash to assume that these geographical contradictions and hectic changes of pace imply that policy-makers were necessarily divided or infirm of purpose. In the first place, as Darwin acknowledges, the challenges they faced were vastly different, ranging from united and prosperous territories where metropolitan and colonial interests meshed easily to divided and alienated societies where they did not. In meeting them, policy-makers were forced to rely upon severely limited and unreliable information. In particular, anticolonial nationalist movements, apparently springing from nowhere, often seemed to the British bewilderingly protean. Where had they come from? What did their leaders want? Did they have a programme or were they merely office-seekers? Whom did they represent? Were they really communists? How wide and deep did their support go? Could they be relied upon to protect British interests? Were there credible alternatives that could be quietly encouraged? Metropolitan policy-makers, mentally confined by Anglocentric conceptions of the political party, relying on secondhand and often outdated information supplied by inadequate and creaking intelligence networks, despaired of finding the answers. Sudden switches of policy, such as the acceleration of pace in the Gold Coast after the 1948 Accra riots, often reflected the policy-makers' judgement that they had miscalculated the odds. Where there were conflicting interests to be reconciled, it was even harder for officials to guess what the parties would accept. Much of the official work of decolonisation thus involved dragging mutually suspicious parties to the negotiating table and forcing them to embrace each other and a British-sponsored solution. Progress came through the successive rejection of alternatives: trying out a plan on one of the parties and making adjustments to suit its objections, then taking it back to the others. Each move required the building and re-working of coalitions sufficiently broad to command support across a wide range of rapidly diverging interests and stable enough to act as a support for British interests. Under such circumstances, it was not merely natural but utterly rational for policy-makers to take swift initiatives to force the pace, or to slow it down with a dose of well-calculated repression. Hence there was great reluctance to tie Britain to a specific plan for decolonisation, and it is perhaps significant that attempts to do this (such as those by Bennett and Cohen in 1947 and Macmillan's 'cost-benefit' exercise a decade later), were never regarded as more than 'mission statements' by policy-makers, who generally found instinct and pragmatism better guides.[11]

But this does not mean that British policy was purposeless, let alone contradictory. In fact, among the policy-making elite, there was broad agreement on the essentials of colonial policy, at least in terms of the response to colonial nationalism.

Some, though not all, of this consensus was forged under the same wartime pressures as its domestic counterpart. Mobilisation was almost as disruptive in the colonies as it was at home, forcing the British into unpopular policies which in more peaceful times they avoided, such as higher taxation, conscription, curfews and rationing.[12] Yet sweeping wartime powers allowed the British to ignore or repress discontent to a degree which would have been inconceivable on the home front. The unpredictable swings of politics in 1940 that pushed reconstruction to the fore in Whitehall left the Colonial Office and its responsibilities largely untouched. Forced to rely on the cooperation of distant and often recalcitrant outposts to implement its policies, and long regarded with scorn by the Treasury and other Whitehall departments, the Colonial Office suffered more heavily than its domestic counterparts from bureaucratic inertia. Unlike other departments of state, it did not suffer an influx of temporary civil servants anxious to plan the postwar world, but instead made do with limited staffing. There was accordingly little in colonial affairs to parallel the masterplans of domestic reconstruction. Left-wing activists, far from pushing reforms at the Coalition as they did in domestic affairs, were cautious on the issue of colonial freedom, while Labour leaders were to be found defending Britain's imperial record to foreign detractors.[13] Despite the desperate efforts of opinion-formers to breathe life into them, popular campaigns of the type that carried Beveridge to prominence had no real equivalent in imperial affairs, which had rarely managed to ignite much enthusiasm.[14] Pressure for statements of intent came largely from the United States, and even this proved resistable once Roosevelt's advisers began to contemplate the instabilities of the postwar order.[15]

Lacking the dynamics that forced reform elsewhere in Whitehall, progress was slow. After 1943, Colonial Office thinking began to turn towards questions of social and economic reconstruction, and many of the favoured methods are familiar to students of the domestic consensus. *Ad hoc* remedial aid for colonies in difficulties was to be replaced by long-term economic planning, private investors by state-dominated planning commissions, and salutary neglect by the provision of welfare to smooth the adjustment to peacetime conditions.[16] Concerning political development, however, the planners were more circumspect. Economic development was a prerequisite of self-government. In enemy-occupied territories such as Malaya, more radical plans were possible, but elsewhere, only piecemeal reforms were envisaged, with the intention of consolidating imperial rule and fending off international critics. In Africa, plans were made under the conservative influence of Hailey to lure traditional allies from their chiefdoms to collaborate with central governments, but self-government was thought a distant prospect.[17] It was not until after the end of the war that the growing influence of Andrew Cohen, the new Head of the African Division, and the Fabian Secretary of State Arthur Creech Jones, coupled with increasing recognition of the inability of existing native authorities in promoting economic development, forced more extensive discussion.

These delays were significant. It is interesting to speculate how much of the domestic consensus would have been enacted had the cold logic of Britain's postwar economic and strategic position been fully understood. By 1947, as the Colonial Office began to plot a new course in Africa, it had become cruelly apparent. To repair her indebted, war-ravaged and dis-located economy, Britain needed to reclaim her foreign markets and sup-pliers, reduce her dependence upon dollars, exploit colonial resources and cut her overseas expenditure. If she was to reach the 'New Jerusalem' rather than 'Starvation Corner', the apostles of full employment and demand management – Beveridge and Keynes – insisted nothing less would do.[18] The new strategic demands of the cold war were equally strin-gent. Containing communism required a firm stand in the Middle East, effective partnership with the United States and strong anti-communist propaganda at the United Nations.

It was within these tight constraints that the new policy towards nation-alists evolved. The growth of movements opposed to direct colonial rule was accepted as an inevitable development, even where (as in Africa) they had yet to threaten British dominance. Authoritarian rule was repeatedly ruled out as anachronistic, partly because it was expensive – given military commitments in Europe and defence cuts – but mostly because it was counter-productive. To resort to force to crush nationalist movements, however satisfyingly drastic it seemed to frustrated politicians, was likely to exacerbate anti-British feeling both in the colony and its neighbours and to expose Britain to criticism both at home and abroad, especially from anti-colonial blocs at the United Nations and in the United States. Where the colonial state could plausibly claim that its tactics were directed against 'extremists' in response to the demands of law-abiding citizens and when its actions were well-targeted, decisive and controlled, it showed little reluctance to use both firepower and imprisonment to deal with its opponents. But policy-makers found conditions were rarely this pleasing, and even when they were, it was recognised that political concessions had to accompany military action. A protracted clash with legitimate national-ists was likely to reduce British authority to that of an overworked and harassed police officer.

Of course, this did not entail surrender to colonial nationalism. On the contrary, as in India before the war, the British remained reluctant to let control over the pace and direction of constitutional advance slip out of their hands and keen to shape nationalist movements to British economic and strategic interests. The key technique in this reshaping was the identification and encouragement of 'authentic' nationalists. India had seemed to show the dangers of the creation of a class of unrepresentative and self-interested pure politicians, able to sway gullible masses through demagoguery. What was needed was to cut rain-channels into the hard earth of colonial society before the nationalist storm broke and floods carried away the flimsy structures of British rule.[19] Accordingly, plans drawn up by members of the Colonial Office to pre-empt similar problems in West Africa fixed on Africanisation of the administration and the establishment of an 'efficient and democratic system of local government' as the solution. Democracy would make irresponsible nationalist leaders answerable to mass electorates for the delivery of practical improvements rather than anti-British slogans. Opportunities of holding executive power at the local level would divert younger Africans from sterile oppositionism into constructive administrative work. At the centre, constitutional advance would follow in gradual stages, as the Legislative Council evolved into a Parliament and the Executive Council into a Cabinet collectively responsible to it. The pace of advance was to be set not by the urgency of nationalist demands, nor by external pressure, but by the colony's supposed 'maturity': the viability of its economy, the mutual tolerance shown by its ethnic groups and the stability of its political life. Progress was to be leisurely – even the most advanced territory, the Gold Coast, was not expected to reach full self-government in under a generation[20] – but the destination unarguable.

Very little of this applied to the so-called 'plural societies' of the Caribbean, East and Central Africa and South-East Asia. Here, the policy-makers fixed on two techniques as the best means of advance: federation and settler-dominated multi-racialism.

Federation was justified by the claim that it would create viable economic – and in the case of South-East Asia defensive – units, without which political independence could not be meaningful. In doing so, moreover, it might undermine the ability of nationalists to exploit postwar economic distress. As in India (once again), federation also offered a means of bringing nationalists into government, but forcing them to share power with loyalists keen to retain links with the imperial power, thereby diluting strident calls for majority rule. Best of all, successful federalism required the presence of an impartial referee at the centre to hold the ring and reconcile the demands of the constituent units, a demanding yet influential part in which the British were anxious to cast themselves.

Multi-racialism offered many of the same advantages. To those who believed that the colonial empire had reached a 'parting of the ways' at which those colonies where the British presence was confined to a handful of administrators might be seized by inexperienced and unready nationalists while areas with entrenched settler populations were dragged into independence under white minority rule, multi-racialism offered a third way. By careful manipulation of the franchise and the electoral system, the creation and sponsorship of multiracial parties and the provision of constitutional safeguards, it was hoped that only those politicians prepared to campaign for support outside their own communities would win elections. This would serve to break up purely racial formations and offer a chance of peaceful progress. The untangling of communal and regional animosities would promote political stability, which in turn would attract investment and foster economic growth and the emergence of prosperous groups likely to lend their British sponsors a sympathetic ear in the years to come. Better still, it could readily be defended to the international critics of colonialism, since it absolved the British of the old charge that empire meant racial discrimination.

The new approach had something for all the policy-makers. To young 'nation-building progressives' in the Colonial Office, it offered a challenging mission. For economic planners, it provided an excuse to tap the supposedly vast dollar-earning resources of the colonial empire. For older sceptics keen to preserve British control, it supplied devolved powers and the opportunity to outsmart nationalist elites. Naturally, some conservatively-minded Governors grumbled. 'The C.O. has got itself into a sort of mystic enchantment', wrote Kenyan Governor Philip Mitchell, 'and sees visions of grateful, independent Utopias beaming at them from all around the world, as if there was – yet – any reason to suppose that any African can be cashier of a village council for 3 weeks without stealing the cash.'[21] Nevertheless, the Colonial Office regarded such attitudes as obstacles to be broken down through persuasion and careful presentation rather than accommodated.[22] Little tolerance was shown to those who showed themselves unwilling to adapt, and the plan swiftly became accepted policy. Diehards were told that they should consider 'whether they can conscientiously serve a Government with whose policy they are in fundamental disagreement. For this policy is clear and there is no prospect of it being changed except in the direction of still faster progress.'[23]

Almost immediately, however, as its expectations were defeated and its timetables shortened, the Whitehall consensus came under strain.

Nationalists proved reluctant to see economic development as an acceptable substitute for political independence.[24] Africanisation of the administrative cadres failed to keep pace with the political reforms, and had failed to divert the energies of the young and ambitious into cooperation with the British.[25] According to a Colonial Office report in 1958, they had largely ignored the lure of local office, preferring to construct territory-wide organisations to make a bid for power at the centre.[26] Indeed, in the opinion of at least one civil servant, the policy of devolving power in stages was itself destabilising, since it encouraged politicians to agitate for the next constitutional change rather than 'getting on with the job'.[27] It proved impossible to seal one colony off from the next: what was offered in one place inevitably sparked off demands for the same or more elsewhere. Thus an official committee concluded in 1954 that while it might be possible to delay constitutional progress a little, 'the pace of constitutional change will be determined by the strength of nationalist feeling and the development of political consciousness in the territory concerned'.[28]

Political agitation had (necessarily, and as had always been intended) been met at first with modest half-measures. But it had proved impossible for the British to control the pace at which such concessions were made. The co-option of moderate African politicians to executive councils left them open to the charge of collaboration. After 1960, radicals outside the council chamber were prepared to point to the rapid successes of French colonies, and even the notoriously backward Belgian Congo, at winning full independence. At the same time, the approach of self-government also deepened the fears of minority communities fearful of being left out of the settlement. It was increasingly appreciated that the unavoidable price of sustaining the 'moderates' against militants and separatists was ever more rapid instalments of constitutional advance.[29] Elections too, far from forcing nationalists to moderate their demands, served to intensify the process. Newly-formed African nationalist parties were exposed to the pressures of party competition, thereby sharpening their determination to wrest control of the administrative machine from the British without delay.

Such instability threatened to undermine the whole purpose of decolonisation (economic, political, diplomatic, strategic), and could only be resolved by luring nationalists into bargaining under British auspices, which meant speeding up political concessions. As the Cabinet noted in 1955 in discussing Singapore, the choice lay between refusing concessions, which could only lead to 'bloody and disastrous consequences' and meeting the demand for constitutional advances fast enough to keep the peace and retain 'a guiding influence over developments'.[30] The criteria for advancement were, at least privately, changed. What mattered was less whether a colony was 'mature' enough, but whether there was a political elite with sufficient popular support to govern effectively. The policy-makers came to calculate a balance of risks: to go slowly was simply riskier than to go quickly. As Colonial Office civil servant Charles Jefferies argued in 1956, the gradual plan had failed to provide stability: 'I think there is too much tendency to consider whether these places are "ready" for Statehood. Of course they are not, any more than the Gold Coast is "ready" for independence, or than one's teenage daughter is "ready" for the proverbial latch-key.'[31] Transfers of power were simply the logical conclusion of the process.

Until historians work through the newly opened archival material, we will not know how easily the policy-makers found it to adapt to the change of pace, or whether the consensus buckled under the strain. The published work on the independence of the Gold Coast in 1957 suggests that there were few objections in Whitehall to the quick independence that the Governor demanded as the best means of strengthening Kwame Nkrumah's Convention People's Party government against its secessionist opponents in Ashanti.[32] It remains to be seen whether Colonial Office civil servants, their counterparts in the Commonwealth Relations Office and colonial proconsuls were more divided in the controversial cases of East and Central Africa.

CONSENSUS AS PARTISAN CONVERGENCE

Support for the Whitehall settlement among party politicians was more heavily qualified. As is well known, until the 1960s, the assumption that Britain must remain a world power was challenged only on the fringes of British political life. But the parties disagreed about the means by which greatness was to be sustained. In particular, they remained fundamentally divided over the question of how colonial nationalism should be handled.

The key to understanding Conservative attitudes to colonial national-ism is India.[33] Contrary to much historical opinion,[34] the majority of Conservatives never reconciled themselves to the transfer of power to Congress nationalists in India. This claim does not depend upon the diehard campaign led by a small and unrepresentative – if highly vocal – minority of ageing MPs and activists which resisted modest advances in the constitutional status of India in the early 1930s. Rather, it rests on the mass of loyal backbenchers, many of whom were strongly critical of gov-ernment policy. Cuthbert Headlam, for example, though never tempted by

Churchill's call for defiance of the Party Whip, was equally unattracted by Indian self-determination, a 'pretty theory' which simply failed to work with 'Eastern races', who were 'not temperamentally fitted to rule themselves'.[35] The support of such men for the 1935 Act was based on the assumption that it would tame Congress, not capitulate to it. Even progressive Conservatives such as Macmillan and Butler regarded Congress leaders as extremist and unreliable and wished to see Britain remain in India until more acceptable successors had emerged.[36]

Thus the War Cabinet's 1942 proposal to promise India freedom at the war's end had been strongly opposed by Conservative backbenchers and had come closer than any issue, other than perhaps the Beveridge Report, to breaking up the Coalition.[37] The Conservatives were deeply unhappy about the policies of the Attlee government towards India, which they saw as tantamount to an abdication of duty and an act of betrayal. From the summer of 1946 until well after Independence Day, they argued that Congress ministers were bent on achieving caste Hindu domination of India, that they lacked the ability to unite the country and to provide effective government, and that Attlee and his colleagues were supine in the face of their agitation.[38]

Thus when the Conservatives came to reformulate their imperial policy in 1948, they were determined to avoid the mistakes of India.[39] Power should not be transferred to 'a small and clamorous political group' out of touch with the masses. The welfare of white minorities in plural societies was of specific importance. It would be wrong to hand them over 'to possible victimisation by politicians incapable of exercising power in accordance with democratic conceptions of justice, toleration and humanity'. Economic stability must come first, progress could only be gradual and 'each constitutional step forward must be accompanied by a growing understanding, not only of the machinery, but also of the spirit of democratic government'. Conservatives, unlike their counterparts on the left, 'did not underestimate the difficulties which surround the application of democratic constitutions and ideas to people whose traditions are wholly different from those of the Western world.'[40] In West Africa, the Conservative Research Department set its face against the transfer of colonial power to an unrepresentative and partial 'black-coated intelligentsia'.[41] A broad range of opinion running from Maxwell-Fyfe through the 1922 Committee to Macmillan (who found 'grave concern' at the Labour's 'liquidation' of empire and wanted a 'strong sentimental appeal') wished for a revived empire policy to be a central plank of the Tory reconstruction.[42]

The return of the Conservatives to office in 1951 is usually taken to be the clinching moment of the case for consensus. In the opinion of the

leading authority on the new administration, commitment to Labour's pro-
gramme of decolonisation formed part of the agenda inherited by the
Conservatives, and 'continuity, not change, was ... the order of the day'.[43]
Although no Colonial Office territory achieved freedom until 1957, con-
stitutional reforms were introduced in East and West Africa and South-
East Asia, and the 74-year 'temporary occupation' of Egypt ended.

But even if as *policy-makers* the Conservative leaders accepted the
necessity for concessions, as *partisans* they were profoundly unhappy
about them. While few now believed that colonial peoples were unsuited
to self-government, almost all held that a lengthy period of apprenticeship
was necessary. Nationalists were accordingly still privately regarded as
unrepresentative troublemakers, bent on securing advantages by agitation.
At best, they were simply unschooled and over-ambitious, at worst
corrupt, authoritarian, anti-Western and probably pro-communist
demagogues.

Accordingly, many senior Conservatives stressed the need to 'keep
change within bounds', or to use the phrase of Salisbury, to 'keep the lid
on' the process of constitutional change. Even the snail's pace of Lyttelton
and Lennox-Boyd had attracted criticism from those in the Party keen for
something more glacial.[44] Unless the pace was slowed to allow time for
the changes to be digested, the colonies would suffer 'at the best the
degradation of Liberia and at the worst the inhumanities of Soviet colonial
rule'.[45] It is unsurprising to find that Churchill himself was personally
deeply unsympathetic to the transfers of power to colonial nationalists.[46]
But these views were shared by a number of his colleagues too. 'Some
well-informed, and by no means reactionary, people', wrote Eden of West
Africa in 1952, 'think that we have been moving at a pretty dangerous
political gallop there lately.'[47] As the Gold Coast neared independence,
Lyttelton expressed his 'great reluctance' to sanction further advances,
while both Home and Macmillan were 'frankly unhappy' and 'full of foreboding' on the chances of it avoiding corruption and authoritarian rule.[48]
'Power to those unused to it', Home believed, was 'heady wine'.[49] 'It was
unfortunate', the Cabinet concluded in December 1954, 'that the policy of
assisting dependent peoples to attain self-government had been carried
forward so fast and so far.'[50]

Thus where it was possible to regain the initiative in controlling the
pace of constitutional advance, Conservative Cabinets were keen to do so.
The incoming Colonial Secretary, Oliver Lyttelton, tellingly compared his
task to that of reviving a near-dead patient.[51] In East and Central Africa,
the Conservatives exhibited an 'almost reckless confidence' in their
attempts to frustrate nationalists who demanded African majorities, in

Kenya to such a degree that no political parties were allowed above the level of the district. In Tanganyika, the multiracial United Tanganyika Party was sponsored to woo Africans away from Julius Nyerere's TANU, while in Uganda, a nationalist movement was created to act as a counter-weight for the separatist ambitions of Buganda. In the Central African Federation, emergency powers were used to imprison anti-federal nationalist leaders and proscribe their organisations.[52] Even in the Gold Coast, where matters had gone so far under their predecessors, and where so little of substance was at stake, the Conservative Cabinet expressed its unhappiness with the concessions demanded by the Governor.[53] In the case of three 'fortresses', where Britain's strategic needs were taken to be paramount, Conservative ministers were prepared to make it plain that independence could never be granted: Cyprus in 1954, Aden in 1956 and Malta in 1961.[54]

The most striking attempt by frustrated partisans to break out of the stifling embrace of the Whitehall settlement came, of course, at Suez in 1956. The new Egyptian policy forced on the British after the Neguib–Nasser coup of 1952 had been deeply unpalatable to the Conservative right. The sacrifice of the Suez Base in 1954 to pacify nationalists, the subsequent humiliations inflicted by Nasser on British allies in Jordan and Iraq and the necessity of coordinating regional strategy with longstanding rivals in the United States were all bitter pills for those who believed, with Eden, that it was Britain's capacity to act independently that defined her foreign policy.[55] Once it had become apparent that Nasser was intent on expelling all British influence from the Middle East, protests from the Conservative backbenches, with goading allusions to 'appeasement',[56] backed by a stiffened amendment at the Party Conference, fuelled Eden's determination to strike 'some blow, somewhere, to counterbalance'.[57] '[T]he alternative', he told Churchill bluntly, 'was a slow bleeding to death.'[58] That the ill-fated decision to collude with the French and Israelis was taken by the narrow circle of Conservative partisans around Eden rather than senior soldiers and officials, most of whom were either not informed or misled, is a fine illustration of the chasm of perception that divided partisans from policy-makers.[59] In Cabinet, at Westminster and in Conservative associations, support for the use of force, indeed, was widespread, and embraced even those such as Home and Macmillan who later sought to distance themselves from it. Epstein estimates that only an informal group of 25–40 MPs opposed the use of force, of whom a mere eight withheld their support in the division lobbies. While five of the eight abstainers suffered politically for their disloyalty to Eden, four of them to the extent of deselection, pro-Suez extremists enjoyed constituency support. Among Conservative voters, moreover, support was 'really immense'.[60]

The violence of Eden's Suez policy allowed a thankful Labour Party a rare moment of unity and obscured the ambivalences of their own response to Nasser, whom Gaitskell too had earlier compared to Hitler and Mussolini. Like the Conservatives, Labour saw colonial nationalist movements in the light of its Indian experiences. Congress, it had been thought, was too closely entwined with the vested interests of local bourgeoisies to be truly democratic, and too reliant upon illegitimate and unparliamentary strategies of direct action and civil disobedience. Much better, it was thought, that it should follow the lines of Labour's own political evolution and adopt the methods that had brought them to prominence: that is, through participation in legislative work and campaigns not merely for political independence, but social and economic reform for the Indian worker and peasant. The failure of Congress to evolve along the lines Labour had set for it irritated the party leaders and led them as late as 1945 to question whether Congress was fit to inherit the Raj.[61]

Among the party leaders, particularly those of the older generation, these instincts still twitched after 1951, especially in relation to Africa.[62] In 1952, while nearly 200 Labour MPs backed the NEC on a motion to open the Kenyan White Highlands to Kikuyu farmers, there was little dissent from the suppression of Mau Mau. Lyttelton's suspension of the constitution of British Guiana in 1953 split the Party largely on the issue of whether to support the popularly-elected but anti-democratic Peoples Progressive Party government. Cold War considerations also enhanced Labour's innate suspicion of communist-backed nationalists. In Malaya, Labour's official spokesmen confined themselves to vigorous protests over police brutality and starvation tactics rather than support for the communist-dominated nationalist movement. Even on the test question of Central Africa, the party leaders, while insistent that the white settlers should sweeten the medicine of federation, still believed it good for dissenting Africans to swallow.[63] Until October 1956, Labour was committed to equality between races in plural societies rather than majoritarian democracy, a stance which was bound to favour white minorities. Even after the 1956 party document *The Plural Society*, which made transfers of power conditional upon the introduction of one man-one vote, Labour refused to support the demands of Banda and Kaunda for the right of Nyasaland and Northern Rhodesia to secede from the Federation.[64]

However, as was often the case in matters of colonial policy (the same happened over Rhodesia with the Conservatives after 1964), moving into opposition allowed partisan considerations their head. After a period of uneasy transition, in which generalised face-saving formulae were devised to hold the Party together, Labour's position on the colonies came increasingly to be defined by the left. Of course, given the depth of strife between Bevanites and the 'revisionist' leadership, there were quarrels over colonial policy, especially over Malaya. But they were much less substantial than those on nuclear weapons and public ownership, and remarkable in that it was the left that won them. The waves of colonial crises in East and Central Africa, the Mediterranean and the Far East in the 1950s found backbench Labour MPs better informed, quicker to respond, and ready to condemn the obsolete imperialism that so embarrassed the right at Suez. In 1957, the Party's *The Smaller Territories* argued that the strategic value of territories such as Cyprus did not trump their right to self-determination.[65] In East Africa and the West Indies, the Party pressed for negotiations and rapid progress to independence. The unexpected dominance of the left was partly due to the vigorous campaigning of Benn and Brockway's Movement for Colonial Freedom, which persuaded a large cohort of Labour MPs that only independence at an early date would avert a series of futile colonial wars. More importantly, perhaps, even party leaders traditionally cautious about the unpopularity of attacking the empire and those bored by colonial affairs saw in anticolonialism a political weapon to divide the Conservatives, win the moral high ground and rally their divided Party. After the 1959 election, the Labour right found itself thoroughly outflanked by the rapid transfers of power effected by British policy-makers in East and Central Africa. The left, by contrast, found itself pushing at a door that was not merely open, but through which Macleod had already passed.[66]

Macleod and Macmillan contemplated the widening racial divide in East and Central Africa as students of international realpolitik, not as partisans. Mounting black unrest could not be crushed without destroying the Commonwealth, destabilising the Anglo-American alliance, and driving the newly liberated states of Africa into the arms of the Soviets. Yet to withdraw too rapidly would leave white settlers dangerously exposed, possibly precipitating unilateral declarations of independence and civil war, thereby destroying all hope of future British influence south of the Sahara. This entailed setting a pace towards black majority rule which Macleod regarded as 'not as fast as the Congo and not as slow as Algiers', but which even the most sympathetic Cabinet ministers saw as 'faster than we would choose'.[67] '[I]n the Federation they are frightened', Macleod told Duncan Sandys, 'and it is very understandable that they should be so. A way of life that seemed utterly safe, remote and secure is now brought suddenly into the frontiers of conflict and for the uncertainty that results they blame the British Government and our policies. But in fact our policies are the only ones thát can save them.'[68]

The starkness of racial divisions in Africa was reflected in partisan polarisation at home, especially on the right where there was much instinctive sympathy for the plight of the settler.[69] He was 'almost entirely responsible for the economic development that [had] taken place' and his leadership was vital to the future of Africa. He was 'not a bird of passage but [was] there to stay and his children after him'.[70] In Kenya, Conservative MPs called for guarantees to protect settler communities from the full implications of devolution and majority rule by granting them an status equal to that of indigenous communities. In Central Africa, they held that Britain had promised to ensure that the Federal experiment survived. Indeed, on all fronts but the political, it had, they felt, been successful. Thus while most of them felt that it should reform its racial policies to create a real partnership with Africans, they were unprepared for the creation of African majorities in Northern Rhodesia which might vote for secession from the Federation in which so much capital – both literal and metaphorical – had been invested.[71] The collapse of the Congo in the wake of precipitate Belgian withdrawal hardened their instinctively gradualist assumptions. Opposition to rapid decolonisation thus found support in the deeply Conservative belief that it amounted to the victory of ideology over common sense and the national interest.[72]

At first, Macleod's accelerated pace won support on the backbenches because its boldness and imagination offered a marked contrast to the ineffectiveness of Lennox-Boyd.[73] From the beginning of 1961, however, party opposition grew over the issue of protection of Roy Welensky's United Federal Party (UFP) interests in Northern Rhodesia, and Macmillan's refusal to offer military help to the pro-Western secessionist regime across the Congolese border in Katanga. The divisions were evident at Cabinet level, where on at least three separate occasions, Macleod was prepared to resign unless concessions were made to Banda and Kaunda.[74] For his part, Home, convinced that the government 'cannot impose political conditions in Northern Rhodesia which would make it impossible for the Europeans to control the country if we left', also threatened to leave.[75] In February 1961, effective lobbying by Welensky paid off when a hostile motion calling for the government of Northern Rhodesia to remain in 'responsible hands' (which Macleod rightly regarded as 'UFP double-talk' for white control)[76] found over 100 signatures, over a third of the backbench party. When Southern Rhodesian premier Edgar Whitehead addressed the Commonwealth Affairs Committee, his proposal that the Rhodesias be amalgamated, with only a devolved assembly to protect the separate interests of the north, was met with strong approval.[77] On the left of the party, the Bow Group campaigned for Macleod.[78] Whatever line was taken, Macmillan gloomily predicted Cabinet resignations and a 'Government and party split in two'.[79]

Amid the death throes of the Federation and the apparently unstoppable rise of Jomo Kenyatta's KANU party, imperial affairs that had once fired the Conservative imagination had come to seem tawdry and dishonourable. Ever since 1951, Powell had told a post-Suez Conservative Study Group in 1957, Conservative colonial policy had been 'on the wrong track': we had used our enemies' thinking, used phrases we did not believe in, accepted arrangements because the alternative was worse or could not be defended in public, and adopted a set of principles and attitudes in which we at best half believed.[80]

Wheedling and pleading with nationalist leaders, diluting the strength of the Commonwealth to attract new members and going cap-in-hand to Washington for support were essential skills for the modern decoloniser, but held little attraction for traditionally-minded Conservatives, many of whom, disgusted by Macleod's craftiness, now gathered in the 1957 Committee and the Monday Club established to commemorate the black day of Macmillan's 'Winds of Change' speech. In April 1961, Salisbury raged against his leaders' decision to release Kenyatta:

> All the glib excuses are trotted out. No doubt he is a murderer, but Makarios was a murderer [and] we've swallowed him. No doubt he encouraged the lowest forms of bestial vice; but, after all, he's already paid the penalty for that. Why not let bygones be bygones? Are these things always to debar him from being Prime Minister? Really, I don't think we've ever fallen so low.[81]

Later the same year, senior party officials reported that over-hasty retreat in Africa was demoralising constituency workers and driving Conservatives to cast protest votes at by-elections.

> [In 1953] ... we envisaged the *steady* progress of colonial territories to self-government – an aim to which 99 per cent of party members subscribed. But swept along by the flood tide of nationalism, we have gone at the gallop, and in doing so, have upset many of our supporters.[82]

That diehard groups found themselves unable to hold the centre of the Party for long is explained less by Macleod's ability to persuade MPs of the merits of his policies than by the size of Macmillan's majority, and the skill of his Party Whips at deploying persuasion, patronage and threats.[83] The preservation of Cabinet unity owed much to the skill of Butler at reminding his Cabinet colleagues of their overriding duty to support the government.[84] As over India in the 1930s, revolt was contained less by ideological conversion of the rebellious than by a combination of factors which hampered the formation and articulation of protest: first, a strongly hierarchical and institutionalised Conservative Party with no serious competitor on its right flank, equipped with the rewards and sanctions provided by government office, functioning in a two-party system which offered strong disincentives to rebellion; and secondly, an imperial system whose agencies (especially the army and colonial civil service) remained firmly under the control of the metropolitan authorities, and in which colonial expatriates, lacking direct representation in the metropolitan legislature, were forced to lobby through intermediaries with other priorities.[85]

The limits of Conservative acceptance of black majority rule are clear from the support won by the demands for immediate independence made by the Field–Smith regime in Southern Rhodesia.[86] The Whips' Office warned the party leaders that on a motion denying independence to Southern Rhodesia 'we might have 100/150 of our own side against us'. This would represent 'sentimental attachment to the last bastion of white government in Africa, and would reflect Conservative opinion in the country'.[87] This was partly because the Rhodesian Front regime and its Conservative allies took great care to draw contrasts between their own successes and the sorry record of authoritarianism and economic collapse in independent African states. But in a less tangible way, it was because white Rhodesian society, at least in the way it was portrayed by Conservatives, encapsulated many of the values of Toryism: hierarchical, anti-communist, Christian, resolute, prizing responsibility, effort, independence and enterprise, with a severely limited role for state ownership or the provision of welfare services.[88] To those angered by what they saw as the moral stagnation of Wilson's Britain, beset by strikes, inflation and high taxation, Rhodesia offered sanctuary from the 'British disease'.[89] Indeed, it does not seem too fanciful to see Conservative support for white Rhodesia as a kind of frustrated reaction against the 'Whitehall' consensus not merely as it had operated in colonial affairs, but in all its works.

CONSENSUS AS POPULAR CONTENTMENT

How far were such attitudes shared in the electorate? In answering this question, vital though it is to establishing the nature of 'consensus', we are handicapped by lack of evidence. The evidence from opinion polls is scanty and often too coarse to permit detailed conclusions to be drawn.

Opinion was complex, often infuriatingly changeable, highly differentiated, even self-contradictory, and conclusions can therefore only be
impressionistic.

It can easily be established that there was widespread public ignorance
about the colonial empire. A 1948 government survey found that half its
sample could not name a single British colony.[90] Even in 1959, when the
parties were at their most divided, colonial matters did not raise much
interest at the polls.[91] But, as Darwin has pointed out, it would be mistaken
to conclude that this meant the public was apathetic about empire. When
British imperial prestige was challenged by the military aggression of supposedly lesser powers (as in the Indonesian Crisis of 1963 or the Falklands
War of 1982), when British economic assets were menaced (as in Iran in
1951 or Suez in 1956) or the livelihoods of British expatriates threatened
(as in Kenya and the Rhodesias after 1950), when British soldiers, especially national service conscripts, died in colonial wars (as in Palestine in
the late 1940s and Malaya in the 1950s), and when the coercive and
violent nature of colonial rule was exposed to public view (as in Kenya
and Nyasaland in 1959), colonial issues proved quite capable of breaking
through the crust of public indifference. Too rapid or too humiliating a
capitulation to the demands of colonial nationalism was likely to expose
Britain's residual interests in the colony to erosion and to undermine
British prestige. But too heavy-handed an assertion of British power, especially if it involved the use of emergency powers, was bound to arouse the
anger of those revolted by colonial violence and the fears of those anxious
to avoid expensive and dangerous military entanglements.[92]

Politicians were therefore far from indifferent to the danger of these
combustible materials catching fire. Attlee and his colleagues were
obsessed by the potential unpopularity of a premature scuttle from their
Indian responsibilities.[93] Dragged into supporting reactionary settlers in
Africa over the Hola Camp atrocities and the Nyasaland Emergency,
Macmillan and Macleod feared losing the moral high ground on colonial
issues to Labour.[94] Given widespread public ignorance, much thus
depended on how colonial issues were presented to the public. Great care
was taken to suggest that losing an empire meant gaining a
Commonwealth, that the loss of formal powers would be more than balanced by the gain in influence, that the economic and strategic substance
of the colonial connection would survive the transfer of power, and therefore that decolonisation, in short, meant not national decline but the
fulfilment of an imperial mission.

The ideal of a 'bipartisan consensus' was itself part of this strategy.
Both Labour and Conservative ministers regularly pleaded with the

Opposition to observe the 'parliamentary tradition' that colonial matters were considered without regard to party advantage. The outward justifications for this were the thoroughly paternalistic claims that bipartisanship was essential to ensure the continuity and stability of colonial policy, without which Britain could not discharge her imperial trust, and that for the Westminster parties to take sides in colonial matters would only encourage 'troublemakers' in the colonies to further intransigence. For ministers anxious to win support for potentially unpopular policies, however, the 'tradition' offered a means by which radical advances could be painted in bipartisan colours, and dissenters pushed to the margins and stigmatised as irresponsible. By claiming that all parties had sanctioned the constitutional advances leading to Indian independence, Attlee artfully concealed the differences between the careful measures of Baldwin, Hoare and Montagu, and Mountbatten's rapid and uncautious disengagement.[95] Macleod too, in placing his own policies in a line that started with India,[96] bound himself into the supposed 'consensus'. Decolonisation, it was made clear, was the work of statesmen, not party politicians.

CONCLUSIONS

What should we make of the claims of 'consensus' outlined at the beginning? At the level of high policy, it is possible to identify the main features of an agreed approach to the challenge posed by anti-colonial nationalist movements, pursued by ministers of both political colourings. However, the main cause of this coincidence of policy was less partisan convergence than the harsh economic and international constraints which all British policy-makers had to face. Where partisan considerations were able to make their influence felt, there were genuine divergences of opinion, especially after the mid-1950s. Indeed, the very fact of policy coincidence fostered partisan dissent, especially on the right. The fear that these discontents might spread to the public at large seems to have been a genuine one, and inspired efforts to insulate the electorate from the implications of colonial collapse.

Like, perhaps, its counterpart in domestic affairs, the 'consensus' on the end of empire was therefore Janus-faced. Among the policy-making elite, it arose from a genuine recognition of the necessity to adapt Britain's colonial system to meet the challenges of nationalism. Had it been possible to control the pace of concessions, it is likely that partisan dissent would have been confined to the political fringes. But the necessary, if largely unforeseen, acceleration in these plans required careful handling. For decolonisation to work to British advantage, policy now had to be pragmatic and flexible. It was vital (as the fate of the French Fourth Republic in its Algerian dealings reminded party leaders) for it to be kept free from the paralysing effects of party strife. In their hands, 'consensus' was a device by which partisan divisions were to be bridged, and popular anxieties contained or even concealed: less, perhaps, the happy product of a people's war than a highly successful exercise in the political management of discontent.

ACKNOWLEDGEMENT

I am grateful to my former colleagues at the University of Durham for the opportunity to try out these ideas at the Department of Politics Research Seminar, and to Dr Philip Murphy, Dr Sîan Nicholas, Dr David Omissi, Bob Williams and the editors of this collection for reading and criticising an earlier draft.

NOTES

1. Paul Addison, 'Epilogue: "The Road to 1945" Revisited', in *The Road to 1945*, 1994, London, Pimlico, 2nd edn, pp. 279–92; Ben Pimlott, 'The Myth of Consensus', in *Frustrate Their Knavish Tricks*, 1994, London, HarperCollins.
2. There are early signs, however, of right-wing revisionism on the question of Europe. See John Charmley, *Churchill's Grand Alliance: The Anglo-American Special Relationship 1940–57*, 1995, London, John Curtis/Hodder and Stoughton.
3. Kenneth O. Morgan, *The People's Peace: British History, 1945–1989*, 1990, Oxford, Oxford University Press, pp. 513–14.
4. See 'The Road from 1945', in Peter Hennessy and Anthony Seldon, eds., *Ruling Performance*, 1987, Oxford, Basil Blackwell, pp. 5–6.
5. Dennis Kavanagh, *Thatcherism and British Politics*, 1987, Oxford, Oxford University Press, pp. 34, 57.
6. Dennis Kavanagh and Peter Morris, *Consensus Politics From Attlee to Major*, 1994, Oxford, Basil Blackwell, 2nd edn, p. 97.
7. David Dutton, *British Politics Since 1945: The Rise and Fall of Consensus*, 1991, Oxford, Basil Blackwell, pp. 48–9.
8. David Goldsworthy, *Colonial Issues in British Politics, 1945–1961*, 1971, Oxford, Clarendon Press.
9. Addison has claimed, with some justice, that his definition of consensus is of the first sort, but has been misconstrued as the other two. See his 'Epilogue', 1994.
10. John Darwin, 'British Decolonization Since 1945: A Pattern or a Puzzle?', *Journal of Imperial and Commonwealth History*, XII, 2, 1984, pp. 187–209.

11. For Bennett's plan, see Ronald Hyam, ed., *The Labour Government and the End of Empire 1945–1951*, 1992, London, Institute of Commonwealth Studies/HMSO, introduction, p. xxxix, and II, 174. For the planning of the new African policy, see John Flint, 'Planned Decolonization and its Failure in British Africa', *African Affairs*, 82, 328, July 1983, pp. 389–411; John W. Cell, 'On the Eve of Decolonization: The Colonial Office's Plans for the Transfer of Power in Africa, 1947', *Journal of Imperial and Commonwealth History*, VII, 3, May 1980, pp. 235–57; R.D. Pearce, 'The Colonial Office in 1947 and the Transfer of Power in Africa: An Addendum to John Cell', *Journal of Imperial and Commonwealth History*, X, 2, January 1982, pp. 211–15; Robert Pearce, *Turning Point in Africa: British Colonial Policy, 1938–1948*, 1982, London, Frank Cass; Robert Pearce, 'The Colonial Office and Planned Decolonization in Africa', *African Affairs*, 83, 330, January 1984, pp. 77–93. For Macmillan, see John Darwin, *Britain and Decolonisation: The Retreat From Empire in the Post-War World*, 1988, Basingstoke, Macmillan, p. 230.
12. See Robert Holland, *European Decolonisation 1918–1981: An Introductory Survey*, 1985, Basingstoke, Macmillan, pp. 37–69 for an excellent summary.
13. Stephen Howe, *Anticolonialism in British Politics: The Left and the End of Empire, 1918–1964*, 1994, Oxford, Clarendon Press, p. 139.
14. Iain McLaine, *Ministry of Morale: Home Front Morale and the Ministry of Information in the Second World War*, 1979, London, George Allen and Unwin, pp. 223–4.
15. Wm R. Louis, *Imperialism at Bay 1941–1945: The United States and the Decolonization of the British Empire*, 1977, Oxford, Clarendon Press.
16. A.N. Porter and A.J. Stockwell, *British Imperial Policy and Decolonization, 1938–1964*, 2 vols, 1987, 1989, Basingstoke, Macmillan, vol. I, pp. 39–45.
17. Pearce, 1984, p. 85.
18. William H. Beveridge, *Full Employment in a Free Society*, 1944, London, George Allen and Unwin, pp. 208–41; J.M. Keynes, 'The Problem of Our External Finance in the Transition' and 'Overseas Financial Policy in Stage III', *The Collected Writings of John Maynard Keynes*, vol. XXIV, *Activities, 1944–46*, 1979, London, Macmillan, pp. 34–65, 256–95.
19. The metaphor comes (slightly adapted) from a memorandum by R.E. Robinson, quoted in Ronald Hyam, 'Africa and the Labour Government, 1945–51', *Journal of Imperial and Commonwealth History*, XVI, 3, 1988, p. 151.
20. Report of the Agenda Committee on the Conference of African Governors, 'Constitutional Development in Africa' (Appendix III), in Hyam, *Labour Government*, I, 59.
21. Diary of Sir Philip Mitchell, 10 November 1947, MSS Afr. r.101, Rhodes House Library, Oxford.
22. See for example, the minutes by Cartland and Robinson linking the new approach to older traditions of native administration. Hyam, *Labour Government*, I, 48, I, 49.
23. Hyam, 1982, IV, 347.
24. Porter and Stockwell, 1989, II, Introduction, p. 48.
25. *Ibid.*, II, 21.
26. *Ibid.*, II, 73.

27. David Goldsworthy, ed., *The Conservative Government and the End of Empire, 1951–1957,* 1994, London, Institute of Commonwealth Studies/HMSO, II, 204.
28. Porter and Stockwell, 1989, II, 37.
29. *Ibid.*, 37.
30. *Ibid.*, 49; Goldsworthy, 1994, II, 351.
31. *Ibid.*, 204.
32. See Richard Rathbone, ed., *Ghana,* 1992, London, Institute of Commonwealth Studies/HMSO.
33. The claims of the following paragraphs are more fully developed in my thesis: 'The Confusions of an Imperialist Inheritance: The British Labour Party and Indian Independence, 1940–1947', 1993, Oxford D.Phil.
34. See, for example, John Ramsden, *The Age of Balfour and Baldwin, 1902–1940,* 1978, London, Longman, p. 336.
35. Headlam Diary, 10 May 1930, 27 June 1932, 29 March 1933, 6 April 1933, 28 June 1933, 6 October 1933, 13 November 1934, 22 March 1935, 27 March 1935, in Stuart Ball, ed., *Parliament and Politics in the Age of Baldwin and MacDonald: The Headlam Diary, 1923–1935,* 1992, London, The Historians' Press, pp. 187, 240, 265, 266, 274, 280, 313, 325, 327, 328.
36. On Macmillan, see Alastair Horne, *Harold Macmillan, 1894–1956,* 1988, London, Macmillan, pp. 282–301, 310. Harold Macmillan, *Tides of Fortune, 1945–1955,* 1969, London, Macmillan, pp. 233–56. On Butler, see 'A Visit to Chequers', 11 March 1943, Butler Papers G18/1–10. Cf. Butler, *The Art of the Possible,* 1979, London, Hamish Hamilton, p. 111; Butler to Attlee, 5 January. 1945, enclosed in India Committee Paper I(45)5, in Nicholas Mansergh *et al.*, eds., *India: Transfer of Power,* 12 vols, 1970–83, London, HMSO, vol. V, doc. 188; Butler to Attlee, 5 April 1945, Butler Papers, F83/41.
37. Owen, 1993, pp. 112–13.
38. *Ibid.*, chapters 7–8.
39. See Philip Murphy, *Party Politics and Decolonization: The Conservative Party and British Colonial Policy in Tropical Africa, 1951–1964,* 1995, Oxford, Clarendon Press, pp. 42–5; Goldsworthy, 1971, pp. 193–8.
40. Conservative Party, *Imperial Policy,* 1949, London, Conservative and Unionist Central Office, pp. 53–5.
41. Conservative Party Archive [CPA], CRD 2/34/10, 'Self-Government in the Colonies', 28 June 1950.
42. CPA CRD 2/50/10–11, 'General Policy, 1946–49'.
43. Anthony Seldon, *Churchill's Indian Summer: The Conservative Government, 1951–55,* 1981, London, Hodder and Stoughton, p. 377.
44. PRO: PREM11/874, 'Alan [Lennox-Boyd] shows signs of giving way all along the line', wrote Salisbury to Eden in 1955. Porter and Stockwell, 1989, II p. 46.
45. Conservative Party, *Report of Annual Conference,* 1950, pp. 34–5.
46. David Goldsworthy, 'Keeping Change Within Bounds: Aspects of Colonial Policy During the Churchill and Eden Governments, 1951–57', *Journal of Imperial and Commonwealth History,* XVIII, 1, 1990, p. 83; Ronald Hyam, 'Churchill and the British Empire', in Robert Blake and Wm. Roger Louis, eds., *Churchill,* 1993, Oxford, Oxford University Press, pp. 167–86.

180   *The Myth of Consensus*

47. Goldsworthy, 1994, II, 175.
48. *Ibid.*, II 265; Home to Lennox-Boyd, 11 July 1956; Home to Macmillan, 29 January 1957, in Rathbone, *Ghana*, II, 237, 284.
49. Lord Home, *Where the Wind Blows*, 1976, London, William Collins, p. 120; CPA CRD 2/53/32, paper for CRD, 'British Colonial Policy in Africa', 23 June 1959.
50. Goldsworthy, 1994, II, 195.
51. Murphy, 1995, p. 53.
52. Darwin, *Britain and Decolonisation*, pp. 183–94.
53. Goldsworthy, 1994, II, 266, 272.
54. *Ibid.*, II, 321; Holland, *The Pursuit of Greatness: Britain and the World Role, 1900–1970*, 1991, London, Fontana Press, pp. 265–6; Darwin, *Britain and Decolonisation*, pp. 279–80. See also Lennox-Boyd on Kenya, quoted in Darwin, *Britain and Decolonisation*, p. 189.
55. Goldsworthy, 1971, pp. 295–300; Leon D. Epstein, *British Politics and the Suez Crisis*, 1964, London, Pall Mall Press, pp. 51–8.
56. Holland, *Pursuit of Greatness*, pp. 267–8.
57. Evelyn Shuckburgh, *Descent to Suez: Diaries, 1951–56*, 1986, London, Weidenfeld and Nicolson, p. 340; Goldsworthy, 1971, p. 299.
58. Robert Rhodes James, *Anthony Eden*, 1986, London, Weidenfeld and Nicolson, p. 567.
59. See W. Scott Lucas, *Divided We Stand: Britain, the US and the Suez Crisis*, 1991, London, Hodder and Stoughton, pp. 325–30.
60. Epstein, *British Politics*, pp. 87–93, 97–122, 146; David Carlton, *Britain and the Suez Crisis*, 1988, Oxford, Basil Blackwell, pp. 57–60.
61. Owen, 1993.
62. See Hyam, 'Africa and the Labour Government', pp. 149, 152, 169.
63. Goldsworthy, 1971, pp. 214–30.
64. *Ibid.*, pp. 339–40.
65. Labour Party, *Labour's Colonial Policy (3) The Smaller Territories*, 1957, London, Labour Party.
66. Howe, *Anticolonialism in British Politics*.
67. PRO: CAB134/1560, CPC(61)1, Iain Macleod, 'Colonial Problems in 1961', 3 January 1961; PRO: CAB134/1560, CPC(61)33, Reginald Maudling, 'Northern Rhodesia', 15 December 1961.
68. PRO: PREM11/3080, Macleod to Sandys, 15 November 1960.
69. Murphy, 1995, p. 180.
70. CRD, *Bi-Monthly Survey of Commonwealth and Colonial Affairs*, 20 June 1952, quoted in Miles Kahler, *Decolonization in Britain and France: The Domestic Consequences of International Relations*, 1984, Princeton, Princeton University Press, p. 143.
71. PRO: PREM11/3943, Commonwealth Affairs Committee, 16 February 1961, CPA; meeting of ministers, 22 January 1962; PRO: PREM11/3495, Cunningham to Macmillan, 16 March 1961; Murphy, 1995, pp. 188–9.
72. See for Julian Amery's revealing comment on Rhodesia: 'We had interests of a very important character. To neglect those interests in favour of *theory* was wrong.' Michael Charlton, *The Last Colony in Africa: Diplomacy and the Independence of Rhodesia*, 1990, Oxford, Basil Blackwell, p. 13.
73. Murphy, 1995, pp. 173–81.

74. Over the release of Banda in February 1960 (see Horne, 1988, pp. 200–1) and twice over Northern Rhodesia (PRO: PREM11/3487, note by Bligh, 17 February 1961; Meeting of ministers, 18 February 1961; PRO: PREM11/3942, Butler to Macmillan, 18 January 1962. Macmillan claimed the threats were a 'daily event', Horne, 1988, p. 397.

75. PRO: PREM11/3486, Home to Macmillan, 3 February 1961; Horne, 1988, p. 396.

76. PRO: PREM11/3490, Macleod to Macmillan, 24 April 1961.

77. PRO: PREM11/3943, Cunningham to Macmillan, 1 March 1962.

78. Murphy, 1995, pp. 212–21.

79. Harold Macmillan, *At the End of the Day*, 1973, London, Macmillan, p. 309.

80. CPA CRD 2/53/28, Policy Study Group, 15 February 1957.

81. Salisbury to Emrys Evans, 16 April 1961, Emrys Evans Papers, British Library ADD MSS 58241.

82. CPA CRD 2/34/26, notes by Sayers, 22 and 24 August 1961. Protest votes on the Rhodesian question were regarded as part of the reason for the Orpington defeat: CPA CRD 2/52/7, paper by Maurice Macmillan, 15 March 1962; CPA CRD 2/52/9, discussion by Peter Goldman and Edward Boyle on Orpington, 19 March 1962.

83. Murphy, 1995, pp. 201–3.

84. PRO: PREM11/3942, Butler to Macmillan, 18 January 1962; PRO: PREM11/3943, Butler to Macmillan, 26 February 1962.

85. Kahler, 1984, John Darwin, 'The Fear of Falling: British Politics and Imperial Decline'; *Transactions of the Royal Historical Society*, 5th series, 36, 1986, pp. 27–44.

86. Horne, 1988, p. 411; Murphy, 1995, p. 200.

87. PRO: PREM11/4420, Redmayne to Alport, 24 April 1963.

88. Andrew Gamble, *The Conservative Nation*, 1974, London, Routledge and Kegan Paul, p. 178; Colin Leys, *European Politics in Southern Rhodesia*, 1959, Oxford, Clarendon Press, chapter 8.

89. Conservatives disgusted by the lack of reward for free enterprise in Britain were encouraged to emigrate to the Rhodesias. See Leys, 1959, p. 248.

90. G.K. Evens, *Public Opinion on Colonial Affairs*, June 1948, London, HMSO NS 119.

91. D.E. Butler and Richard Rose, *The British General Election of 1959*, 1960, London, Macmillan, pp. 71–2, 198.

92. John Darwin, *The End of the British Empire: The Historical Debate*, 1991, Oxford, Basil Blackwell, pp. 16–24.

93. Nicholas Owen, 'Responsibility Without Power: The Attlee Governments and the End of British Rule in India', in Nick Tiratsoo, ed., *The Attlee Years*, 1991, London, Pinter.

94. Murphy, 1993, p. 174; PRO: PREM11/2538, Macleod to Macmillan, 25 May 1959; Horne, 1988, pp. 183–5.

95. Nicholas Owen, 'More Than a Transfer of Power: Independence Day Ceremonies in India, 15 August 1947', *Contemporary Record*, 6, 3 (Winter 1992), pp. 415–51.

96. Iain Macleod, 'Trouble in Africa', *The Spectator*, 31 January 1964.

Index

Index